DIGITAL EMBROIDERY

PAINTING WITH THREADS

David Morrish

DIGITAL EMBROIDERY

PAINTING WITH THREADS

THE CROWOOD PRESS

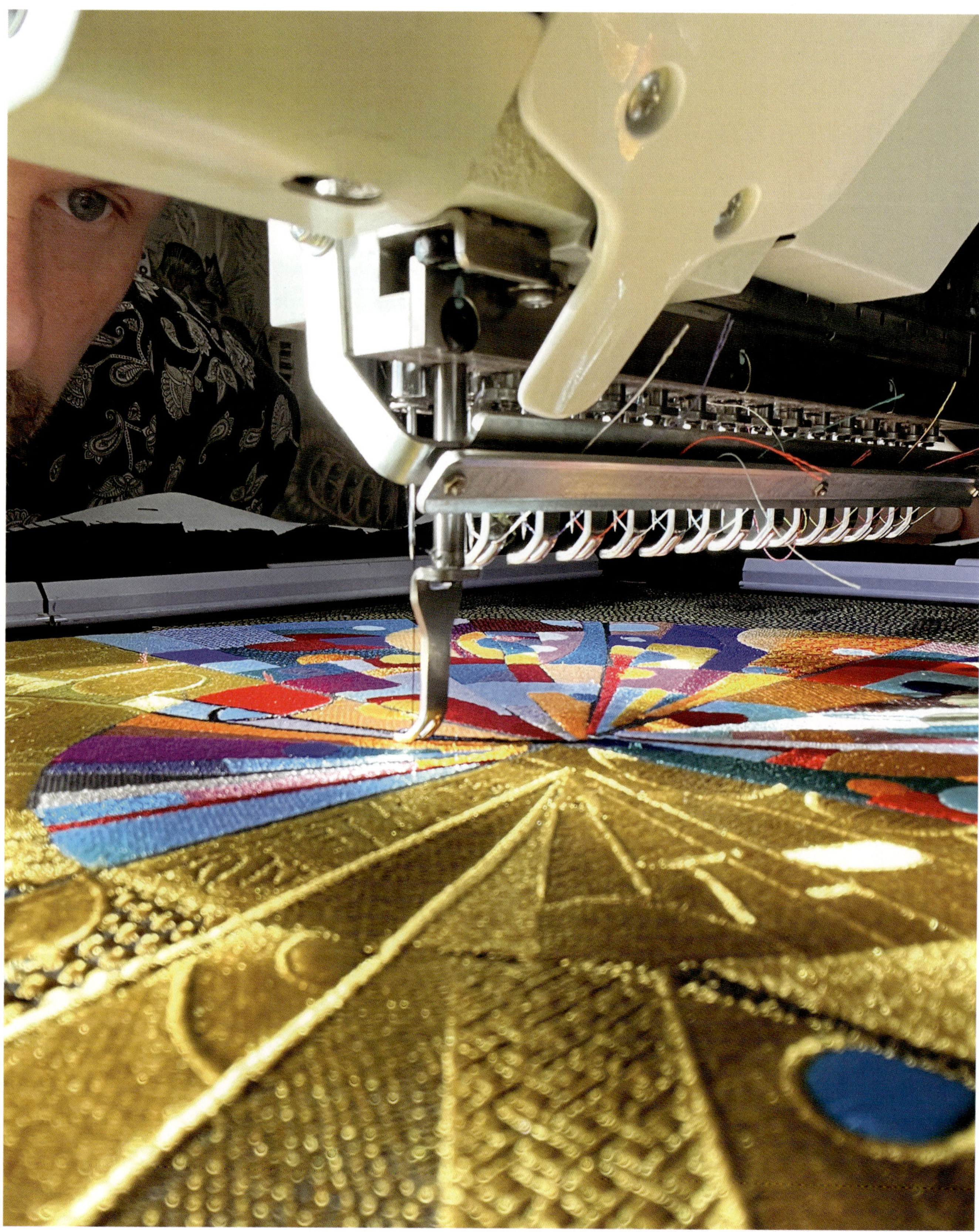

CONTENTS

FOREWORD

David brings my two favourite subjects, art, and needlework, together to create exciting, vibrant, colourful and impactful embroidery designs. Both subjects have been part of my lifelong journey. Drawing in stitches is now a dream come true and meeting David brought everything to the surface again.

Digital embroidery has been in home sewing since Janome introduced the first home embroidery machine with the Memory Craft 8000 in 1990, the world's first home-use computerised sewing machine with embroidery functions. Janome technology made users' dreams come true and opened up a new sewing machine market in hobby use.

As Creative Director of Janome UK, I see a lot of stitching talent. Meeting David and his work was an instant trigger; I knew I had to see more, hear more and learn why, how, and what makes him tick, what drives his stitch ambition.

I've heard many people comment as they pass our digital embroidery machines stitching away at shows saying, 'That's cheating'. My instinct is to shout 'No, it's so much more!' It's a tool to visualise your dreams, just like pen and paper, paint, and print. It's not just a matter of what perfect stitch can come out of the machine (obviously the stitch quality matters, but that is a given with Janome): it's what went into creating the embroidery, what the designer imparts, and gives of themselves.

Design is a journey taking you through many stages. In this book, David shares his journey and extensive underpinning knowledge of digital embroidery software application through his projects. It's always inspiring to meet like-minded people who want to translate their vision as an artist into stitches. David's hoop is his canvas, his thread is his paint, and his needle is his paintbrush. David isn't confined by the hoop parameter limits; what he creates is so much bolder, he gives of himself to help explore digital stitch as an art form in vibrant colour and texture. Digital stitch is his medium to translate his message. In this book, his generous nature shares his thoughts, tips, and vision to help you develop your own style and realise your visions in stitch.

This essential digital stitch book is for those looking to enjoy, explore and experiment, for those who want to go beyond the motif and take risks. David imparts his passion for sketching with thread, he tells his stories in stitch, in a beautiful way. The software opens up endless possibilities, sparks the imagination and revitalises the soul as we share David's digital journey and see him push the boundaries and dispel preconceived perceptions.

Deborah Shepherd
Creative Director Janome UK

OPPOSITE: Embroidered self portrait of the author.

INTRODUCTION

Digital embroidery is a test of patience and resilience; don't give up and keep striving forward.

For generations, embroidery has been a favoured form of ornamentation and embellishment. It is a way of creating art, telling stories, preserving culture, expressing personal beliefs, religion, affiliation, identity, military rank, social class and even a way of passing on secret coded messages. Embroidery can be both commercial and creative, crossing disciplines and topics. Embroidery allows the wearer to show their allegiance to a sporting club or membership of a school or society through proudly displayed badges and logos, but it can also be seen dominating royal ceremonial events or haute couture catwalk shows, whether on clothing, banners or even anointment screens as seen at King Charles III's coronation in 2023.

For me, embroidery is the ultimate timeless fine art, crossing all subject matters, disciplines, languages, ages and genders. Embroidery pushes the artist in many ways, asking them not only to consider the visual aesthetic of the image, but also the tactile qualities and the technical and practical complications in its creation. Embroidery can evoke an array of emotional responses. The flexibility and adaptability of embroidery make it a truly fascinating and important art form.

In recent years, embroidery has undergone a transformation with the advent of digital embroidery.

Throughout history we can see recurring patterns of traditional handcrafts being impacted by technological and scientific advances, which often results in what were once time-consuming and sometimes elitist art forms, becoming easier, faster and cheaper to produce, thus becoming more accessible and affordable. Digital embroidery is a process where a machine is used to create embroidered designs using specialised computerised software. This exciting medium has revolutionised the world of embroidery, opening it up to new possibilities for creativity and innovation.

Machine embroidery has been around for over 200 years, but it wasn't until the 1980s that digital embroidery became a reality. The first computerised embroidery machine was invented by Wilcom and Melco in the 1980s. Since then, technology has advanced at a rapid pace, allowing for more complex designs and faster production times. Today, digital embroidery is used in fashion, home décor, advertising, medical, military, engineering, sports and more.

One of the most exciting things about digital embroidery is its versatility. With a digital embroidery machine, you can create intricate designs with ease. You can use a variety of threads and fabrics, and the machine can stitch different types of stitches, including fills, running stitches and motifs. Digital embroidery also allows you to create designs with multiple colours, shading and gradients, which can be difficult to achieve with traditional embroidery methods. In today's fast-paced society, digital embroidery gives those who have limited free time, dexterity in their hands or lack the patience to work on a piece of hand embroidery over many months or years, an opportunity to enter this incredible multi-sensory world. Whether creating a simple design for a T-shirt or a large inspirational art piece, digital embroidery can be adapted to suit many requirements. With specialist attachments available on some machines, digital embroidery goes beyond just threads, enabling you to embroider with sequins and beads, as well as bore holes or add cording and other materials to create dramatic 3D effects.

Despite the innovation of digital embroidery, many similarities exist between hand, free machine, and digital embroidery. All three methods require a design or pattern, base material, thread and a needle. They all involve the use of stitches to create a design. Additionally, hand, free and digital embroidery all rely on a hoop to hold the fabric in place during the stitching process.

I hope that this book will act as a comprehensive guide to digital embroidery and that it will inspire you to develop your own skills and create beautiful designs.

OPPOSITE: Close-up detailing of the tactical textures created by digital embroidery.

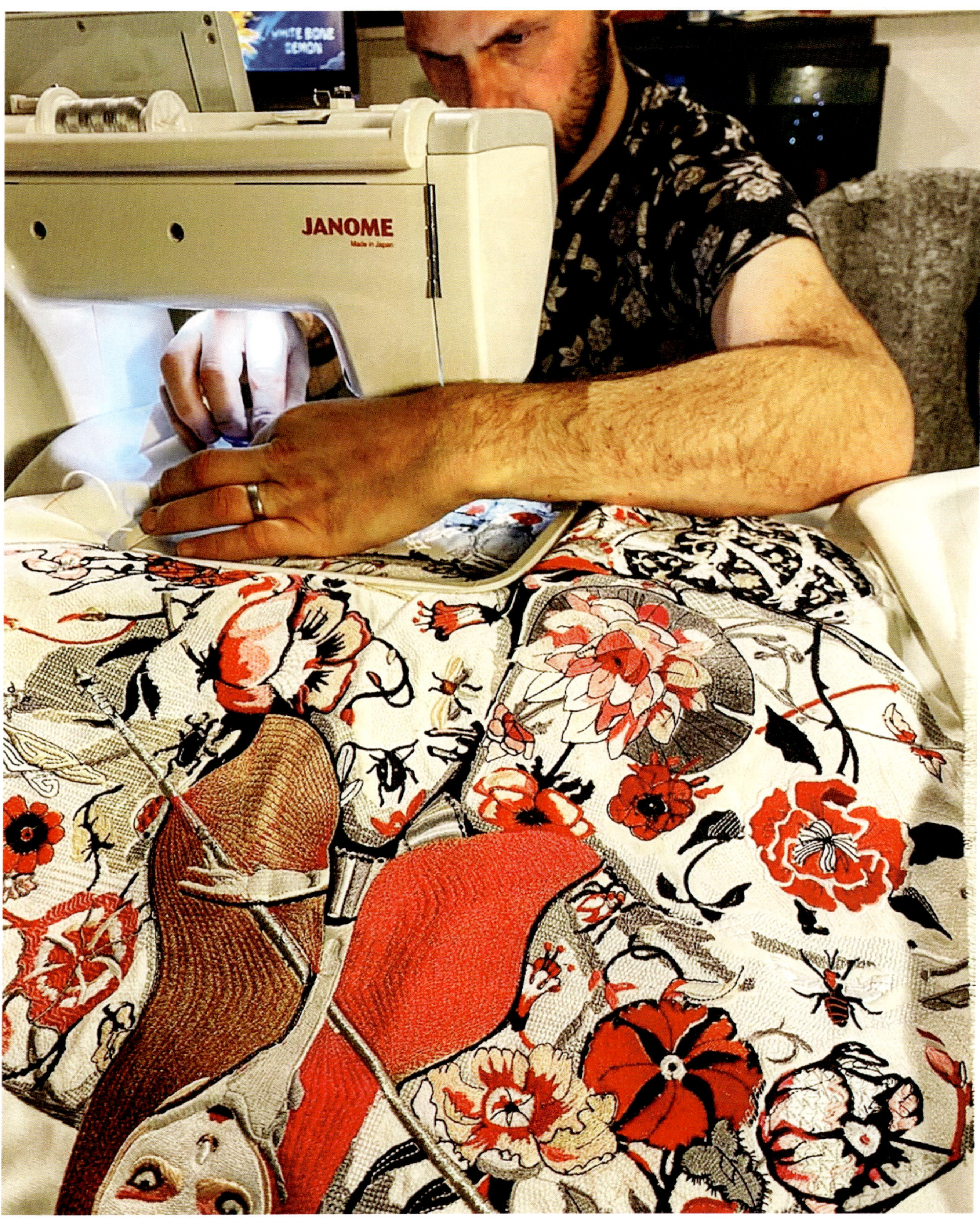
WHITE BONE DEMON
JANOME
Made in Japan

CHAPTER 1

MATERIALS AND EQUIPMENT: SETTING UP YOUR WORKSTATION

Know that with each stitch and pattern, you are crafting not just a piece of art, but also a piece of yourself into your creations.

Like all arts and crafts, in order to carry out your passion, there are key pieces of equipment that you need to have access to. Digital embroidery is no exception. Initial investment can be quite costly, so it is important you source the right embroidery machine, computer, software and materials (threads, fabric, stabilisers, and so on). What is right for one person's needs may not be right for someone else's, and with so much choice available to you, it can become a minefield. Buying an unsuitable machine could set you back in terms of money and time, whilst the wrong threads or backings will give you issues with quality and productivity. In this chapter, I will cover the different types of machines and software available, as well as explain the different needles, threads and backings at your disposal. By the end of this chapter, you should be informed enough to be able to make considered purchases for your needs.

DIGITAL EMBROIDERY MACHINES

Most likely your biggest investment will be the embroidery machine itself. With lots on the market, it can be difficult to determine which is best for you. When the salesperson starts talking about multi-heads, attachments, laser guidance, multi-tension dials, speeds, embroidery areas and so on, it can become all too confusing and in some cases off-putting altogether.

However, you can generally split digital embroidery machines into two categories: domestic and industrial. Let's look a bit closer at both.

Domestic Embroidery Machines

These tend to be more affordable to the general hobbyist and enthusiast, consisting of a single needle and flat bed. They may look very similar in appearance to a normal sewing machine, with the addition of a digital display screen built into the front and a hoop holder either to the left- or right-hand side of the needle. These machines are often portable, and some are hybrids, enabling you to machine sew, free machine embroider and even quilt. The main disadvantages (compared to industrial embroidery machines) are the hoop sizes, which tend to be significantly smaller; the flat bed, which can restrict or hinder the ability to embroider on tubular items, for example, garments (without unpicking a seam to lie flat); less choice on specialist attachments and the need for the user to change the thread manually for each colour change. The speed at which the machine embroiders (stitches per minute or SPM) is comparable to industrial machines, though the top-end industrial machines are able to run a little faster. The time lost changing threads and with the bed limitations means it is not the best choice of machine for mass-produced items. Prices generally range from £600–£10,000.

OPPOSITE: David machine embroidering a section of a large fashion illustration by Laura Laine (canvas 150 × 80cm – over 1.5 million stitches).

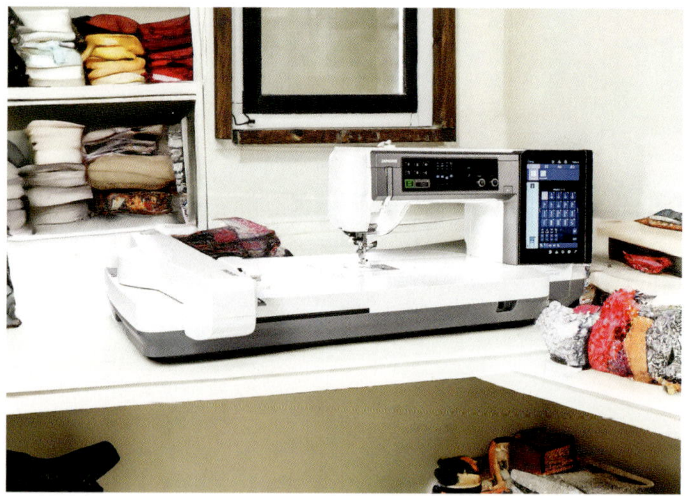
The new Janome Continental M17 embroidery, quilting and sewing machine, which has a massive hooping area and specialist features.

A HappyJapan multi-needle, single-head industrial embroidery machine.

There are, however, a few domestic machines new to the market (2024) that are really challenging the lower-end industrial machines in terms of embroidery area size, speed and quality, and these can start from £11,000 upwards. When you are considering these machines you may wish to compare the machine against an introductory industrial embroidery machine to best determine which is better value for money for you and your needs.

Popular brand names for domestic embroidery machines include Janome, Brother, Bernina, Pfaff, Babylock, Bernette, Husqvarna and Singer.

Industrial Embroidery Machines

These are often multi-needle machines which can embroider larger areas in one hoop and can embroider on flat and tubular fabrics (perfect for garments). Industrial machines are generally much larger, heavier and robust, making them perfect for mass production and more demanding embroidery pieces. Multi-needle machines can vary in the number of needles they have, ranging from 6 to 24+; this saves time in rethreading the needle for each colour change, as the needles are threaded at the beginning of the stitch-out stage (this is when you transfer the design to fabric and actually begin embroidering), with the machine automatically selecting the correct needle based on the colour assigned. It is possible to replace some of the needles with special attachments, enabling the user to embroider with sequins, beads, cord or even bore holes to create a lace effect. Additional specialist attachments can be added to these machines allowing for easy embroidery on caps, shoes and belts, for example. Prices can start from £7,000 up to £100,000 or more for very large, custom-built machines.

Popular brand names include HappyJapan, ZSK, Tajima, Brother, Toyota, SWF, Ricoma and Merlin.

Different Types of Digital Embroidery Machines

Single-head machines: these are the most common type of embroidery machines and are designed for one person to operate. They are ideal for small businesses and home use.

Excellent German engineering – The ZSK 7XL Sprint – a multi-needle industrial embroidery machine with an impressive embroidery area (140 x 40cm) and 18 needles.

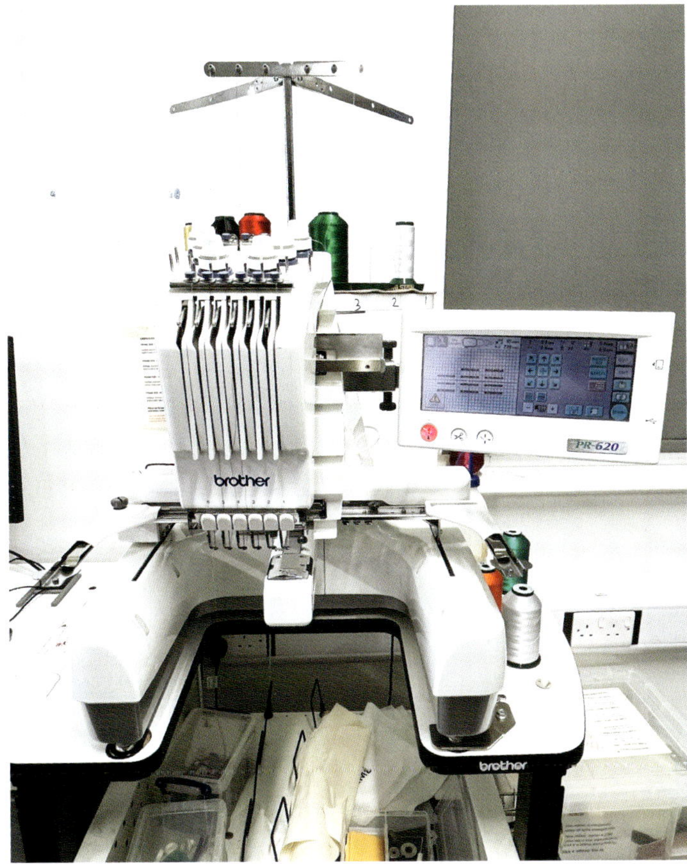

A Brother PR600 Semi - industrial embroidery machine, with 6 needles. A popular choice for schools, colleges, universities, hobbyists, and small businesses.

A Janome MC550E domestic embroidery machine, single head and single needle. This machine has a large hooping areas for a single-needle machine and has an affordable purchase price.

A multi-head, multi-needle ZSK industrial embroidery machine with cap attachments. This setup is common in factories for mass production.

The Janome Atelier 9, a hybrid sewing and embroidery machine, giving you more sewing options in one device.

David's studio with both his industrial and domestic embroidery machines.

Multi-head machines: these machines have several sewing heads, which allow them to embroider multiple items at once. They are best for large-scale commercial embroidery jobs.

Single-needle machines: common in domestic embroidery machines, these machines will have only one sewing needle attached to the machine.

Multi-needle machines: common in industry and mass production – these machines will have more than one needle that can be utilised.

Combination (hybrid) machines: these machines can both sew and embroider (and sometimes quilt), allowing for more versatility in the types of projects that can be completed.

When you talk to a dealer about embroidery machines, they will be trying to assess what the best machine is for what you need it to do. If your aim is to embroider on lots of sweatshirts and caps, for example, the machine and attachments will differ from someone who wants to create small monograms and logos on tea towels. In my studio, I have a portable domestic single-needle embroidery machine, which I use for creating one-off, flat, creative art pieces, small embroideries and for embroidering outside my studio (yes, I do embroider at events or in the garden on a sunny day – it's one of the advantages of having a portable machine). To complement my domestic machine, I have a single-head, multi-needle industrial embroidery machine which I use for larger pieces, embroidering on garments, creating multiples of a design and using attachments to add other decorative features to my work.

HOOPS, CLAMPS AND ATTACHMENTS

Your machine will most likely come with one or two embroidery hoops that are specific to your particular machine model. If you require other compatible hoops, you will need to search the model brand and purchase them separately. Be warned; larger and more specialist hoops and attachments can be expensive to purchase, and you need to factor this into your plans if you are working to budget. Machine hoops vary in shape, size, material, tightening mechanism and how they physically connect to the machine. For this reason, hoops are not often compatible with other machine types.

When buying a machine, it is worth researching what hoop types, sizes and attachments are available to that specific machine model, as this could have a significant impact on your decision-making. You don't want to invest in a machine only to realise it cannot do what you need it to do! Here are a few common types of digital embroidery hoops and attachments on the market today.

Standard Hoop

These are the most commonly used hoops for digital embroidery and can be circular, square or rectangular. They typically consist of an inner and outer ring that holds the fabric in place during the embroidery process. The securing mechanism is often a corner lever mechanism, or bolt and screw.

Magnetic Hoop

These hoops use magnets to hold the fabric in place instead of traditional screw or clamp mechanisms. They provide a strong and even hold, reducing the chances of fabric shifting during embroidery.

Cap Hoop (Cap Frame)

These specialised hoops are designed specifically for embroidering on caps. They have a curved shape that accommodates the curvature of the cap, allowing for precise and accurate embroidery. They can be very expensive to purchase and are not available on all types of machines.

Boot/Belt Clamp

Boot and belt clamps are specialised attachments or clamping systems used in the embroidery industry to secure boots and belts (or similarly shaped items) in place, allowing them to be embroidered with precision. These attachments ensure that the material stays taut and in the correct position while the embroidery machine does its work. I have also used these on knitted beanies. These

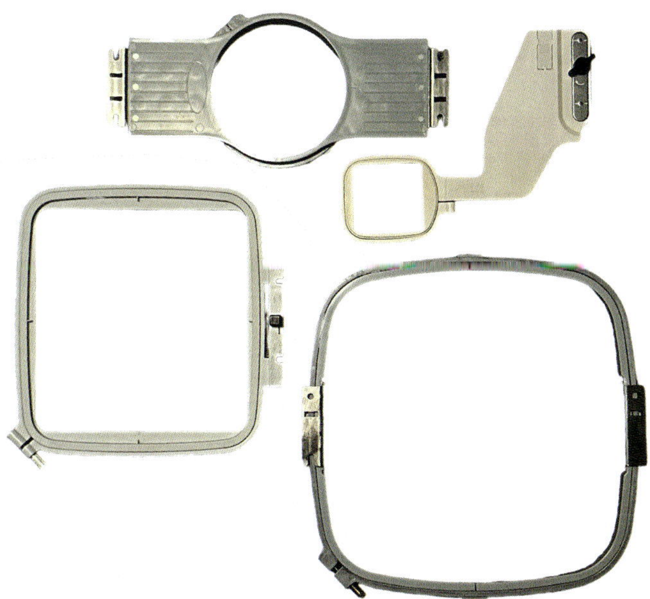

Four standard embroidery hoops for industrial and domestic embroidery machines showing variety in sizes and shapes.

A magnetic frame used to embroider a cat design.

A cap being embroidered on an industrial machine using a specialist attachment.

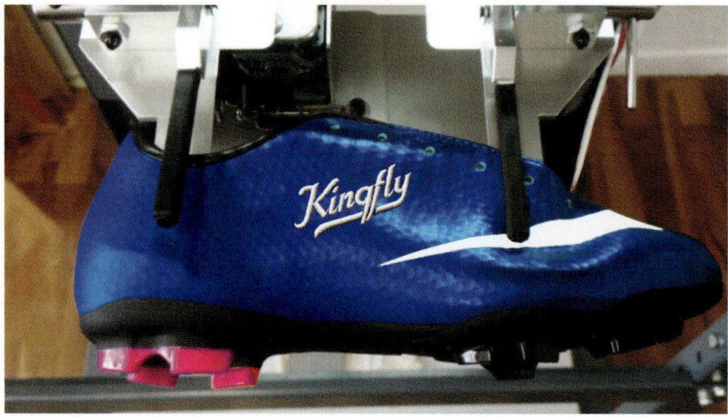

Kingfly name embroidered on a football boot, still held in place by the boot clamp. This clamp is also great for embroidering on belts, straps, collars and more.

are only available on machines that allow for tubular embroidery (not flat bed).

Border Hoop (Frame)

Border hoops, also known as border frames, are specialised embroidery hoops designed to simplify the process of embroidering on edges, borders or seams of various materials. They're particularly useful for items such as towels, sheets, shirts, and more where you might want to embroider directly along a border or edge.

Features and Benefits of Border Hoops

Design: these hoops are generally rectangular or long and thin, making them ideal for border designs.
Easy repositioning: border hoops often come with a mechanism that allows the embroiderer to reposition the fabric without unhooping, ensuring continuity in long border designs.
Stability: by holding the material taut and flat, border hoops ensure even and consistent embroidery along the edges.
Reduced fabric handling: because you can embroider longer stretches without rehooping, you handle the fabric less, reducing the chances of leaving marks or stretching the material.

Tips for Using Border Hoops

Material prep: ensure the material is clean and ironed. Wrinkles or creases can affect the quality of the embroidery.
Alignment: proper alignment is crucial. Before starting, ensure the design is straight and positioned where you want it.
Stabilisation: even with the hoop, you might need a stabiliser depending on the material you're embroidering. This helps maintain design integrity.
Tension: make sure the fabric is taut in the hoop, but not overly stretched, which can distort the design.
Test first: always do a test run on scrap material or an inconspicuous area to ensure the design looks right and the settings are correct.
Machine settings: ensure your embroidery machine settings (such as speed, tension, and so on) are appropriate for the material and the design's size and complexity.

Buying Considerations

Compatibility: make sure the border hoop is compatible with your specific embroidery machine model.

Size: border hoops come in various sizes. Choose one that fits the scale of your projects.

Material: look for hoops made of sturdy materials that can withstand repeated use without warping.

Adjustability: some hoops offer more adjustability in terms of tension and positioning, which can be a bonus for varied projects.

Border hoops can be a valuable addition to an embroiderer's toolkit, particularly for those who frequently work on projects where border or edge designs are desired. They can significantly enhance the professional finish and ease the embroidery process for such items.

A Parisian-inspired colourful embroidery art piece created in a border frame attached to a multi-needle embroidery machine. (Canvas 60 × 40cm)

Free-motion Hoop

These hoops are used for free-motion embroidery, where the fabric is moved freely under the needle by the operator to create artistic designs. They typically have a larger hoop size to allow for more movement and flexibility. Not all digital embroidery machines allow for free machine embroidery.

Sequin Attachment

Sequin attachments for embroidery machines allow the user to incorporate sequins into their embroidery designs automatically. Instead of manually sewing on each sequin, the attachment and the machine do it for you, saving time and ensuring precision. This is a wonderful tool to add some sparkle to your artwork!

How the Sequin Attachment Works

Feeding mechanism: the sequin attachment usually features a reel or spool where you place a string of sequins. This feeds the sequins into the attachment.

Punch and stitch: as the embroidery machine operates, the attachment picks up individual sequins and places

Free machine embroidery, where the hoop is controlled by hand to create the image. Dropping the feeder dog allows the hoop to move freely, though this is not always possible on all domestic embroidery machines.

them onto the fabric. The machine then punches a hole and uses a stitch to secure the sequin in place.
Cutting: some advanced attachments can cut the sequin string after each sequin is placed, allowing for individual sequin placement, rather than a continuous line.

Benefits of a Sequin Attachment

Efficiency: instead of manually sewing each sequin, the machine automates the process, significantly speeding up the task.
Precision: automated placement ensures each sequin is placed uniformly and consistently.
Complex designs: with software assistance, it's possible to create intricate sequin designs that would be challenging and time-consuming to do by hand. Not all digitising software programs allow for sequin design.

Multi-head industrial machine with sequin attachments added.

Things to Consider

Compatibility: not all embroidery machines are compatible with sequin attachments. Before purchasing, ensure that your machine can support it.
Learning curve: while the attachment automates the process, there's a learning curve involved. You'll need to understand how to set it up, feed the sequins and troubleshoot any issues.
Maintenance: just as with the main embroidery machine, the sequin attachment will require regular cleaning and occasional maintenance to keep it running smoothly.
Design software: for maximum flexibility in design, you might want embroidery software that supports sequin design. This allows you to digitise custom patterns and integrate sequins seamlessly.

Tips for Using Sequin Attachments

Test first: always do a test run on scrap fabric to ensure the sequins are being fed correctly, and the design looks as expected.
Watch tension: ensure that the tension on the sequin reel or spool is consistent so that the sequins feed correctly.
Quality matters: use high-quality sequins to avoid jams or breaks in the sequin string.
Regular checks: periodically check the attachment for any jamming or issues, especially if you're running a long embroidery job.

Embroidered piranha fish with sequined underbody.

Bead Attachment

Bead attachments for embroidery machines allow for the automated addition of beads to embroidery designs. This can provide a unique texture, depth, and sparkle to a project, elevating the overall design. Automated beading through machine attachments can be more consistent and faster than manual beading.

How the Bead Attachment Works

Bead feed: the bead attachment typically has a mechanism for feeding individual beads from a reservoir or spool.
Placement and stitching: the embroidery machine, guided by the design input, positions the needle over the desired bead placement spot. The bead attachment places a bead, and the machine stitches it in place, securing it to the fabric.
Multiple sizes: some advanced bead attachments can handle beads of different sizes, while others may be designed for a specific bead size.

Benefits of Using a Bead Attachment

Efficiency: automating the beading process can save a considerable amount of time compared to manual beading.
Precision: automated placement ensures beads are placed uniformly and according to the digitised design.
Versatility: allows for the integration of beading into a wide range of embroidery projects, from clothing to home décor.

Things to Keep in Mind

Compatibility: ensure that the bead attachment is compatible with your specific embroidery machine model.
Bead quality: use high-quality beads that are uniform in size for the best results.
Design limitations: the complexity of designs might be limited by the capabilities of the bead attachment and the embroidery machine.
Stabilisation: the added weight and texture of beads may require the use of a stabiliser to ensure the fabric remains taut and the design retains its shape.
Maintenance: regularly clean and maintain the bead attachment to ensure smooth operation and prevent jams.

Tips for Using Bead Attachments

Test Runs: always test a new design or bead type on scrap fabric first to ensure proper placement, tension and overall look.
Spacing: ensure beads are spaced in a way that the fabric remains flexible (if needed) and the beads are secured without too much tension.
Digitising designs: when creating or choosing designs for beading, ensure they are optimised for the bead attachment's capabilities.
Thread choice: consider using a stronger or speciality thread when working with beads to ensure they're securely attached and resist wear over time.
Backup supplies: always have backup beads on hand in case of breaks, losses or discrepancies in bead counts.

Bead attachments can significantly expand the capabilities of an embroidery machine, allowing crafters and professionals to create intricate, textured designs that stand out. However, like any tool or attachment, it requires practice and understanding to utilise it to its full potential.

Industrial ZSK industrial machine with beading attachment.

Cording Attachment

The cording attachment for digital embroidery machines is designed to feed cords, yarns, or similar materials into the embroidery process, allowing the machine to stitch them directly onto the fabric. This results in raised, textured designs that stand out and add a tactile dimension to your embroidery projects.

How the Cording Attachment Works

The cording attachment typically attaches to the embroidery machine's presser foot area. Once in place:

Cord feeding: the user threads the chosen cord, yarn or thin ribbon through the cording attachment's guide, ensuring it feeds smoothly.
Design selection: the machine is set to a design compatible with cording. Some machines may have specific cording stitch settings.
Embroidery process: as the machine stitches, the cording attachment feeds the cord onto the fabric. The needle then goes over the cord, securing it to the fabric, resulting in a raised design.
Finishing: once the design is complete, any excess cord is carefully trimmed and secured.

Benefits of Using the Cording Attachment

Texture and dimension: cording introduces a unique 3D texture to embroidery, making designs stand out.
Versatility: the attachment works with various materials, from cords and yarns to thin ribbons, allowing for diverse design outcomes.
Enhanced aesthetics: cording can add an elegant or rustic touch, depending on the chosen material, elevating the overall look of the embroidery.
Durability: the added cord provides reinforcement to the embroidery, often making it more robust and long-lasting.
Creativity boost: incorporating cording pushes the boundaries of traditional embroidery, allowing for a broader range of artistic expression.
Economic: utilising cords, especially if you have leftover yarns or materials, can be a cost-effective way to enhance designs without investing in more expensive embroidery materials.

Things to Keep in Mind

Cord thickness: the cording attachment is designed to accommodate cords of certain diameters. Ensure the cord or yarn you're using fits comfortably.
Tension: adjusting the tension is crucial – too tight, and the cord may break or not feed properly; too loose, and the cord might not be secured firmly to the fabric.
Stabilisation: given the added weight and texture of the cord, using an appropriate stabiliser is essential to prevent fabric puckering or distortion.
Compatible designs: not all embroidery designs are suitable for cording. Opt for designs specifically made or adjusted for the cording technique.

Tips for Using the Cording Attachment

Preparation is key: before starting, ensure the cord is free from tangles and is fed correctly into the attachment.
Test run: always test the cording on a scrap piece of fabric, especially if it's your first time or if you're using a new type of cord or yarn.
Keep an eye on the cord: while embroidering, monitor the cord's feed to ensure it doesn't snag, tangle or run out.
Trimming: after the design is complete, trim any excess cord carefully to ensure a clean finish without cutting the stitches.
Experiment: don't be afraid to experiment with different types of cords, yarns, or even thin ribbons. The varied textures and colours can produce unique and stunning results.

Incorporating cording into your embroidery projects can add depth, texture and a touch of creativity. With patience and practice, the cording attachment can become an indispensable tool in your embroidery arsenal.

Boring Device

A boring device for digital embroidery machines is a specialised attachment designed to create controlled holes in fabrics, which are then embellished with embroidery stitches. These holes can range from small, subtle punctures to larger, more pronounced cuts, depending on the design and intent.

How It Works

The boring attachment is specially designed to create controlled holes or cuts in the fabric, which are then embellished with embroidery stitches. Here's how it operates:

Attachment setup: the boring attachment replaces or attaches to the regular embroidery machine's needle or presser foot area.
Design selection: set the machine to a design made specifically for boring. This will ensure the machine knows when to cut and when to embroider.
Boring process: as the design progresses, the boring tool punctures or cuts the fabric in specific areas according to the design.
Embroidery enhancement: after the boring process, the machine then switches back to embroidering, usually outlining or embellishing around the holes made.
Finishing: once the embroidery is complete, carefully remove any small fabric remnants from the bored areas, if necessary.

Benefits of Using the Boring Attachment

Unique design element: boring adds a unique design element, allowing for eyelet embroidery, cutwork, and other decorative hole techniques.
Versatility: allows for the creation of intricate lace-like effects, perfect for projects such as table linens, garments and heirloom sewing.
Enhanced texture and look: the combination of holes and embroidery gives a multi-dimensional look to the design, making it stand out.
Creativity boost: the boring attachment expands design possibilities beyond traditional embroidery, paving the way for a myriad of artistic expressions.
Professional finish: achieve professional-looking cutwork embroidery without the need for manual cutting or tedious handwork.
Time efficiency: automates the process of creating decorative holes, saving significant time compared to manual methods.

Things to Keep in Mind

Fabric choice: not all fabrics are suitable for boring. Opt for stable fabrics that can withstand the process without fraying excessively.
Stabilisation: always use a suitable stabiliser beneath your fabric. This helps in ensuring clean cuts and prevents the fabric from puckering.
Regular maintenance: the boring tool's blade can become dull over time. Ensure it's sharp to get clean cuts.
Test first: always do a test run on a scrap piece of your chosen fabric to ensure the desired effect is achieved.

Tips for Using the Boring Device

Design selection: choose designs specifically made for boring to get optimal results. Trying to adapt a regular embroidery design may not produce the desired effect.
Watch your speed: running the machine at a slower speed can provide more control and precision when using the boring device.
Clean cuts: after the boring process, you may find small fabric remnants. Use tweezers or a similar tool to remove these gently.
Protect your fabric: if working with delicate fabrics, consider using a water-soluble topper to prevent any snagging or undue stress on the fabric.
Master the basics first: before attempting intricate designs, start with simpler ones to get a feel for the tool and how it interacts with different fabrics.

When used correctly, the boring device can elevate the look of your embroidery projects, adding a touch of sophistication and depth. Practice makes perfect, so take your time to get familiar with the tool and its capabilities.

These are just a few examples of the types of hoops and attachments available for digital embroidery. The choice of hoop/clamp or attachment depends on the specific project requirements and the machine being used for embroidery.

CAD AND DIGITISING SOFTWARE

Embarking on digital embroidery will require three significant investments: your embroidery machine, your digitising software and a device to run your software. The latter two are crucial for creating and editing designs and this is a decision you need to consider carefully. There are

Close-up of boring device tool and fabric with hole created and embroidered with satin stitch to finish.

several digitising software options available, each offering different features at varying costs. Your choice should be guided by two main factors: your budget and the specific tools you need for your embroidery projects.

Creating your own unique designs demands dedicated software. However, you might consider outsourcing your digitising tasks to a third party to save time. Nevertheless, owning your software still has its benefits. For instance, it will allow you to tweak designs more efficiently, bringing your vision to life without constantly returning to a third-party digitiser for adjustments, which can impact your time, patience and bank balance.

The cost of embroidery software can fluctuate greatly. Some require an annual renewal fee, others require a one-time payment. The price range can span from free to over £1,500 per annum. Therefore, it's wise to take your time researching, trying out free trials and asking around for recommendations before committing to a purchase. This way, you'll make an informed decision that suits your needs and budget.

Wilcom Embroidery Studio and Janome Artistic Digitiser are my go-to software programs and they each offer something different and collectively fulfil all my needs. There are others on the market for you to consider.

Wilcom E4.5 Embroidery Studio

Wilcom is a widely recognised brand in the embroidery industry, offering professional-grade digitising software. Their software, such as Wilcom EmbroideryStudio e4, provides advanced tools for designing, editing and digitising embroidery designs. It supports various file formats and offers precise control over stitch settings. This version currently comes with the Coral Draw package to allow you to edit your original artwork before digitising.

Hatch Embroidery

Hatch Embroidery, developed by Wilcom, is a user-friendly embroidery digitising software suitable for both beginners and professionals. It offers different levels of functionality, from basic to advanced, allowing users to choose the features that best meet their needs. It includes design editing tools, lettering options and a vast library of built-in designs.

Janome Artistic Digitiser

Relatively new to the market, this software is aimed more at graphic designers and artists as opposed to technical digitisers. The Janome Artistic Digitiser sets itself apart with its seamless integration with Janome embroidery machines, ensuring optimal compatibility and smooth operation. It stands out by offering a user-friendly interface that caters to both novices and professionals, combining advanced editing features with the simplicity needed for beginners.

Exclusive to this software are design features that cater specifically to the unique functions of Janome machines, such as their stitch composition and design formatting, providing users with a tailored experience that enhances the capabilities of their Janome embroidery hardware.

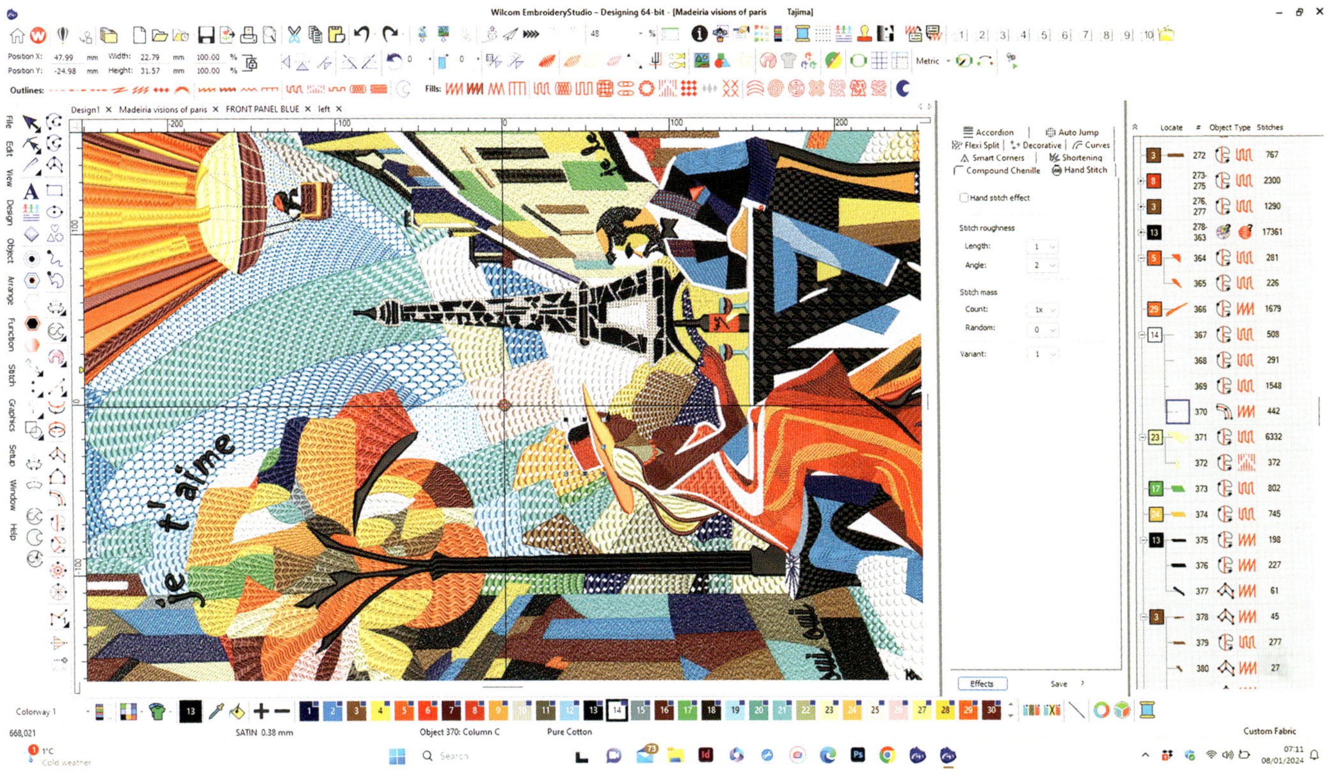

The Wilcom software; working area with tools around the edges and design in the centre.

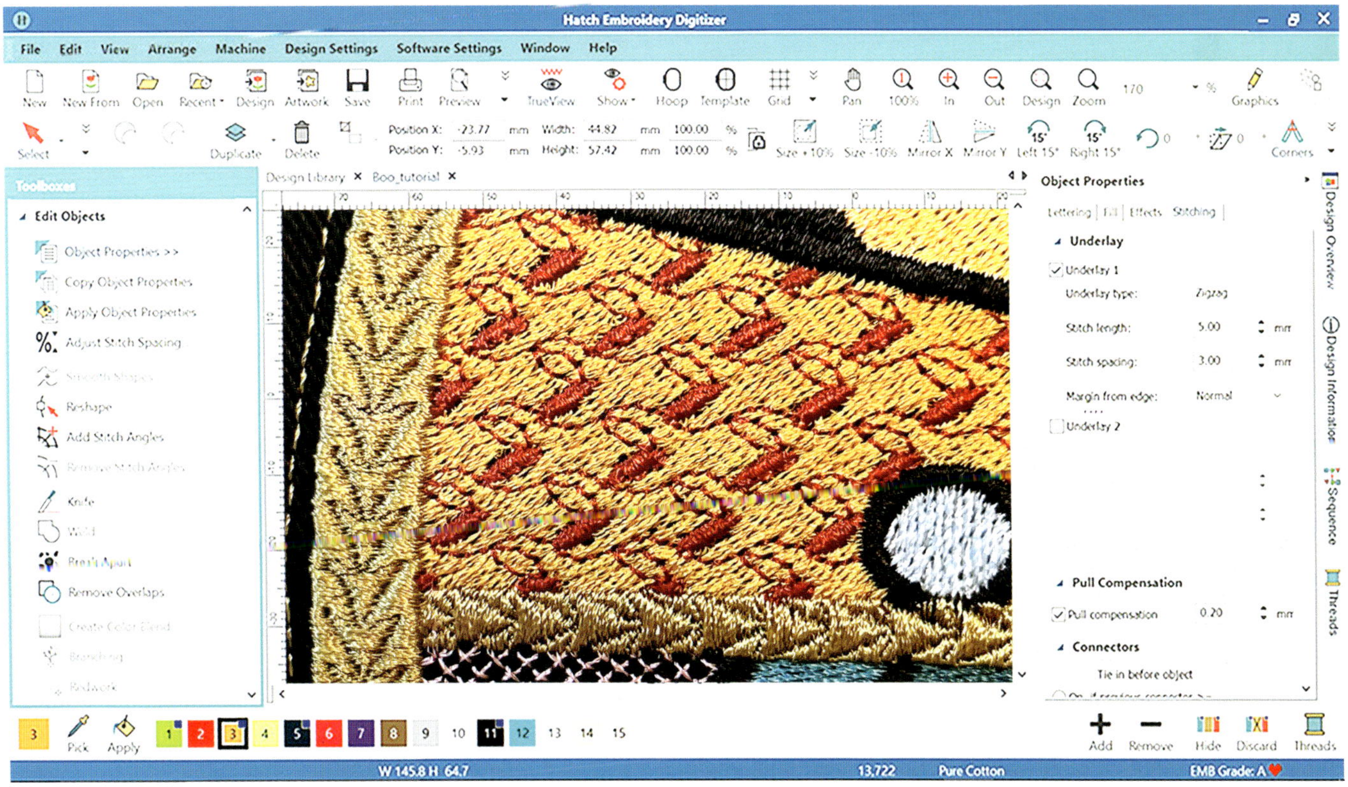

The Hatch working screen with close-up detail of embroidery design.

Janome Artistic working screen with close-up detail of Old English Sheepdog artwork.

Bernina Embroidery Software

This software is designed for Bernina embroidery machines and offers features such as automatic digitising, advanced lettering and monogramming.

Embird

This software offers digitising features, such as auto digitising, splitting, stitching order control and stitch editor. Reasonably priced, it allows you to purchase add on modules to make your software more appropriate to your needs.

Brother PE-Design

This software is designed for Brother embroidery machines and offers advanced features such as automatic digitising, advanced lettering and monogramming.

Embrilliance

This embroidery software has a focus on ease of use and affordability. Their products, such as Embrilliance Essentials and StitchArtist, provide basic to intermediate digitising capabilities. They offer features such as design manipulation, lettering and stitch editing.

PulseID

Pulse is another prominent provider of embroidery digitising software. Their software suite, including Pulse Signature, Tajima DG/ML by Pulse, and PulseID, offers a range of features for digitising and customising embroidery designs. They provide powerful editing tools, lettering options and integration with various embroidery machine formats. A great feature is the ability to communicate rendered designs for customer sign-off.

Floriani Total Control U

This is a comprehensive embroidery digitising software with advanced tools for creating and editing embroidery designs. It offers a wide range of stitch types, automatic digitising features and precise control over stitch settings. It supports multiple file formats and integrates with various embroidery machine brands.

Sierra Embroidery Office

Sierra Embroidery Office is a feature-rich embroidery software with tools for digitising, editing and managing embroidery designs. It offers advanced digitising options, lettering capabilities and extensive stitch editing tools. It supports multiple machine formats and offers compatibility with various embroidery machines.

Design Doodler – The Deer's Embroidery Legacy

Design Doodler is a new software program available on PC and iPad, enabling the user to sketch, trace or doodle designs without the technical aspect of digitising.

These are just a few examples of embroidery digitising software programs available on the market. When choosing a software, consider factors such as your skill level, desired features, compatibility with your embroidery machine and budget. It's recommended to explore different options, read reviews, and, if possible, use trial versions to find the software that best suits your needs and workflow.

OUTSOURCING DIGITISING TO THIRD-PARTY PROFESSIONALS

Outsourcing your digitising is an option you could consider if you do not want to invest in software or if you have no interest or time in learning the skills required to convert your art into stitches. There are plenty of digitisers out there, all with various levels of expertise and styles. The internet enables you to employ the services of experts overseas as files are often emailed to the buyer upon completion. Finding a digitiser is relatively easy as many advertise their services on popular social media sites, such as Facebook groups; however, finding the right digitiser for your work may require a bit of trial and error. You may end up having several digitisers you can turn to, each with their own strengths and weaknesses. A digitiser maybe excellent at animal portraits but may not be as good at human portraits, for example. Having two or three digitisers you can outsource to is a manageable number and enough to build up good relationships and trust.

There are advantages and disadvantages to outsourcing your artwork which you need to consider.

Advantages

On the positive side, outsourcing can save considerable time and energy for businesses or individuals unfamiliar with the intricacies of digitisation. This enables them to focus on their core competencies, such as design, making or marketing. Additionally, professional digitising companies often have access to state-of-the-art software and skilled experts, ensuring high-quality outcomes and potentially faster turnaround times. Moreover, it can be cost-effective in the short run, eliminating the need for expensive software purchases or training sessions. The speed and accuracy of using an expert digitiser can far outweigh a novice who is attempting to digitise and making many mistakes affecting stitch-out and overall quality.

Disadvantages

On the downside, outsourcing introduces a dependency on external entities, which can sometimes result in miscommunications or misunderstandings regarding design specifics. This can lead to iterations or revisions, delaying the final output. There's also the risk of intellectual property breaches; sharing designs with third parties always carries the danger of unauthorised reproduction or leaks. Lastly, while outsourcing may be cost-effective initially, repeated services could accumulate costs over time, which might outweigh the benefits for businesses producing designs regularly. Thus, while outsourcing digitising offers immediate convenience and expertise, it comes with potential challenges that businesses must consider carefully. Many digitisers I have used tend to be abroad and language issues can be problematic, especially when you are trying to explain specific changes you would like them make.

Engaging with a third-party digitiser typically unfolds in a structured, step-by-step manner:

1. **Identify an appropriate digitiser for your work**
   Start by sourcing a reputable digitisation specialist, often based on recommendations, reviews, or industry credentials. Does their style match what you need? Are they reliable? Can they do what you need them to do?
2. **Submit your artwork**
   Forward your design or artwork to the digitiser, which can be done via email, a social media platform, or even instant messaging apps like WhatsApp.
3. **Detail your specifications**
   Clearly convey your needs, including the type of fabric, desired size, intended use (be it for a garment or a standalone art piece), and the make of your embroidery machine, so they send you the digitised file in a compatible format.

4. **Request a preliminary quote**
   Before any work begins, ensure you obtain a cost estimate to avoid any surprises.
5. **Authorise the project**
   If the quote is within your budget and you're confident in the digitiser's expertise, give the green light for the digitisation process to commence.
6. **Receive the final outputs**
   Upon completion, you'll be provided with a master file, allowing for modifications if you possess the necessary software. Additionally, you may also receive a PDF production sheet, a jpeg representation of the digitised embroidery, and an exported file tailored to be compatible with your specific embroidery machine.
7. **Settle the invoice**
   Conclude the process by processing payment through the agreed-upon methods, such as bank transfers, PayPal, or other secure platforms.

Amendments after digitising is completed

This phase can occasionally present challenges, especially when modifications to the original design are wanted. Precision in communication is crucial, particularly if you're liaising with an international digitiser where language barriers might exist. Articulating the desired changes with utmost clarity can minimise misunderstandings and iterations. It's also important to be familiar with the revision policies of the digitiser. While some may offer a set number of complimentary edits, others might impose a fee for each individual alteration. To sidestep potential complications, it's advisable to settle on the terms of revisions during the initial job negotiations. This proactive approach ensures both parties are aligned in their expectations and minimises the possibility of disputes or unforeseen costs.

Based on my own experience, outsourcing embroidery digitising can save a lot of time. However, many outsourcers I've encountered tend to use only two basic stitch types: tatami and satin. This approach often results in a design that appears relatively flat and lacks the textural qualities that come from a diverse range of stitches or techniques such as appliqué. Digitisers are skilled technicians, not necessarily creative artists, so they may not always be able to infuse the design with the creative vision needed to enhance its textural impact. That said, if you have access to digitising software and are skilled in its use, outsourcing the initial digitising to a third party can get you most of the way to your goal. The digitised outcome will be logically organised for stitch-out. This allows you to open the master file in your software, adjust stitch types and shapes to better meet your creative needs, and refine the textural elements, all without having to digitise the design from scratch.

COMPUTER OR LAPTOP

If you have decided to invest in digitising software, you will need a device to run it from. Choosing a computer or laptop for digitising software requires careful consideration of several key factors. I have listed some points below to help you make an informed choice.

Purpose and Software Needs
First, identify the specific digitising software you plan to use. Different software applications have varying system requirements. Look at the recommended requirements (not just the minimum) of the software to ensure optimal performance.

Processor (CPU)
Most digitising software is processor-intensive. Opt for a high-performance CPU, preferably quad-core or better. Intel i5 or i7, or AMD Ryzen series are generally considered robust choices.

Memory (RAM)
A minimum of 8GB RAM is recommended for basic tasks, but 16GB or more can offer smoother multitasking and better handling of complex designs. If you are digitising very large art pieces, then more RAM is recommended.

Storage
Solid State Drives (SSD) offer faster data access speeds than traditional Hard Disk Drives (HDD). This means quicker boot times and faster software performance. Aim for at least 256GB SSD or a combination of SSD (for operating

system and software) and HDD (for data storage). I store all my files in a cloud format, enabling me to open the files on different devices if need be.

Graphics Card (GPU)

While many digitising tasks are CPU-intensive, a good GPU can aid in rendering graphics smoothly. Dedicated graphics cards from NVIDIA or AMD with at least 2GB VRAM are ideal, especially if the software leverages GPU acceleration.

Display

A larger screen (15 inches or more) with high resolution (Full HD or better) will offer clearer visuals and more workspace. If colour accuracy is critical, consider screens with good colour calibration capabilities. Opting for multiple displays can also help with your productivity.

Ports and Connectivity

Ensure the device has sufficient USB ports for dongles, external drives and other peripherals. Also, check for other connection types you might need, such as HDMI for external displays.

Operating System

Most digitising software is designed for Windows, though some programs work on macOS. Ensure compatibility with your chosen OS. If using macOS, you might need to run a Windows partition or emulator for certain software.

Battery Life (for laptops)

If portability is essential and you're leaning towards a laptop, consider battery life, especially if you plan to work on the go.

Brand and Support

Opt for reputable brands with good customer reviews. Ensure they offer sound customer support and warranty services, especially if you encounter hardware or compatibility issues.

Budget

Higher-end specifications often come at a premium. Determine your budget and prioritise features that are most crucial for your digitising tasks.

Future-proofing

Technology evolves rapidly. Consider purchasing a device that is slightly ahead of your current needs to ensure it remains relevant and efficient for a few years.

In conclusion, researching and comparing various models based on the above criteria will help you find the perfect computer or laptop for your digitising software needs. If possible, seek recommendations from fellow digitisers or relevant forums for real-world insights. There are popular digital embroidery Facebook groups you can join and most people will happily offer advice and recommendations based on their set up.

My personal preference is to work on a laptop (allows for portability), large screen size, fast processor speed and RAM. A good graphics card helps the digitising process to be smooth and less troublesome. I invested in a gaming Alienware machine and, although I do not use it for gaming, I find it is perfect for digitising, especially large art pieces.

David's Alienware laptop used for digitising.

Embroidered laptop art piece for the Hand & Lock, The Prize – Wilcom Digital Award – winning entry piece, 2021.

EMBROIDERY NEEDLES

Choosing the appropriate embroidery needle is a crucial factor in enhancing both productivity and the overall quality of the embroidery. The selection of the embroidery needle – both the needle point and needle size – depends on several factors. These include the type of fabric to be embroidered upon (and the stabiliser), the embroidery thread in terms of both its material and thickness, and the complexity of the embroidery pattern, particularly its stitch density. Accurately aligning these factors guarantees the best outcomes when it comes to the embroidery stitch-out.

There are a lot of needles on the market for both domestic and industrial embroidery machines and it can be confusing as to which is best for your machine and the task at hand. Generally, needles can be categorised in terms of their material type, point type, needle size and whether they are suitable for domestic or industrial machines.

Material: most needles are chrome-plated steel and are silver in appearance with a groove along one edge. Titanium needles appear golden and are more robust, making them ideal for bulky and tough-to-penetrate materials.
Needle point type: there are generally three main types of points available: sharp, ball point and cutting.
Needle size: all the needle point types are available in a range of sizes, from fine to large and the one you choose is determined by your thread and fabric selection and the stitch density of your design.

Needle Anatomy

The anatomy of an embroidery needle consists of several integral components: the eye, shaft, shank, point, groove and scarf. At the needle's end, the eye serves as the passageway for the embroidery thread, typically oriented forward when inserted into the machine. The needle's shaft, which gauges its size and length, extends to the shank – a broader section fitted into the machine's needle holder to ensure stability. The point, found at the extremity of the needle, is finely crafted for smooth fabric penetration. Along the shaft lies the groove, a path that directs the thread towards the eye during the stitching process and should face forward when the needle is mounted. The scarf, a subtle notch just above the eye on the needle's reverse, facilitates the bobbin hook's access to the thread, thereby minimising skipped stitches in machine sewing. It is crucial to remember that incorrect needle insertion can impede proper stitching, leading to inferior stitch quality or thread breakage.

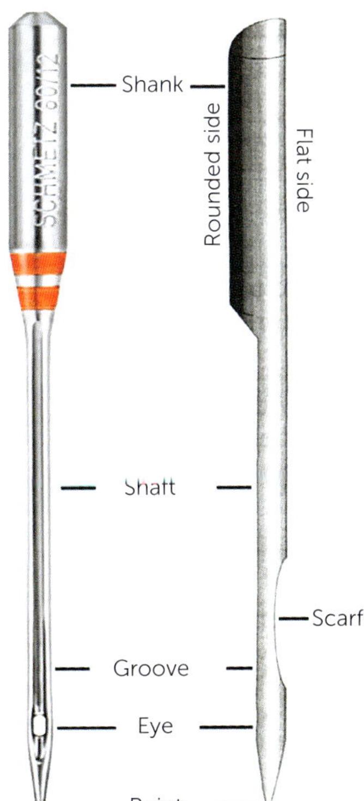

Machine embroidery needle anatomy, identifying the key elements and terminology.

Here are the main needle types available

Sharp (universal) needles: these are the most commonly used needles in digital embroidery. They have a sharp point and work well with a wide range of fabrics, including woven and knitted fabrics. Sharp needles are suitable for general embroidery projects and come in a range of sizes from 60/8 to 110/18.

Ball point needles: ball point needles are designed specifically for knitted and stretch fabrics. They have a rounded tip that slides between the fabric's fibres, reducing the risk of damaging or breaking delicate knitted threads. Ball point needles are ideal for embroidering on T-shirts, jerseys and other stretchy fabrics.

Cutting needles: these are needles that have an extra-sharp point that easily penetrates dense fabrics. Some cutting needles are specifically for non-wovens such as leathers, and some are suitable for fine wovens such as silks. Leather needles will cut through the skin, creating a cleaner hole than a sharp needle would.

Cutwork needles: many of the domestic embroidery brands (Janome, Brother, and so on) offer a cutwork set of needles for their domestic embroidery machines which will cut holes in fabric, similar to the boring device on an industrial embroidery machine.

Metallic needles: metallic needles are specially designed for embroidering with metallic or speciality threads. They have a larger eye and longer groove to accommodate the thicker metallic threads and a smooth, polished surface that reduces friction. Metallic needles help prevent thread breakage and ensure smooth stitching.

Twin needles: twin needles consist of two needles mounted on a single shank, placed side by side. They are used to create parallel rows of stitching or decorative effects, such as double lines or parallel fills. Twin needles come in various sizes and can add interesting textures to embroidery designs.

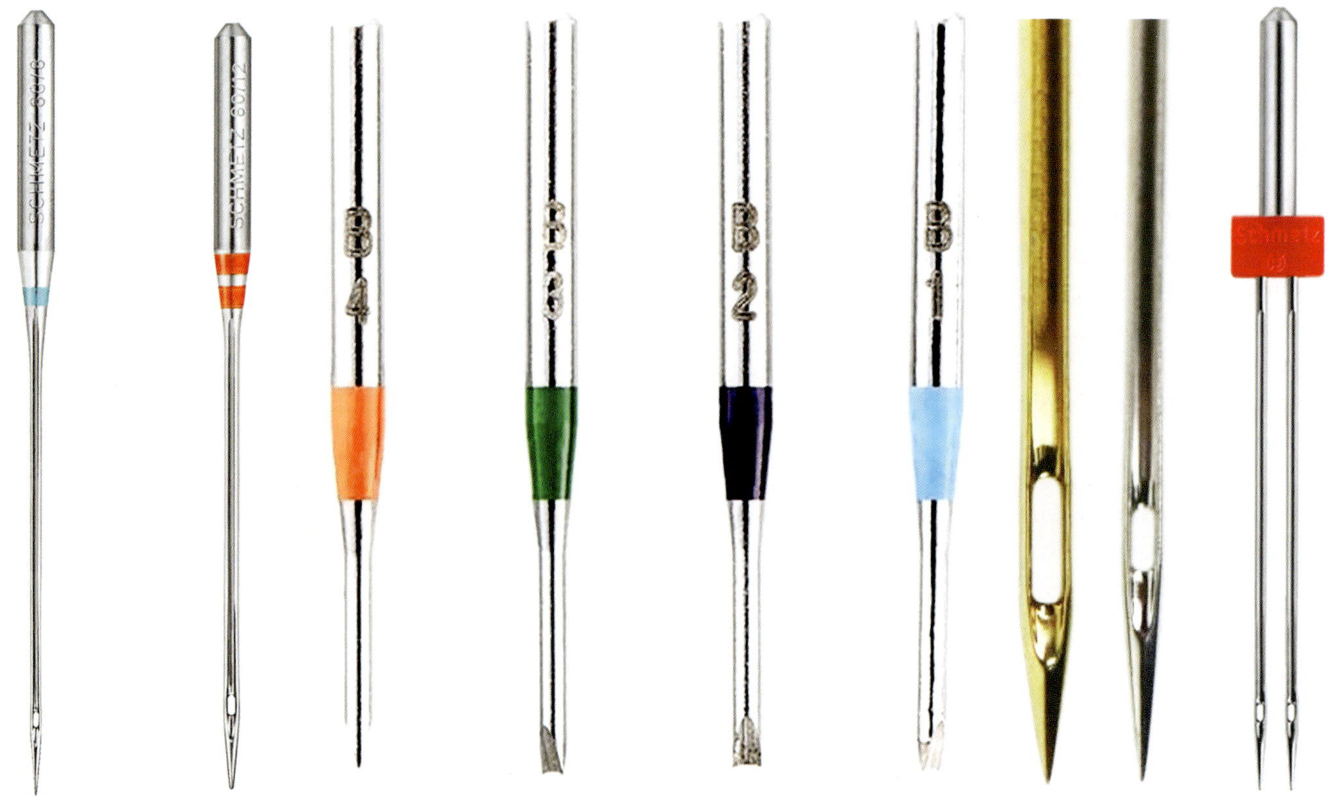

Universal machine embroidery needle.

A ball point machine embroidery needle.

Cutwork needle set for domestic embroidery machines.

Close-up of a metallic needle next to a standard needle.

A twin needle for a domestic embroidery machine enables two rows to be stitched simultaneously.

A wing embroidery needle.

A pack of titanium needles, ideal for embroidering with metallic threads.

Wing needles: wing needles have wide, flared wings on the sides of the needle shaft. These needles are used to create heirloom-style embroidery, often found in techniques like drawn thread work or openwork embroidery. Wing needles produce decorative holes or cutouts in the fabric while stitching.

Titanium-coated needles: titanium-coated needles are more durable and last longer than regular needles, suitable for thicker fabrics and items such as belts, dog collars, bag straps and so on.

It's essential to select the appropriate needle based on the fabric type, thread type and the design you're working on to ensure optimal stitching results and minimise the risk of fabric damage, thread breakage or poor stitch-out quality. Always refer to the machine's manual and consider the recommendations of the embroidery machine manufacturer for the best needle selection.

EMBROIDERY NEEDLE SIZES

Also referred to as needle count, digital embroidery needle sizes are typically specified using a numbering system, which can vary depending on the manufacturer. This can be confusing!

The needle size determines the thickness of the needle shaft and the size of the needle eye, which can affect the stitching quality and the compatibility with different fabrics and threads. Below are some key points to understand about digital embroidery needle sizes.

Needle size numbering system: needles are labelled with numbers such as 75/11, 80/12, 90/14, and so on. The first number represents the European metric sizing system, while the second number represents the American sizing system. These numbers indicate the diameter of the needle shaft in hundredths of a millimetres or thousandths of an inch, respectively.

Metric (European)	*65*	*70*	*75*	*80*	*85*	*90*	*95*	*100*
American	*9*	*10*	*11*	*12*	*13*	*14*	*15*	*16*

Smaller vs larger needle sizes: smaller needle sizes have a thinner shaft, while larger needle sizes have a thicker shaft. For example, a 75/11 needle is smaller and thinner than a 90/14 needle. Smaller needle sizes are suitable for lightweight fabrics and delicate designs, while larger needle sizes are better for thicker fabrics or dense embroidery designs.

The bigger the needle, shaft, eye and number are, the more suitable the needle is for thicker threads and thicker fabrics. The smaller the needle, shaft, eye and number are, the more suitable the needle is for finer threads and finer fabrics.

Fabric compatibility: the choice of needle size depends on the fabric being embroidered. Lightweight fabrics such as silk or organza may require smaller needle sizes to avoid leaving visible holes or causing damage. Medium-weight fabrics such as cotton or linen often work well with standard needle sizes, such as 75/11 and 80/12. Thicker or denser fabrics such as denim or canvas may require larger needle sizes, such as 90/14 or higher, to penetrate the fabric properly.

Thread compatibility: needle size also affects thread compatibility. Thinner threads generally work well with smaller needle sizes, while thicker threads may require larger needle sizes to accommodate their size. It's important to ensure that the needle eye is large enough to accommodate the thread without causing friction or breakage. If your thread keeps breaking during production, it's worth checking the suitability of the needle in the first instance. Some metallic and specialist threads are very fussy about the type of needle they prefer, so it's always worth doing some research and testing on scrap fabric if you are not sure.

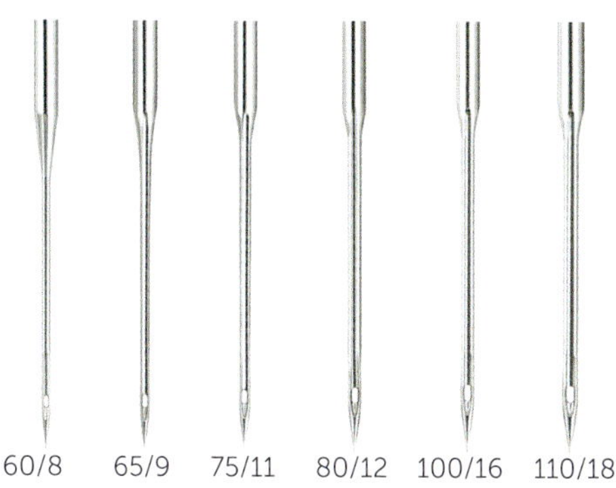

Machine embroidery needles from smallest (left) to largest (right).

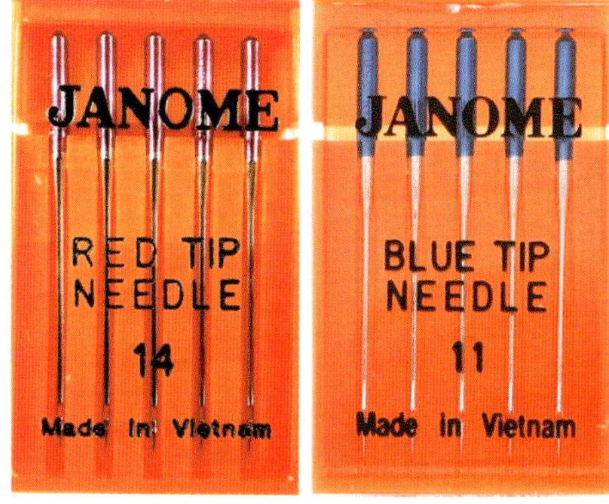

Packs of Janome red and blue tip needles.

Design complexity: the complexity of the embroidery design can also influence the choice of needle size. Intricate or densely stitched designs may require smaller needle sizes to achieve precise stitching and prevent thread build-up.

It's important to refer to your embroidery machine's user manual or consult with the manufacturer to determine the recommended needle sizes for your specific machine. Additionally, it's advisable to test different needle sizes on a fabric swatch before starting a full embroidery project, to ensure optimal results and minimize the risk of needle damage or fabric distortion.

Janome Needles: Red, Blue and Purple Needles

As a regular user of Janome embroidery machines, I often have to remind myself what the colour labelling on the needles and packaging means. Simply put, it refers to the needle size and it affects its usage. The blue tip needle is a size 11 and is thinner, making it an excellent choice for all-purpose use, including machine embroidery and general sewing on a variety of medium-weight fabrics. It has a larger eye which is great for preventing thread breakage and easing the threading process. The red tip needle is a size 14, which is thicker, offering extra strength and durability. This needle is best suited for dense embroidery and working with thick fabrics, as its design can handle heavier material without causing thread breakage.

For those working on particularly heavy fabrics or high-density embroidery designs, Janome also offers the purple tip needle, which has a special 'cobra' head to prevent skipped stitches and is recommended for use with fluffier threads such as cotton, and for sewing knits and synthetic fabrics.

How to Fit an Embroidery Needle to Your Machine

It is vital that the needle is fitted correctly, otherwise it simply won't embroider, or the quality will be jeopardised. The groove of the needle needs to be at the front, with the eye of the needle facing forwards or slightly to the right (as you face it). There is a debate on this, but if in doubt, face it forward and see what the stitch outcome is. The following image shows the left needle, which is correctly inserted, and the right needle, which has been inserted so the eye is facing left; this is incorrect and will result in stitch-out problems (thread breaking, skipped stitches, thread fraying and so on).

When to Change the Needle

It is very easy to overlook the importance of the needle and its condition, replacing only when it breaks in the machine. No doubt we have all been there – it is easy to do! However, to maintain productivity and stitch quality it is important to break this habit and begin regularly analysing the stitching to best determine when a needle needs replacing. Blunt, bent or damaged needles can cause unsightly stitch issues such as looping, unevenness, misalignment, thread snapping or nesting (gathering of threads underneath the fabric, causing a bulk, like a nest). Sometimes you may not visually see any damage, but if you are having stitching issues, replacing the needle may solve your problems.

The needle may need replacing a long time before it breaks. As a guide, I change my needles:

- every two or three weeks
- when starting an important new project
- working on delicate, precious or expensive fabric
- working with bulk or raised embroidery effects, for example, foam or denser 3D fills
- change in the weight of yarn being used
- change in the type of yarn being used, especially metallics or thicker wool types.

If you have multiple needles on your machine, consider allocating a needle for a specific purpose; for example, one needle for metallic thread, one for fine detailing and so on. Label your machine accordingly to remind yourself

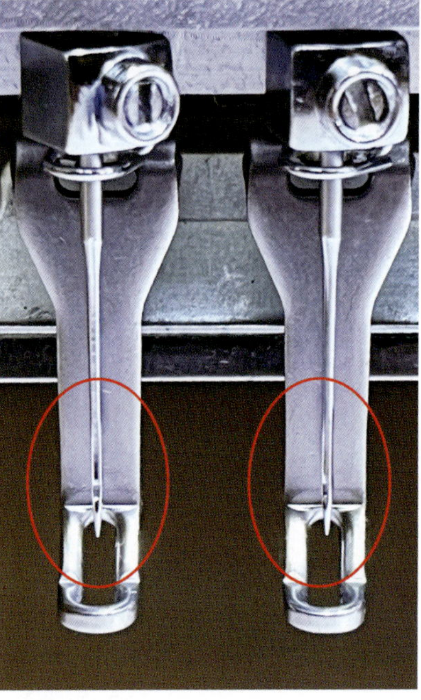

A correctly (left) and incorrectly fitted needle (right).

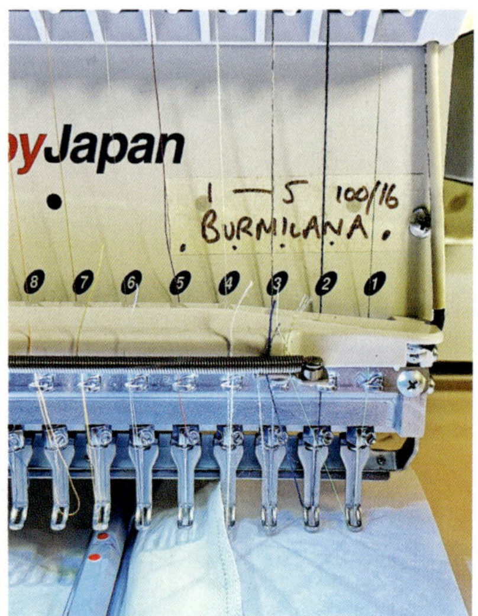

A multi-needle embroidery machine labelled to show larger needle sizes are inserted for a specific thread thickness and type.

which each needle is and what it is for. Avoid using these needles for regular embroidery so they don't become blunt or damaged. Here I have allocated needles 1 to 5 on my machine for Burmilana thread, which is three times thicker and softer than a standard machine thread, therefore requiring a larger needle size. I have opted for 100/16 needles whilst keeping the others at 75/11.

Selecting the Correct Needle for Your Fabric

Wovens:

Linens 70/10 to 80/12 Sharp needles (Universal)
Cotton Canvas 75/11 or 80/12 Sharp needles (Universal)
Denim Jeans 75/11 Sharp needles (Universal)
Cotton Shirts 70/10 to 80/12 Sharp needles (Universal)
Silk 60/8 to 75/11 Sharp needles (Universal)
Organza 65/9 Sharp needles (Universal)
Satin 75/11 Sharp needles (Universal)
Sweatshirts 70/10 to 80/12 Medium ball point or Big ball point
Taffeta 65/9 Sharp needles (Universal)
Velvet 65/9 Medium ball point

Knitwear:

Knitwear 70/10 to 80/12 Medium ball point
Chunky Knitwear 90/14 to 100/16 Big ball point

Non-Woven:

Leather 80/12 Sharp (Universal) or cutting point
Lycra, Spandex 70/10 to 80/12 Medium ball point
Vinyl 75/11 Sharp needles (Universal)

Remember, that some fabrics are very unforgiving. Once you have punctured a hole with the needle, it will remain as a hole and be visible. Leathers particularly can be problematic and fall under this category. It is always worth testing fabrics before you start your project as you may need to change the thread, needle and backing type and also the digitising settings for your design. Take extra care around non-wovens, knits, stretch and delicates.

DIGITAL EMBROIDERY THREADS

Threads excite me and have a massive impact on a design and the outcome. There are various types of threads available for digital embroidery, each offering unique characteristics and suitability for different applications. Digital embroidery threads differ from hand embroidery threads and normal sewing threads, and you may need to buy them from specialist stores. There are several good online stores for you to purchase threads and other materials, with ease (*see* Useful Resources on page 188). Embroidery threads often

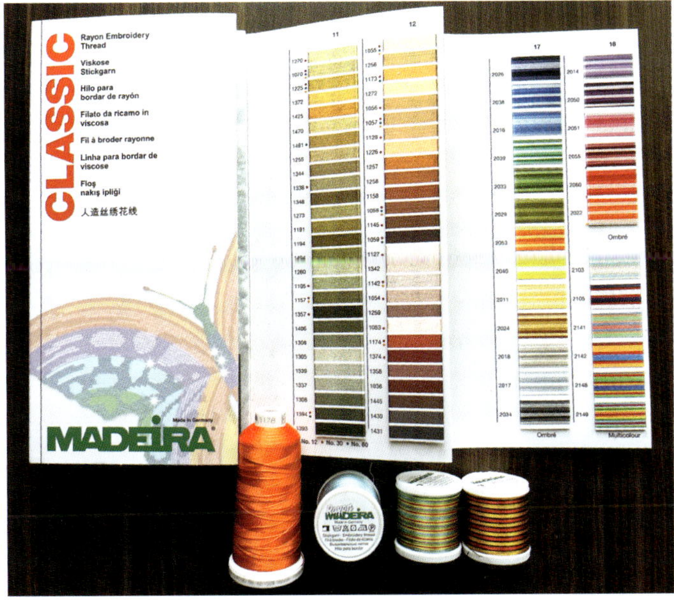

Madeira Classic Rayon threads shade card and thread cones.

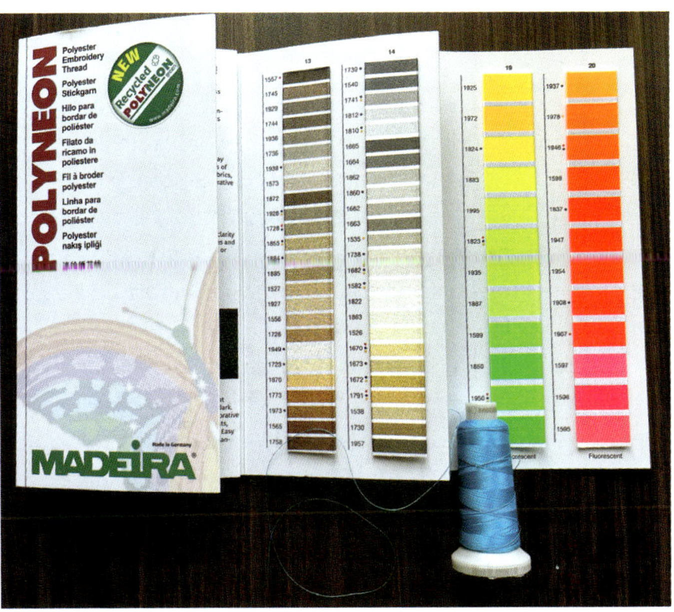

Madeira Polyester threads (Polyneon) shade card and thread cone.

Madeira Metallic threads shade card and thread cones.

come in cones of 5,000m (5,470yd) or cops (mini-cones) of 1,000m (1,095yd). Depending on your machine type, you may be restricted by the size of thread you can use.

Here are some commonly used types of digital embroidery threads:

Rayon thread: rayon thread is one of the most popular choices for embroidery. It is known for its vibrant colours, high sheen and smooth texture. Rayon thread is versatile and works well on a wide range of fabrics, providing a luxurious appearance to the embroidered designs.

Polyester thread: polyester thread is another widely used option for digital embroidery. It offers excellent colourfastness, durability and resistance to fading and shrinkage. Polyester thread is known for its strength and ability to withstand frequent washing and abrasion, making it suitable for various applications, fabrics and product items. This is my go-to thread due to its reliability, strength and vast array of colour options.

Metallic thread: metallic threads are used to add a touch of shimmer and sparkle to embroidery designs. They are composed of a polyester core wrapped with metallic foil or metallic fibres. Metallic threads require special attention during stitching to avoid thread breakage, such as using a metallic needle and adjusting tension settings.

Cotton thread: cotton thread is a natural fibre thread suitable for embroidery on natural fabrics such as cotton, linen, and denim. It offers a matte finish and a soft, natural appearance. Cotton thread is often chosen for vintage or rustic-style embroidery projects. Cotton thread is more likely to break compared to polyester thread if the settings, needles and backing are not appropriate.

Silk thread: silk thread is a luxurious option for embroidery, known for its smoothness and lustrous sheen. It is commonly used for high-end or speciality embroidery projects where a refined and delicate appearance is desired. Silk thread is suitable for fine fabrics and intricate designs.

Variegated (ombre) thread: variegated threads have colour changes along their length, creating a multicoloured or gradient effect in embroidery designs. They add visual interest and dimension to the stitched designs and are available in various thread types such as rayon, polyester or cotton.

Wool-effect thread: Burmilana thread (by Madeira) is a 50 per cent acrylic—50 per cent wool mix, three times thicker than standard embroidery thread. It is a strong, thick thread which fills designs quickly and has a hand-crafted wool look. Filane by Gunold is 100 per cent acrylic and also gives a wool effect.

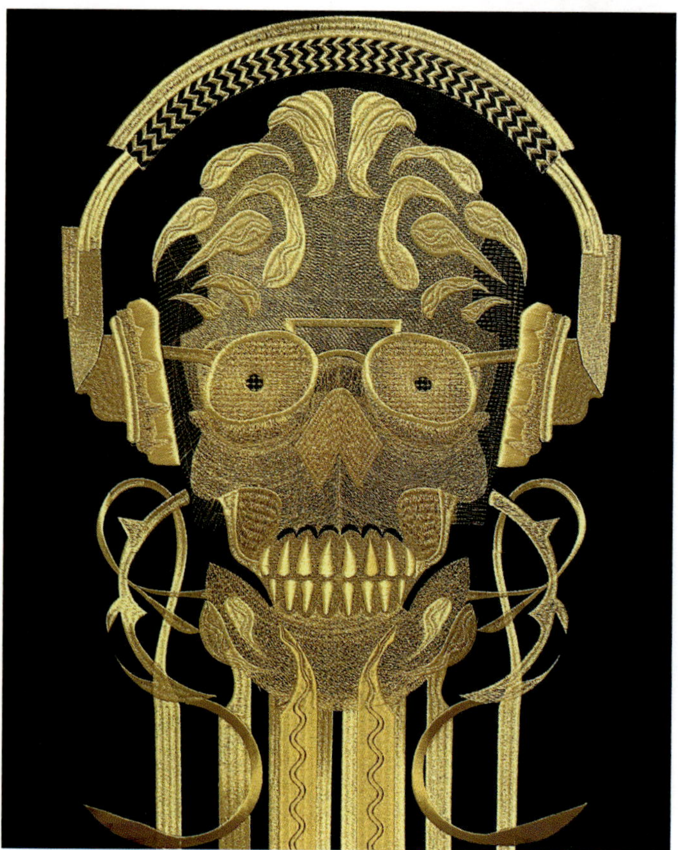
Large skull embroidered with metallic golden threads.

Gunold Cotton threads shade card and thread cones.

Madeira Rayon Ombré threads shade card and thread cones in a drawer.

A spool of silk machine embroidery thread.

Speciality threads (smart threads): there are speciality threads available for specific embroidery effects or applications. This includes glow-in-the-dark threads, glitter, invisible, fluorescent, textured, electro-conductive, light reactive, fire resistant, heat reactive, sustainable

Madeira Burmilana wool-effect threads shade card and thread cones.

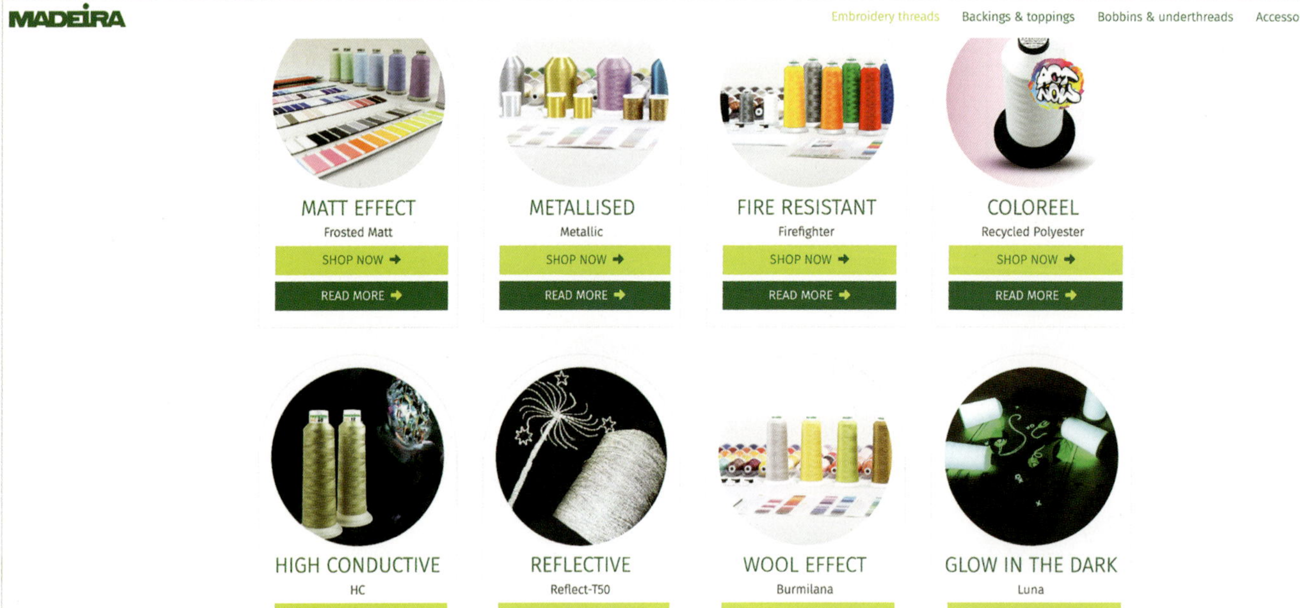

Madeira website showing range of specialist threads you can purchase.

and more. These threads are used to create unique and eye-catching effects in embroidery designs, and can be used within the medical, scientific, engineering and sports industries to create products with specialist functional properties.

It's important to consider the purpose, fabric type, design complexity, desired appearance, and durability requirements when choosing the appropriate thread for digital embroidery. Experimenting with different thread types and brands can help you discover the ones that work best for your specific projects and achieve the desired results. Some threads work better on one machine than others.

THICKNESS OF DIGITAL EMBROIDERY THREADS

Digital embroidery thread sizing can vary depending on the manufacturer and the type of thread. Understanding thread sizing is important for selecting the appropriate thread for your embroidery projects. Here are some key points to understand about digital embroidery thread sizing.

Thread weight: thread weight refers to the thickness or fineness of the thread. It is usually denoted by a number, such as 40wt, 50wt or 60wt. The higher the number, the finer and thinner the thread. For example, 40wt is thicker than 50wt. Thread weight affects the appearance and strength of the stitching.

My go-to thread weight for my average project type is 40wt. For fine detailing, I lean towards 60wt and if I need slightly thicker thread, I choose 30wt.

Tex size: tex is another measurement used to indicate the size of embroidery threads. It is denoted by a number followed by the letter 'T,' such as 30T, 40T or 60T. In the tex system, a higher number represents a thicker thread. For example, 40T is thicker than 30T. The tex measurement is based on the weight in grams of 1,000 metres of thread.

Number of ply: the number of ply refers to the number of strands twisted together to form the thread. Most embroidery threads are available in two-ply or three-ply options. Two-ply threads are thinner, while three-ply threads are slightly thicker and offer more coverage.

Compatibility with needle and fabric: thread sizing is important to consider in relation to the needle size and the fabric being embroidered. Thicker threads may require a larger needle size with a wider eye to prevent thread breakage or tension issues. Similarly, the choice of thread size should be compatible with the fabric's weight and density to ensure proper stitch formation and avoid fabric damage.

A close-up of an embroidered art piece using Burmilana, frosted matt and polyester threads.

Design considerations: the thread size can also affect the appearance and detail of the embroidered design. Finer threads, such as 50wt or 60wt, are often used for intricate or detailed designs where finer stitching is desired. Thicker threads, such as 30wt or 40wt, can provide more visibility and impact in designs or for decorative purposes. Mixing thread types within a design can result in striking outcomes that can add more depth and interest to the outcome. The following image shows an art piece consisting of three different types of embroidery thread, used to add depth, texture and a sense of handcraft and age to the piece.

If you are new to digital embroidery, I recommend starting with a polyester 40wt thread as it is very durable, robust and forgiving. Some of the speciality threads may require a specific needle type or a change in machine tension settings, and so on. Once you start changing machine tension settings, you can potentially cause unwanted stitch issues which may be hard to correct. If this happens, it is worth consulting your manufacturer's instruction manual, or even an embroidery machine specialist who would be able to reset your machine to factory defaults.

STABILISERS

Embroidery backing, also known as stabiliser, or backing material, is a crucial component in the embroidery process. It is a material that is placed underneath the fabric during embroidery to provide support, stability, and prevent distortion or puckering of the design. Placing a stabiliser on top of the fabric can prevent the embroidery stitches sinking into the fabric and becoming invisible; this is particularly useful for fabrics with a pile, such as towelling or velvet. Bear in mind, though, that you do not want to see any stabiliser after you have finished embroidering, therefore you need to select a suitable stabiliser that can be easily removed if used on top of the fabric.

Following are some key purposes of using digital embroidery backing.

Stability: embroidery machines create stitches by penetrating the fabric with a needle, the upper thread looping with the bobbin thread and pulling both threads back through the fabrics. The backing material acts as a stabiliser, holding the fabric in place and preventing it from shifting during the stitching process. Stability ensures that the design is stitched accurately and prevents any misalignment and reduces distortion. (Some heavier fabrics may not require additional stabilising as they are already stable enough, adding additional stabiliser would have no additional benefits.)

Tension: backing helps maintain proper tension while the machine is embroidering, reducing the chance of the fabric puckering or wrinkling. It supports the stitches, allowing them to lie flat and evenly on the fabric surface.

Preventing show-through: in some cases, the design's thread colours may be vibrant or dense and, without backing, they could show through on the reverse side of the fabric. Backing material adds an extra layer between the fabric and the stitches, preventing the design from being visible on the other side.

Reinforcement: backing provides additional strength to the fabric during the embroidery process. It helps stabilise delicate or stretchy fabrics, preventing them

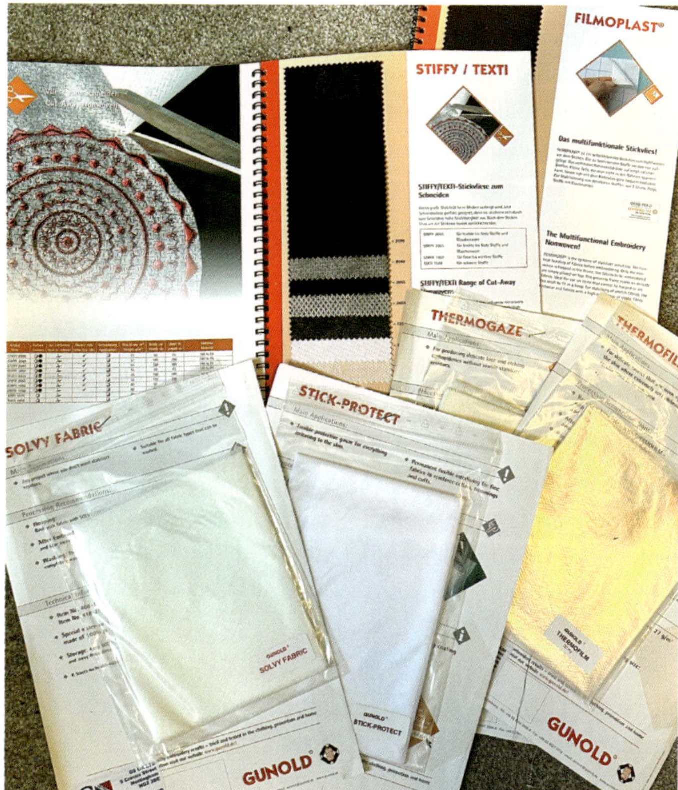

A selection of stabilisers that can help support your embroidery projects.

from stretching or distorting under the tension of the stitches.

Clean finish: once the embroidery is complete, the backing material is often trimmed away to remove excess, leaving behind a clean finish. This allows the design to appear crisp and professional without any visible traces of the stabiliser.

It's important to choose the appropriate type and weight of backing material based on the fabric type, design complexity and desired outcome. It is also possible to use more than one layer of backing, or multiple types of backing in a design. The more backing, the stiffer and more rigid the fabric becomes.

Different backing types include tear-away, cut-away, wash-away, fusible, adhesive and sustainable, each suited for different fabrics and applications.

Tear-Away Stabiliser

A tear-away stabiliser is a type of embroidery backing designed to provide temporary support to fabric during the embroidery process. Once the embroidery is complete, the stabiliser can be torn away, leaving only the fabric and the embroidery design. Weights generally range from 40gm to 75gm.

Characteristics:

Temporary support: unlike cut-away stabilisers that remain with the fabric indefinitely, tear-away stabilisers are meant to be removed after embroidery.
Less dense: generally less dense than cut-away stabilisers, making them easier to tear.
Fibrous texture: the texture aids in the tearing process without stressing or distorting the stitches.

Common uses:

Woven fabrics: especially effective for stable, woven fabrics that require minimal stretch support.
Logos and monograms: ideal for simple designs or text-based embroidery that doesn't have a high stitch count.
Short-term projects: useful for projects that don't necessitate a lasting backing, such as promotional items or event giveaways.

How to Use:

1. **Hoop the stabiliser**
   Place the tear-away stabiliser in the embroidery hoop together with the fabric, ensuring it's smooth and taut.
2. **Embroider the design**
   Complete the embroidery as you typically would.
3. **Remove the stabiliser**
   Gently tear away the stabiliser from the fabric (by hand), working close to the embroidery stitches. Be careful not to distort or pull the design while doing so. A way to avoid this is by pressing the stitches of the design down with one hand, whilst tearing away the stabiliser with the other. Do not rush this or be too rough, and keep an eye on the stitches around the removal areas. If in doubt, use some scissors to help.

Advantages:

Easy removal: offers a quicker clean-up post-embroidery compared to cut-away stabilisers.
Versatility: suitable for a wide range of fabrics, especially those that don't stretch.
Smooth finish: leaves a clean, residue-free finish on the reverse side of the embroidery.

Tear-away stabiliser being torn from the back of a completed design.

Drawbacks:

Limited support: not ideal for fabrics with stretch or designs with a high stitch count, as they may not provide enough stabilisation.

Potential distortion: if not torn away gently, the stabiliser can cause the fabric or embroidery to become distorted.

For designs with denser stitch counts on lighter fabrics, consider using multiple layers of tear-away stabiliser for added support.

Test a small section first to ensure that the stabiliser tears away cleanly without affecting the embroidery.

In conclusion, tear-away stabilisers are a popular choice for many embroiderers due to their ease of use and clean finish. However, as with any tool or material in the world of embroidery, it's vital to choose the right stabiliser based on the specific needs of your project.

Cut-Away Stabiliser

This is my favourite backing. A cut-away stabiliser is a type of embroidery backing designed to provide permanent support to fabrics during and after the embroidery process. Unlike tear-away stabilisers, cut-away stabilisers remain with the fabric after the embroidery is completed, with only the excess being trimmed away with scissors. Weights range from 34gm–160gm.

Characteristics:

Permanent support: provides ongoing reinforcement to the embroidered design.

Dense construction: generally denser and more stable than tear-away stabilisers.

Non-woven: often made of a non-woven material that doesn't stretch.

Common uses:

Knitted fabrics: ideal for stretchy fabrics like jerseys, as it prevents distortion both during the embroidery process and in subsequent use/wear.

Dense designs: supports intricate or heavy stitch designs without tearing.

Delicate fabrics: offers support and ensures the fabric doesn't get pulled or puckered by the embroidery machine.

How to use:

1. **Hoop the stabiliser**
   Position the cut-away stabiliser and fabric in the embroidery hoop, ensuring both are taut and smooth.
2. **Embroider the design**
   Proceed with the embroidery as intended.
3. **Trim the excess**
   Once embroidery is complete, use scissors to trim away the excess stabiliser from around the design. However, a small margin should remain around the embroidery to ensure ongoing support (a couple of millimetres is sufficient).

Advantages:

Lasting support: provides ongoing reinforcement, ensuring the design remains stable even after multiple washes.

Versatile: suitable for a broad range of fabrics, especially those prone to stretching or distortion.
Prevents puckering: helps to keep the fabric smooth during the embroidery process, preventing puckering or warping of the design.

Drawbacks:
Visibility: since it remains with the fabric, it may be visible on the reverse side of lighter or sheer fabrics.
Bulkiness: can add some thickness or rigidity to the back of the design, which might be an issue for certain garments or projects.

Choose the weight of your cut-away stabiliser based on the fabric and design. Lightweight stabilisers are available for sheer fabrics, while heavier weights can be used for dense designs on sturdier fabrics. For garments, consider using a fusible mesh cut-away stabiliser, which offers support but feels softer against the skin.

In summary, cut-away stabilisers are an excellent choice when enduring stability is paramount. They're especially beneficial for fabrics and designs that demand a higher level of support, ensuring longevity and maintaining the integrity of the embroidered artwork. My go-to stabiliser is a cut-away type which I much prefer over the tear-away type.

Cut-away stabiliser being cut from the back of a design using scissors.

Water-soluble Stabiliser (WSS)

Water-soluble stabiliser is a material used to support and stabilise fabric during embroidery from either the top side or underneath the fabric. The unique property of WSS is its ability to completely dissolve in water after the embroidery process, leaving no residue or trace behind on the finished product. This property allows for creative exploration, especially when you are considering lace effects, delicate projects or designs with many holes; available between 20–300 microns.

Types:
Film type: this is clear and plastic-like. It's excellent for lace or any project where both sides of the embroidery will be visible.
Fabric type: this resembles a lightweight interfacing and can be used for a wider range of projects, including those with higher stitch counts.

Common uses:
Freestanding lace: this embroidery technique creates designs that are not sewn onto fabric. Instead, they're stitched on WSS, which is then dissolved, leaving only the lace design.
Towels and fleece: the stabiliser prevents stitches from sinking into high-loft fabrics.
Sheer fabrics: using a WSS ensures that there's no visible stabiliser on the finished piece.

How to use:

1. **Hoop the stabiliser**
   Place the WSS in the embroidery hoop either alone (as for freestanding lace) or behind the fabric (as a backing) or on top of the fabric to prevent stitch sinkage.
2. **Embroider the design**
   Complete the embroidery as usual.
3. **Remove excess stabiliser**
   After embroidery, trim away any excess stabiliser around the design.
4. **Dissolve the stabiliser**
   Gently submerge the embroidered item in warm water, agitating it until the stabiliser dissolves. You may need to rinse it a couple of times to ensure all residues are gone. Some embroiderers use a spray bottle for smaller projects. (This can be quite messy, so take care.)

Advantages:

Versatility: ideal for projects where a traditional stabiliser would be visible or hard to remove.

Neat finish: leaves a clean, professional look since there's no stabiliser residue.

Drawbacks:

Not suitable for all fabrics: obviously, fabrics that are sensitive to water or could be damaged by it are not suitable candidates for WSS.

Temporary support: WSS provides temporary support. For projects that need lasting stabilisation, a permanent stabiliser would be more appropriate.

In summary, water-soluble stabilisers are invaluable for specific embroidery projects, especially when a clean finish without residue is desired. As with any tool or material, understanding its properties and best-use cases is key to achieving optimal results.

Water-soluble stabiliser used in a boot clamp to prevent stitches sinking into the thick knitted beanie hat. The stitches will float on top of the stabiliser.

Fusible Cut-Away Stabiliser

A fusible cut-away stabiliser is a type of embroidery backing designed to be fused (or ironed on) to the back of the fabric. It provides permanent support and stability, especially beneficial for stretchy or delicate fabrics, all while maintaining a soft feel against the skin.

Characteristics:

Permanent support: remains with the fabric after embroidery, ensuring durability and longevity of the design.

Mesh texture: lightweight and soft, making it ideal for garments.

Fusible: features an adhesive side that can be ironed onto the fabric, eliminating the need to hoop the stabiliser separately.

Common uses:

Knitted and stretchy fabrics: provides essential stability while maintaining the fabric's inherent stretch and drape.

Delicate fabrics: offers support without adding bulk, ensuring that the fabric doesn't get distorted or damaged.

Wearables: especially suitable for clothing items because of its soft texture, which ensures comfort when worn.

How to use:

1. **Prepare the fabric**
   Lay the fabric flat, with the back side facing up.
2. **Position the stabiliser**
   Place the fusible side (usually the rougher side) of the stabiliser onto the fabric.
3. **Fuse with an iron**
   Use a warm iron to fuse the stabiliser to the fabric. Ensure even heat application across the stabiliser.
4. **Hoop the fabric**
   Once fused, place the fabric into the embroidery hoop and proceed with the embroidery process.
5. **Trim the excess**
   After embroidery, trim away the excess stabiliser around the design, leaving a small border for continued support.

Advantages:

Soft feel: the mesh texture ensures the stabiliser remains soft and flexible, even after embroidery.

No slippage: the fusible attribute ensures the stabiliser stays in place during embroidery.

Prevents puckering: helps keep the fabric smooth and prevents puckering during the embroidery process.

Drawbacks:

Heat sensitivity: not suitable for fabrics that may be damaged by heat, such as certain synthetics or delicate textiles.
Permanent adhesion: once fused, it cannot be repositioned, so care should be taken during initial placement.

Always test a small piece of the stabiliser on a fabric scrap before using it on the main project to ensure compatibility and proper adhesion. Follow the manufacturer's guidelines for temperature settings and fusing time to ensure optimal results.

In summary, fusible mesh cut-away stabilisers are invaluable for projects that demand stability without sacrificing comfort or the natural drape of the fabric. By understanding its properties and best-use cases, you can achieve professional-grade results in your embroidery endeavours.

Iron-on (fusible) stabilisers, with a shiny (glue) side and a non-shiny (non-glue) side.

Adhesive Stabiliser Backing

An adhesive stabiliser backing is a type of embroidery stabiliser that has a sticky side. This sticky side allows the stabiliser to adhere directly to the fabric or item being embroidered, eliminating the need for hooping the fabric itself in some cases. This stabiliser is perfect when embroidering on items or fabric that cannot be hooped and require the floating method (*see* Chapter 2).

Types:

Pressure-sensitive adhesive stabilisers: these become tacky when pressure is applied, and they're often covered with a protective paper that you peel off to expose the sticky side.
Heat-activated adhesive stabilisers: these are activated by heat, typically using an iron, to adhere to the fabric.

Common uses:

Challenging fabrics: great for fabrics that are hard to hoop or damaged by hooping, such as velvets, leathers, silks or very thin materials.
Small items: ideal for items that can't be hooped traditionally, such as collars, socks or caps.
Delicate fabrics: reduces the risk of hoop burn, which is a mark left on sensitive fabrics after hooping.

How to use: (Floating method)

1. **Positioning**
   Secure the adhesive backing only into the hoop, ensuring the sticky side is facing up.
2. **Application**
   For pressure-sensitive adhesive stabilisers, peel off the protective paper to reveal the sticky adhesive layer.
3. **Press**
   The fabric onto the stabiliser carefully. For heat-activated versions, use an iron to adhere the stabiliser to the fabric and hoop together.
4. **Embroidery**
   Proceed with embroidery process.
5. **Completion**
   Once the embroidery is done, carefully tear away any excess stabiliser from the fabric.

Advantages:

Flexibility: allows embroidery on items and fabrics that are traditionally challenging to hoop.

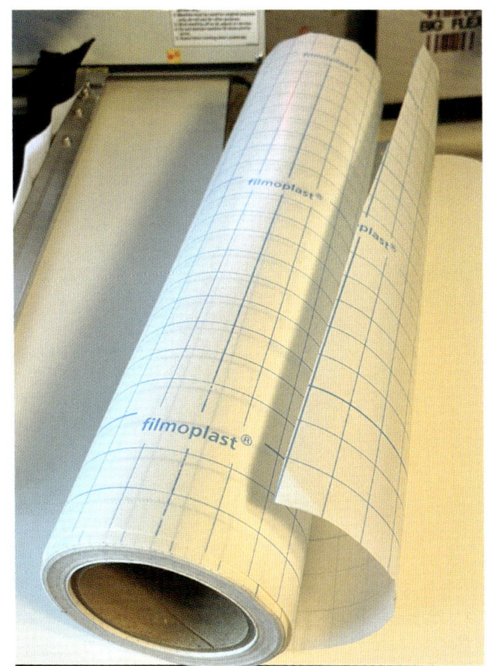

A roll of Filmoplast adhesive stabiliser.

Adhesive stabiliser hooped only. Jacket sits on top using the floating method. The adhesive holds it in place ready to embroider.

Protection: reduces the risk of damaging or marking delicate fabrics.
Stability: offers additional support to fabrics, ensuring the embroidery process runs smoothly.

Drawbacks:
Residue: some adhesive stabilisers may leave a sticky residue on fabrics. Always test on a fabric scrap before using on the main project.
Limited repositioning: once adhered, repositioning can be difficult without damaging the fabric or the stabiliser. For medium and heavier weight fabrics, repositioning is less of a problem, however the more times you remove the fabric, the more likely the stickiness of the adhesive stabiliser reduces.

Tips:
If you're working with a fabric or item for the first time, always do a test run with a small piece to see how it reacts to the adhesive.
For items that can't be hooped, use the adhesive stabiliser as a bridge between the item and another stabiliser that's been hooped. This ensures the embroidery machine can still move freely.

In summary, adhesive stabiliser backing is a versatile tool in an embroiderer's toolkit, especially when dealing with challenging fabrics or items. By understanding its properties and applications, one can achieve professional results even on difficult projects. *Warning*: Adhesive backing can attract unwanted loose threads, for example, lint and debris on areas not covered by the fabric; make sure it doesn't cause interference with your embroidery.

Instead of investing in specialist adhesive backings, you can create a makeshift alternative by spraying a temporary adhesive onto a cut-away or tear-away stabiliser. While this method may not be as robust as dedicated adhesive backings, it often serves a similar purpose. However, for added security, consider using pins or basting stitches to hold the layers firmly in place.

Sustainable Stabiliser Backings

The movement towards sustainability has touched every industry, including embroidery and sewing. The development and use of sustainable stabiliser backings are

Sustainable stabilisers available by Madeira.

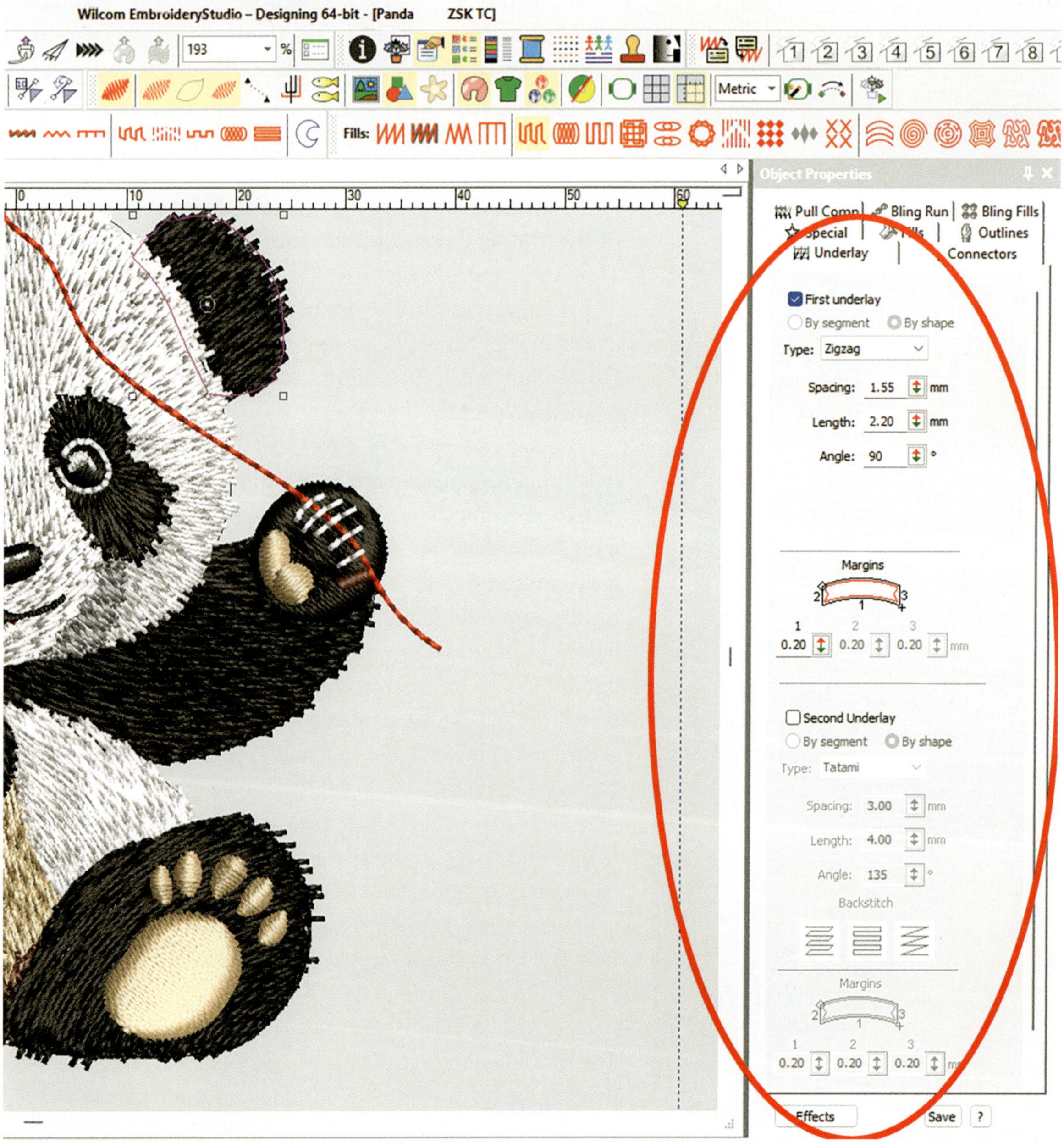

Screenshot of the underlayer settings on Wilcom Software digitising software.

a response to the growing demand for environmentally friendly products. Here's a breakdown of sustainable stabiliser backings and their significance.

Sustainable stabiliser backings are those created from eco-friendly materials or processes. They are designed to degrade faster than traditional stabilisers, have a reduced carbon footprint, or are sourced from renewable resources.

Types:

Organic cotton or bamboo stabilisers: produced without harmful chemicals or pesticides, these stabilisers are biodegradable and soft to the touch.

Recycled material stabilisers: made from recycled fibres, they reduce waste and reuse resources.

Biodegradable synthetic stabilisers: though synthetic, they are designed to break down faster than traditional materials.

Common uses:

Eco-friendly embroidery: for businesses or individuals emphasising sustainable practices.

Sensitive applications: for products that will be in close contact with the skin, such as baby clothing or eco-conscious apparel.

Advantages:

Environmental impact: reduced carbon footprint and waste in the environment.

Consumer appeal: an increasing number of consumers prefer eco-friendly products.

Skin-friendly: organic and sustainable materials are often gentler on the skin, making them ideal for sensitive applications.

Drawbacks:

Cost: sustainable stabilisers can sometimes be more expensive due to the cost of sourcing or producing eco-friendly materials.

Availability: not as widely available as traditional stabilisers, though this is rapidly changing.

Tips for use:

Always pre-test sustainable stabilisers just as you would with any new stabiliser type to ensure compatibility with your fabric and design.

Store in a cool, dry place, as some sustainable stabilisers might be more sensitive to environmental conditions.

Sourcing sustainable stabilisers:

Certifications: look for certifications like GOTS (Global Organic Textile Standard) to ensure the product's organic status.

Supplier transparency: choose suppliers who are transparent about their sourcing and manufacturing processes.

Local sourcing: if possible, source locally to reduce the carbon footprint associated with transportation.

In summary, as the world pivots towards more sustainable practices, the embroidery and sewing industry is keeping pace. Sustainable stabiliser backings not only offer environmental benefits, but also cater to a growing market of consumers dedicated to eco-friendly choices. By integrating these stabilisers into your projects, you contribute to a more sustainable future while delivering high-quality embroidery or sewing products.

When selecting a stabiliser, the fabric type and design density are paramount. The inherent stability or stretchiness of the fabric dictates the extent of added support needed. Ensure you don't exceed three layers; otherwise, consider opting for a denser backing.

If you're facing significant fabric instability, before resorting to multiple layers or a thicker stabiliser, re-examine your digitised design. Adjusting the underlayer settings can help. By reducing the underlayer spacing and stitch length, you increase the stitch count on the underlayer, which acts as its own form of stabilisation; in essence, it can do the same job as a stabiliser fabric.

FABRICS

The majority of your embroidery projects will most likely involve a fabric of some kind, whether you are creating an embroidered art piece for a wall display, creating a patch or embellishing a garment. Embroidery can be carried out on a variety of fabrics, but each type has specific characteristics to consider. The following is a list of commonly used fabrics for embroidery and what to be mindful of.

Cotton

Cotton is a natural fabric that's often quite easy to embroider on, thanks to its durability and stable weave. It's a popular choice for beginners and experienced embroiderers alike. Cotton is my go-to cloth and preferred fabric to embroider on as it gives you fewer problems than other fabrics. Here's what to keep in mind when embroidering on cotton:

Needle selection: a universal (or sharp) needle of size 75/11 or 80/12 is typically a good choice for cotton, depending on the fabric's weight.

Design considerations: cotton is quite versatile and can handle a variety of designs from light and open to more dense. However, extremely dense designs can cause puckering, so they may require additional stabilisation.

Machine-embroidered front corset panel on a medium-weight cotton calico using a medium-weight cut-away stabiliser.

Stabiliser use: a tear-away stabiliser is usually sufficient for cotton, although a cut-away stabiliser might be better for denser, heavier designs or stretchy cotton like jersey.

Hooping: cotton fabric can usually be hooped directly, but be careful not to overstretch it in the hoop, as this can cause distortion or puckering.

Test first: as always, it's a good idea to test your design on a scrap piece of fabric first to make sure your settings, needle and stabiliser are right for your design and fabric.

Embroidering on cotton can produce excellent results, making it a favourite choice for many projects.

Linen

Linen is a natural fabric known for its durability and breathability. Its weave is looser than cotton, which gives it a unique texture that can add a beautiful depth to your embroidery. Here's what to keep in mind when embroidering on linen:

Needle selection: a universal or sharp needle of size 75/11 or 80/12 usually works well for linen. If the linen is particularly loose-weave or heavy, you might need a larger needle.

Design considerations: because of its loose weave, linen is well-suited to open designs, but it can also handle

An Anne Zielinski-Old illustration embroidered on a linen fabric.

medium-density designs. Dense designs, however, may cause puckering or distortion.

Stabiliser use: a tear-away stabiliser is typically good for most linen embroidery, but a cut-away stabiliser may be used for designs with higher stitch density.

Hooping: hoop linen carefully to avoid overstretching, which can cause the fabric to distort. If your linen is prone to creasing or marking from the hoop, consider hooping your stabiliser and then floating the fabric on top, secured with pins or temporary adhesive.

Test first: always do a test run on a scrap piece of linen before you start on your final project.

With its rich texture and natural look, linen can give your embroidery projects a classic and elegant feel.

Silk

Silk (not suitable for beginners) is a luxurious, lightweight fabric with a lustrous sheen, favoured for its beauty and elegance in embroidery. Its delicate nature requires very careful handling, especially when embroidering directly onto the fabric. Here's what to keep in mind when embroidering on silk:

Needle selection: a fine, sharp needle such as a 69/9 or 70/10 is ideal to prevent damage and minimise visible needle holes.

Threads: a finer thread may be required; try using a 60wt.

Design considerations: silk accommodates intricate and delicate designs well, showcasing detailed work beautifully due to its fine weave.

Stabiliser use: a light-to medium-weight tear-away stabiliser works best, providing support without adding unwanted bulk.

Hooping: gentle hooping is crucial to avoid puckering; consider using a hoop with a soft grip or hooping the stabiliser only and then floating the silk on top.

Test first: conduct a test on a silk scrap to ensure tension, needle and stabiliser compatibility, preserving the integrity and appearance of the fabric.

Silk's refined texture is perfect for creating sophisticated, ornate embroidery pieces, making it a favourite for heirloom and bridal work.

An embroidery design on a silk fabric.

Denim

Denim is a sturdy, twill weave fabric that's perfect for embroidery, especially for items like jeans or jackets that need to withstand heavy wear. However, its thickness and varying weights can present some challenges. Here's what to keep in mind when embroidering on denim:

Needle selection: denim is a heavy fabric and needs a strong needle. A denim or jeans needle, typically sized 90/14 or 100/16, is designed to penetrate thick fabrics without breaking.

Design considerations: denim can handle a variety of designs, from simple to complex. However, very dense designs can make the fabric rigid or cause puckering.

Stabiliser use: a cut-away stabiliser is usually recommended for denim because of its strength and stability. It helps to prevent distortion during and after embroidery.

An embroidered allover design on a denim jacket for interior designer Siobhan Murphy.

Hooping: you can typically hoop denim directly, but be cautious not to stretch or distort it in the hoop. If the denim is very thick, you might need to hoop your stabiliser and then use pins or temporary adhesive to secure the fabric on top.
Test first: as with any fabric, it's a good idea to test your design on a scrap piece of denim first to fine-tune your settings and approach.

Embroidering on denim can give a unique, personalised touch to your garments or accessories. With the right technique, you can achieve beautiful, durable results.

Canvas

Canvas is a medium to heavy-duty fabric typically used for tapestry and needlepoint work. It can handle heavier threads and yarns, and it's durable enough to withstand the wear and tear of being used for things like upholstery. However, its thickness and coarse texture can make it more difficult to embroider with a machine. Canvas (approximately 215gm) is my go-to fabric for embroidered wall-mounted art pieces of large scale, used with a medium-weight cut-away stabiliser. Here's what to keep in mind when embroidering on canvas:

Needle selection: on medium canvas you can embroider with a 75/11 Sharp needle, whilst a heavyweight canvas is tougher, so you'll need a stronger needle to penetrate it without breaking. A denim or jeans needle (around size 90/14 or 100/16) can work well.
Design considerations: canvas can handle heavier, denser designs better than many other fabrics. However, you'll still want to avoid designs with very small, intricate details, as they can get lost in the fabric's texture.
Stabiliser use: a cut-away stabiliser is a good choice for canvas. It provides sturdy support during embroidery and helps maintain the design's shape over time. Opt for a medium-weight stabiliser initially.
Hooping: canvas can often be hooped directly but be careful not to stretch or distort the fabric in the hoop. If you are embroidering multiple sections and joining them

Close-up detail of a floral design on a canvas fabric.

together (like a jigsaw puzzle), hooping can become a problem because of the increased bulk created by the stitches, therefore the floating method might be more suitable.
Test first: as with any fabric, it's a good idea to test your design on a scrap piece of canvas first to make sure your machine settings, needle and stabiliser are appropriate for the fabric and design.

With its durability and versatility, medium-weight canvas is a great material for a wide variety of embroidery projects and great for a beginner to experiment with.

Felt

This fabric is great for beginners because it is easy to work with. Felt is a non-woven textile that is produced by matting, condensing and pressing fibres together. It is known for its soft texture and its ability to be easily cut into shapes without fraying, making it popular for craft and design work and giving an interesting dimension to your embroidery. Felt's density and fibre composition make it suitable for projects that require a sturdy yet pliable material. Here's what to keep in mind when embroidering on felt:

Needle selection: when embroidering on felt, a 75/11 or 80/12 embroidery needle is usually sufficient. The needle should be sharp to penetrate the dense felt cleanly.
Design considerations: felt is quite forgiving and can support a range of embroidery designs, from simple to complex. It's particularly good for appliqué work due to its clean edges when cut. Intricate details can be achieved, but it's important to consider the felt's thickness and texture, as very fine details may not be as sharp as on woven fabrics.
Stabiliser use: using a tear-away stabiliser is often recommended for felt, as it provides adequate support during embroidery, but can be easily removed afterward. For heavier designs, a medium-weight cut-away stabiliser can be used to ensure the design holds its shape.
Hooping: hooping felt can be straightforward because of its structure; it typically stays in place without slipping. However, care should be taken not to stretch the felt out of shape. The 'floating' method, where the felt is placed on top of the hooped stabiliser, can be used to avoid hoop burn on delicate felt surfaces.
Test first: always perform a test run on a scrap piece of felt. This helps to adjust the embroidery machine's tension settings and needle choice to ensure the best outcome for your design.

A stylised gangster cat design embroidered on a felt fabric.

Felt is an excellent material for both novices and experienced crafters. Its forgiving nature and structural integrity make it a versatile choice for a variety of projects and a go-to when applying it as appliqué.

Synthetic Fabrics

This category includes a wide variety of materials, such as polyester, nylon, rayon and spandex, among others. Synthetic fabrics are man-made and can vary greatly in texture, weight and stretch. Here's what to keep in mind when embroidering on synthetic fabrics:

Needle selection: the needle size and type will depend on the specific fabric. Light- to medium-weight synthetics typically require a size 70/10 or 75/11 needle. Heavier weight synthetics may need a size 80/12 or 90/14 needle. If the fabric is stretchy, a ball point needle is usually the best choice.

An embroidery design on synthetic fabric.

Design considerations: avoid dense designs on lightweight synthetics, as these can cause puckering or distortion. For stretchy synthetics, designs should also be flexible to move with the fabric.
Stabiliser use: a cut-away stabiliser is usually recommended for stretchy synthetics to prevent distortion. Tear-away can be used for stable synthetics. Lighter-weight, delicate synthetics may benefit from a wash-away stabiliser to avoid damaging the fabric when removing the stabiliser.
Hooping: be careful when hooping synthetic fabrics, particularly delicate or stretchy ones. It may be beneficial to hoop your stabiliser and then float the fabric on top, securing it with pins or temporary adhesive.
Test first: always do a test run on a scrap of your synthetic fabric before starting on your final project. This will allow you to fine-tune your needle, stabiliser and design choices for the specific fabric.

With their wide variety, synthetic fabrics can offer a lot of versatility for embroidery projects. However, they also require careful handling and specific techniques to get the best results.

Leather

Embroidering on leather (not suitable for beginners) gives your designs a high-quality and sophisticated appearance, but it can be a bit challenging because it requires a special approach. Here's what to keep in mind when embroidering on leather:

Needle selection: leather requires a specialised leather needle. These needles have a cutting point that creates a clean hole as it penetrates the material. The size of the needle will depend on the thickness of the leather, but generally, a 90/14 or 100/16 leather needle works well.
Design considerations: avoid designs that are dense or have small, intricate details. Leather does not have a weave for the thread to hold onto, so too many stitches can cut the leather, causing it to tear. Simple, open designs usually work best. If your design has a stain border around the edge it is really important you double-check your digitising settings before stitch-out; if your stitch density is too dense (or even left at default settings) it is likely you will see holes, or in the worst case, your embroidery will fall out of the leather altogether, leaving a larger hole.
Stabiliser use: a sturdy cut-away stabiliser is a good choice. Adhesive stabilisers are also commonly used, as they can help prevent the leather from shifting during embroidery and are perfect to help float the fabric on the hoop.
Hooping: hooping can leave burn marks on the leather, and thick leather can be very problematic to frame, so many embroiderers choose to hoop their stabiliser and then use adhesive spray to hold the leather in place on top of the hooped stabiliser. Adhesive stabiliser does the same job as an adhesive spray; however, it is more expensive and can be difficult to remove excess material afterwards.
Test first: this is vital. Testing your design on a scrap piece of leather first can help you fine-tune your settings and approach. If your design is small, I recommend embroidering all of it to double-check the settings; you will be surprised how easy it is to overlook a shape's settings and next minute you have a visible hole! If you are creating a large embroidery piece or are unable to sample all the design, at least sample areas of it, and

A geometric shooting star and planet embroidery on the back of a leather jacket.

check the settings for the remainder of the design two or three times. Once embroidered, hold your fabric up to the light and gently pull it taut (don't over pull it); if you see a lot of light around the edges and it looks as if it can rip, then you might want to review your settings, especially if you are embroidering on a garment, as body movement and usage can cause fragile areas to wear easily. If it is for an art piece, then it is not so important, but care would need to be taken if mounting and framing. Avoid using pins as pin holes may be visible after removal.

For leather embroidery with heavy fills, opt for appliqué to maintain durability and achieve a visually appealing finish.

Vinyl

Vinyl (not suitable for beginners) is a synthetic material known for its durability and leather-like appearance. It's widely used in various projects, such as bags, upholstery and accessories. While it can be challenging to embroider due to its non-porous and often thick nature, it's not impossible. It requires extensive testing in order to identify the correct machine and digitising settings. Here's what to keep in mind when embroidering on vinyl:

Needle selection: a sharp needle is best for vinyl. The size (usually 80/12 or 90/14) will depend on the thickness of the vinyl. A sharp needle can cleanly penetrate the vinyl without tearing it.
Design considerations: light- to medium-density designs tend to work better on vinyl. Dense designs can puncture the vinyl too much, causing it to tear.
Stabiliser use: a cut-away stabiliser is generally recommended for vinyl to provide sufficient stability. Tear-away stabilisers can be more difficult to remove and may stress the vinyl.
Hooping: hooping vinyl can be tricky due to its thickness and risk of hoop burn. It's often better to hoop the stabiliser alone and then float the vinyl on top, securing it with temporary adhesive.
Thread considerations: polyester thread is usually recommended when working with vinyl because of its strength and durability.

An embroidery design on a vinyl fabric.

Test first: doing a test run on a scrap piece of vinyl before you begin your project is highly recommended.

Embroidering on vinyl can add a professional touch to your projects. With careful handling and the right materials, it's a great way to personalise and enhance your creations. Avoid using pins as pin holes may be visible after removal.

Fur

Embroidering on fur (not suitable for beginners), whether real or faux, can present some unique challenges due to the pile's height and density. However, with the right techniques, it's certainly possible to achieve great results. Here's what to keep in mind when embroidering on fur:

Needle selection: a sharp needle is best for fur, and the size (usually 80/12 or 90/14) will depend on the density and thickness of the fur. A sharp needle will cleanly cut through the fur and backing.

Embroidery design on a fur fabric.

Design considerations: heavier designs featuring robust columns and bold lettering are most effective for managing these fabrics. Additionally, employing a base layer of fill stitching can help in flattening the fabric's pile beneath your design. Using appliqué is also a great strategy for covering larger areas to restrain the nap, providing a smooth surface for embroidery work.
Stabiliser use: a cut-away stabiliser is typically recommended for fur to provide sufficient stability. Additionally, a water-soluble or heat (melt away) topper may be used to prevent stitches from sinking into the fur and keeping the pile flat during stitching.
Hooping: hooping fur can be difficult due to its thickness. It's often better to hoop the stabiliser alone and then float the fur on top, securing it with pins or temporary adhesive. Adhesive stabilisers work well on fur.
Trimming: if the fur's pile is too long, it may be necessary to trim it in the area where you plan to embroider. This can help prevent the fur from getting caught in the stitches and makes your design more visible.
Test first: as always, doing a test run on a scrap piece of fur before you begin your project is highly recommended.

Embroidery on fur can create a unique and luxurious look. While it may require a bit of extra preparation and care, the results can be well worth it.

Knitted Fabrics

Knitted fabrics (not suitable for beginners), such as jersey or interlock, are made from one continuous yarn, looped repeatedly to create a braided look. This results in a fabric that's stretchy and comfortable, but also potentially challenging for embroidery due to its elasticity. Here's what to keep in mind when embroidering on knitted fabric:

Needle selection: a ball point needle is best for knitted fabrics, as it slips between the fabric's threads, rather than piercing them. This can help prevent damage to the fabric and the knitted loops from unravelling. The size will depend on the fabric's weight, but generally, a 70/10 or 75/11 needle works well for lighter and standard knits, and 80/12 for double and heavier knits.

Design considerations: lighter, more open designs are typically a better choice for knitted fabrics. Be careful of heavy, dense designs as they can stretch and distort the fabric and end up looking like a stuck-on patch or badge. Lighter, more open designs are typically a better choice for knitted fabrics.

Stabiliser use: a soft cut-away stabiliser is usually the best choice for knitted fabrics, as it provides the necessary stability and prevents the design from stretching out over time and reduces the risk of the outline showing through the cloth on the right side. A water-soluble topper can be used to prevent stitches sinking into the fabric.

Hooping: hoop the fabric and stabiliser together, being careful not to stretch the fabric in the hoop. Alternatively, use the floating method, by hooping the stabiliser and applying a temporary adhesive to secure the fabric. If using the floating method, secure in place with pins around the edge or basting stitches (put in by hand or machine, if it has this feature).

Test first: always do a test run on a scrap of your knitted fabric to ensure your settings, needle and stabiliser choices work well with your fabric and design.

Dense embroidery designs on knitted beanie hats.

If you are embroidering on items of clothing that are intended to be stretched when worn, then you need to consider how the embroidery design will look when worn (stretched) and not worn (unstretched). If you embroider on a knitted beanie hat for example, it may look visually perfect when not worn, but once stretched on someone's head, the embroidery design may look distorted and undesirable. This happens the other way around as well, where the beanie can look perfect when worn, but looks unappealing when not worn (would you buy a beanie that doesn't look appealing?). To overcome this, you have to find the middle ground – the right balance between the two ends of the spectrum (distortion when worn and distortion when unworn). When hooping the knitted fabric, you will need to slightly stretch it, so when embroidered you may see slight distortion when not worn and slight distortion when worn. The amount you stretch it when hooping will swing the distortion either close up towards worn (stretched) or closer to not worn (unstretched). Notice the distortion around the spoon in the cat's hand in the photo. It won't prevent anyone from buying the beanie, and when worn this straightens out a little, therefore looking better when worn. Embroidering on knitted fabric can be a big challenge due to its stretch, but with careful handling and the right materials, you can achieve beautiful results. If you are mass-producing the same product, make a note of how much you stretched the knitted fabric, so all the products are the same.

Woven Wools

Woven wool fabrics come in various weights and textures, from lightweight worsteds to heavy meltons or tweeds. They are durable and generally quite easy to embroider on, with their own specific considerations. Wool also reacts to heat and steam, causing it to shrink or reshape. As a result, any areas of fluting or puckering after embroidery can often be steamed away. Here's what to keep in mind when embroidering on woven wool fabrics:

Needle selection: a universal or sharp needle, usually of size 80/12 or 90/14, is typically used for woven wool, depending on the fabric's weight.

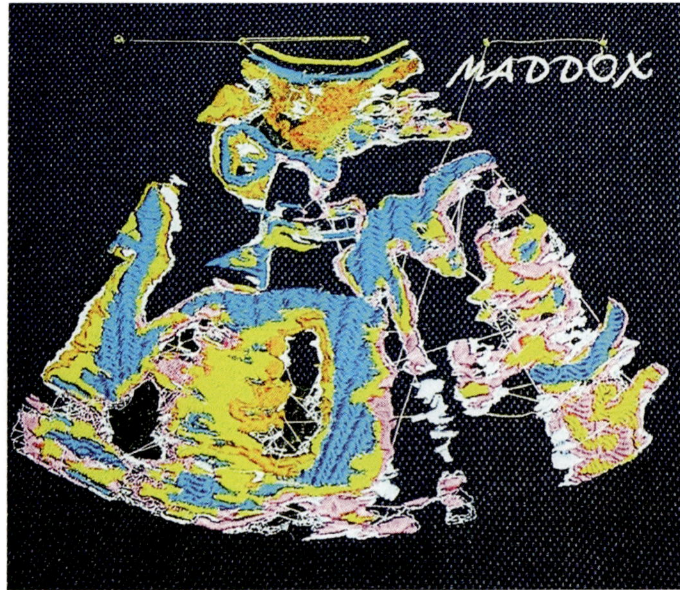

Embroidered baby scan on a woven wool fabric.

Design considerations: woven wool can handle a variety of designs, from simple to complex, but very dense designs may cause puckering or distortion. The fabric's texture might obscure fine details, so bold, simple designs usually work best.
Stabiliser use: a cut-away or tear-away stabiliser can work, depending on the design's density and the fabric's weight. Cut-away is generally better for heavier designs or stretchy wools, while tear-away can be used for simpler designs or stable wools.
Hooping: wool fabric can usually be hooped directly but be careful not to stretch or distort it in the hoop. If your wool is prone to creasing or marking from the hoop, consider hooping your stabiliser and then floating the fabric on top, secured with pins, temporary adhesive or basting stitches.
Test first: always do a test run on a scrap piece of wool before you start on your final project. Given the vast variety of woven wool clothes available, they won't all react in the same way, so testing is very important if you are to maximise the quality of your design on your selected wool cloth.

Embroidering on woven wool can give your projects a warm, classic look. With the right techniques, you can create beautiful, durable embroidery on this versatile fabric.

Velvet

Velvet (not suitable for beginners) is a lush fabric with a dense, soft pile that can give your embroidery an extra touch of luxury. However, it's also quite challenging to embroider on because of its texture and tendency to mark easily. Here's what to keep in mind when embroidering on velvet:

Needle selection: a sharp needle is best for velvet, and the size (usually 75/11 or 80/12) will depend on the weight of the velvet. A sharp needle will cleanly cut through the pile and backing of the fabric.
Design considerations: avoid designs that are very dense, as they can crush the velvet's pile and look heavy. Lighter, more open designs tend to work better.
Stabiliser use: a light, water-soluble topper is often used in addition to a cut-away stabiliser. The water-soluble topper helps prevent the stitches from sinking into the pile and getting lost, while the cut-away stabiliser supports the fabric.
Hooping: velvet can be permanently marked by an embroidery hoop, so it's often recommended to hoop your stabiliser and then float the velvet on top, securing it with pins, temporary adhesive or basting stitches around the edge. Be sure to remove the water-soluble stabiliser carefully to avoid crushing the pile.
Test first: as always, it's recommended to do a test run on a scrap piece of velvet before embroidering your final piece.

Remember to handle velvet with care, as it can be easily damaged or marked. But with the right techniques, you can create a gorgeous, luxurious finished piece.

Satin

Satin (not suitable for beginners) is a sleek and glossy fabric that's perfect for adding a touch of elegance to your embroidery projects. However, its slippery, delicate nature and tendency to show needle marks can make it a challenging material to work with. I often find this cloth will embroider well; however, when removed from the hoop it starts to pull in on itself, creating visible fluting around the edge of the embroidery and/or in between embroidered areas. Here's what to keep in mind when embroidering on satin:

Needle selection: use a sharp, fine needle (70/10 or 75/11) to ensure clean punctures and to prevent snagging or

A basting edge stitch applied around the edge of a design to hold the velvet fabric in place whilst floating on a stabiliser backing.

damaging the fabric. Given the weave of satin fabric, it can be easy to cause visible damage lines if fibres are pulled too much.

Design considerations: opt for designs that aren't too dense, as they can cause puckering or distortion in the fabric. Also, keep in mind that every needle hole will be visible in this fabric, so repositioning your hoop or ripping out stitches can leave permanent marks.

Stabiliser use: a lightweight, tear-away stabiliser is typically a good choice. This can provide some support during the embroidery process without adding unnecessary bulk.

Hooping: be very careful when hooping satin. It's better to float the stabiliser and use a temporary adhesive to hold the fabric in place. Applying the floating method will help prevent hoop burn, which is a permanent crease or mark left by the embroidery hoop.

Test first: due to the delicate nature of satin, it's a good idea to test your design on a scrap piece first to ensure the best possible result.

Embroidering on satin can be a bit tricky, so do not be surprised if you need to test several times in order to find the optimal settings for your fabric and design.

Allover rose design embroidered on a duchess satin fabric.

Chiffon and Organza

Chiffon and organza (not suitable for beginners) are very lightweight, sheer fabrics often made from silk, nylon or polyester. They are delicate in nature and their slippery texture can make them quite challenging to embroider. They are also prone to fraying and puckering, but the results can be quite beautiful and elegant. Here's what to keep in mind when embroidering on chiffon:

Needle selection: use a small, sharp needle. A fine, sharp needle (size 69/9 or 70/10) will make cleaner punctures in these delicate fabrics, reducing the risk of snagging, tearing or leaving holes in the fabric.

Embroidered feather on an organza fabric.

Design considerations: less is more. Opt for simple, open designs rather than dense ones, as heavy designs can weigh down the fabric.

Stabiliser use: a lightweight, water-soluble stabiliser is usually the best choice. It provides support during embroidery but can be completely removed afterwards, preserving the fabric's sheer appearance.

Hooping: hoop the fabric together with the stabiliser, making sure it is taut but not overly stretched. If floating the fabric, consider using temporary adhesive to hold it in place.

Thread: choose a lightweight thread (60wt). This prevents creating too much tension that can pucker the fabric.

Test first: due to the delicate nature of these fabrics, always do a test run on a scrap piece of fabric first to ensure your chosen design, stabiliser and thread work well together.

Sweatshirts and Hoodies

These are arguably amongst some of the most popular product choices to be embroidered on and common garment types in a lot of fashion brands' product ranges. This may vary from chest logos for school uniforms and sports tops to larger, more visible designs located on the front or back of the garment. Premade garments are classed as tubular, meaning when you open the garment up it creates a tube effect (which you place over your head). Tubular products can be problematic to embroider on for domestic embroidery machines, as the flat bed of the machine restricts hooping. Unpicking a side seam may be necessary in order to get round this. Tubular garments are easier to embroider on an industrial machine, as the flat bed is removed and replaced with a prong system.

Sweatshirts and hoodies are commonly made from cotton or polyester fabric of varying weights with a varying amount of stretch. Fabrics may be a blend of natural and synthetic fibres and there is a move towards organic and sustainable fabrics, which adds more complications for embroiderers. Here's what to keep in mind when embroidering on sweatshirts and hoodies:

Needle selection: a 75/11 Sharp needle is a good choice to start with and can handle the majority of these fabrics with ease. After testing, adjust your needle choice if you need to.

Design considerations: heavier sweatshirt fabrics can handle the dense designs but avoid these designs on lighter

A large, stylised cat design on the front of a black hoodie.

weight cloth as it will affect the hang of the cloth and could cause fluting around the edge.

Stabiliser use: cut-away stabilisers work best; trim the excess around the edge after stitching. Choose the weight of the stabiliser based on the fabric thickness and stretch of the cloth. Stiffer stabilisers will cause garments to become more rigid and affect the fabric properties and visual appearance, whilst softer stabilisers will allow the garment to retain more of its natural appearance.

Hooping: hooping or floating methods both work well, though hooping is the most common choice. If hooping, be careful of hoop burn and do not overstretch the fabric as it will cause distortion.

Test: given the variety of fabric types that could be used to make sweatshirts and hoodies, it is always worth testing the cloth prior to embroidering on your final product. Any errors in digitising or improvements in the quality of the outcome can be identified after testing, before applying to the final garment. This could save you time and money!

Consider investing in a test sweatshirt, a garment you can use to test elements of your design – it can be used time and time again until there is no fabric left.

T-shirts

Another popular garment among fashion brands is the T-shirt. These are typically made from a light-to medium-weight knitted fabric, often cotton, polyester or a blend of the two. The key characteristic of T-shirt fabric is that it's stretchy, which makes it comfortable to wear, but can pose some challenges for embroidery. Like sweatshirts and hoodies, if purchased premade, these will be tubular and you may find difficulties with hooping, depending on your machine type. Here's what to keep in mind when embroidering on T-shirts:

Needle selection: a ball point needle is ideal for t-shirt fabric. It will pass between the fabric threads, rather than piercing them, which helps prevent damage to the fabric. A 70/10 and 75/11 needle is a good choice.

Design considerations: keep in mind that lighter, less dense designs often work better on T-shirt fabric, as they are less likely to cause distortion or puckering.

Stabiliser: a stabiliser is a must when embroidering on stretchy fabric. A lightweight cut-away stabiliser is generally recommended for T-shirt fabric as it remains with the fabric after stitching, helping to keep the design stable even after wearing and washing. This garment is worn next to the skin, so adding a protective soft mesh after embroidering will prevent the stabiliser rubbing against the skin.

Hooping: when hooping, make sure the fabric is flat and smooth, but not overly stretched, as this can cause puckering once the hoop is removed.

Test: always test your design on a similar piece of fabric before starting on your actual project. This will give you an opportunity to adjust your tension, stabiliser, needle or design as necessary.

Embroidered feather on a T-shirt jersey fabric.

OTHER TOOLS AND USEFUL EQUIPMENT

Some other useful items in my toolbox include the following:

- Snips, fine cutters
- Scissors: fabric, backing and paper
- Tweezers: pointy and flat tip
- Screwdrivers
- Cleaners (wipes)
- Paint brushes: various sizes for cleaning
- Spools
- Unpicker
- Pens and pencils

- Fixion pens (ink disappears with heat)
- Sharpe pens
- Pins, thimble and hand sewing needles
- Rulers and tape measure
- Bull dog clips
- USB storage devices
- Machine oil and cloth

OVERVIEW

As we conclude this chapter, it's my sincere hope that the insights shared here have equipped you with a deeper understanding of the essential principles required to embark on your digital embroidery adventure. With this newfound knowledge, you should feel empowered to make informed decisions about the specific tools and paraphernalia that will best suit the projects you envision.

As you turn the page and begin the next chapter, anticipate expanding on this foundation with more advanced techniques and creative explorations. The journey ahead is not just about mastering the mechanics of digital embroidery, but also about unleashing your creativity and bringing your unique visions to life. I encourage you to approach each subsequent lesson with an open mind and a willingness to experiment.

Embrace the challenges and the learning opportunities they present, knowing that with each stitch and pattern, you are crafting not just a piece of art, but also a piece of yourself into your creations. So, take a deep breath, gather your materials, and let's continue this exciting journey together into the next chapter, where your skills will grow and your embroidery will take on new dimensions of complexity and beauty.

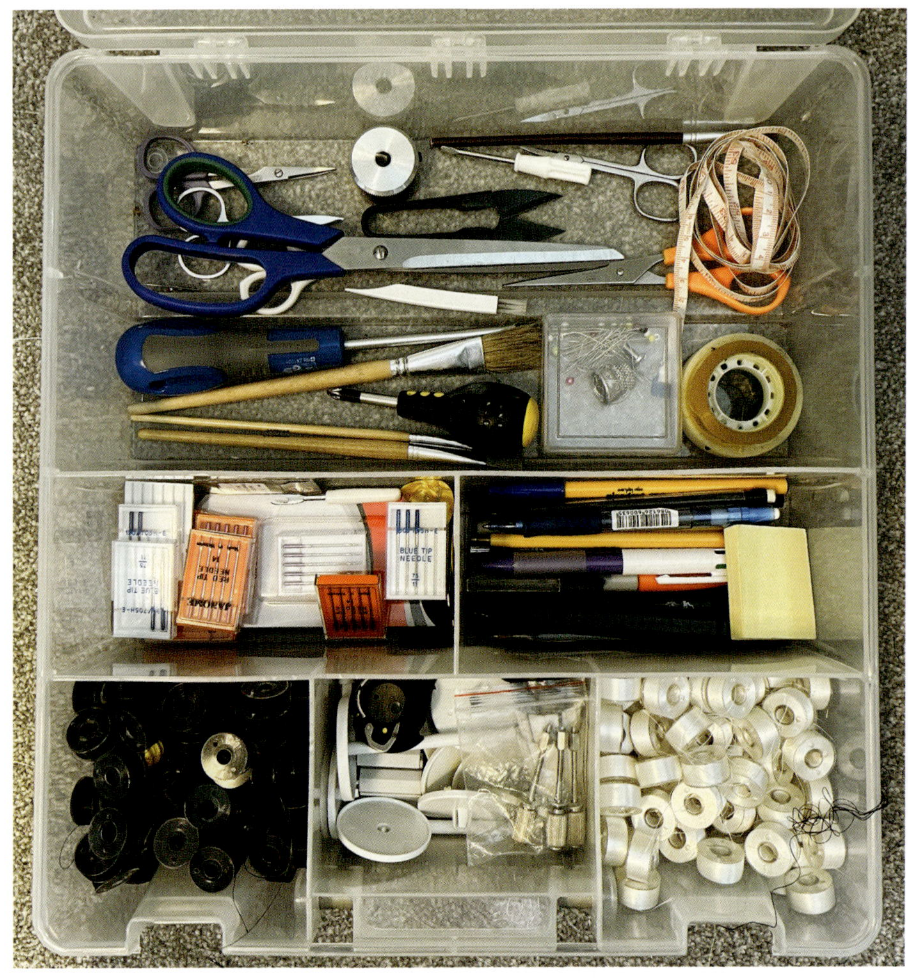

My toolbox, with regularly used equipment – not always this tidy.

CASE STUDY: GS UK LTD

GS UK Ltd has established itself as a beacon in the textile industry, providing a spectrum of embroidery services and products. With over 30 years of expertise, they offer an array of embroidery machines, including the Merlin Pro range and the Brother Industrial series, exclusive to the UK and Ireland. Their comprehensive selection includes not just machinery, but also essential consumables and supplies like threads, backings and software. GS UK prides itself on delivering a full package, from sales to embroidery services, backed by experienced technicians ensuring seamless installation and aftercare. Their new website, part of a broader rebranding, reflects their dedication to quality and customer service, making it simpler for clients to access their vast product range and services. As a leader in garment decoration, GS UK continues to evolve, driving the industry forward through innovation and a commitment to excellence.

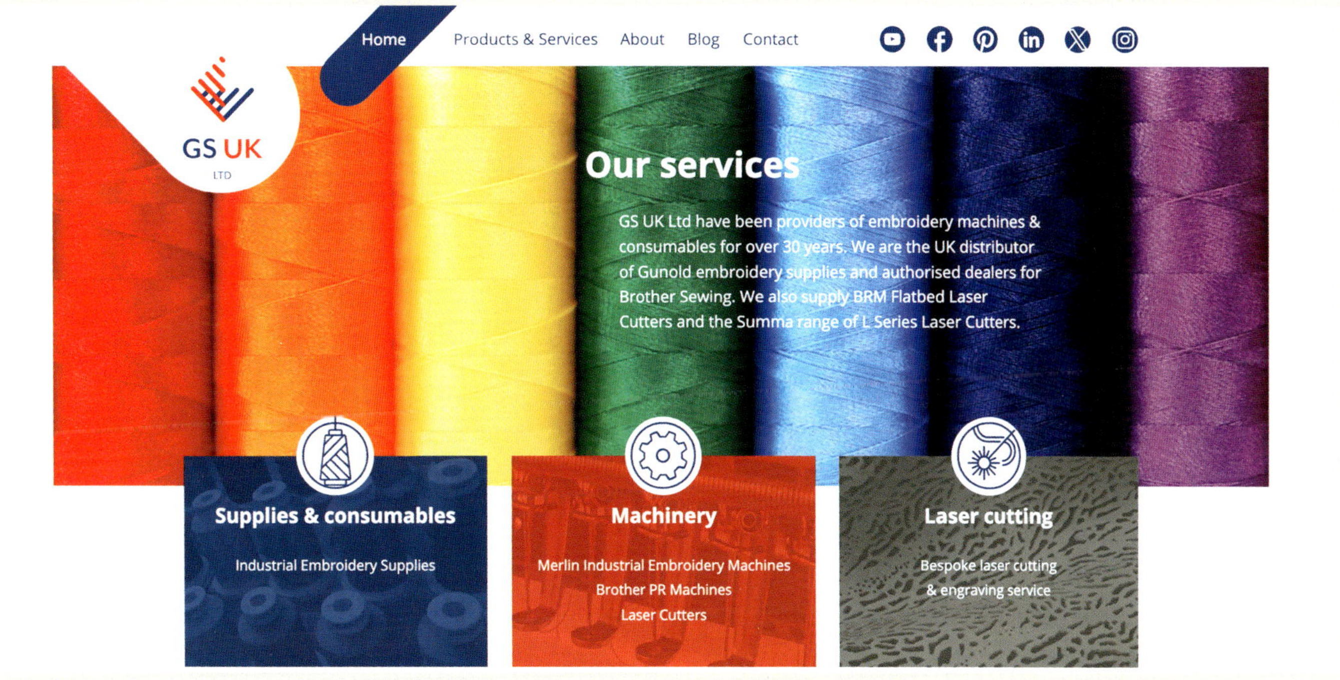

GS UK Ltd website screenshot – material and equipment suppliers.

TROUBLESHOOTING

What to do when things go don't go as planned? Here are the two most common questions I get asked by beginners starting out on their digital embroidery journey.

QUESTION 1: The quality of my embroidery is poor, what do I do to improve it?

Poor stitch quality can result for various reasons. Here are some steps and adjustments you can make to improve your work.

Needle check: first, ensure the needle is not bent, blunt or damaged. A fresh needle can make a significant difference in stitch quality. Also ensure that you have inserted the needle correctly and it is of a suitable size.

Thread quality: use high-quality embroidery thread. Cheap or old thread can break easily or cause uneven stitches.

Machine threading: double-check you have threaded the machine correctly and it is still correctly threaded. Occasionally threads may catch on things around them, making a difference to the thread tension.

Thread tension: incorrect thread tension can lead to puckering or looped stitches. Check the machine's upper and bobbin thread tension and adjust as necessary.

Stabilisers: ensure you're using the correct type and weight of stabiliser for your fabric and design; an inappropriate stabiliser can lead to poor stitch definition or puckering.

Hoop tension: ensure the fabric is hooped tautly without being overstretched. Slack in the fabric can cause misalignment and uneven stitching.

Machine maintenance: regularly clean and oil your embroidery machine. Lint and dust can build up, affecting stitch quality, especially around the needles and bobbin.

Design density: ensure the design's stitch density is appropriate for the fabric you're using. Designs that are too dense can cause puckering or needle breaks on lightweight fabrics.

Speed: try reducing the stitching speed. Sometimes, running the machine at a very high speed can compromise stitch quality.

Software: if you're using digitising software, ensure that the design has been digitised correctly. Poor digitisation can lead to subpar stitch-outs. Check your underlayer and pull compensation settings.

By addressing these factors and making the necessary adjustments, you should see a noticeable improvement in your stitch-out quality.

QUESTION 2: Why does my thread keep breaking or shredding during embroidery?

Breaking and shredding thread is quite common and can be frustrating. Here are some steps and adjustments you can make to help prevent this happening. Like the previous question, there is no one answer, so you have to apply a process of elimination. Here are my recommendations on what to check.

Needle check: first, ensure the needle is not bent, blunt or damaged. Ensure you have inserted the needle correctly and it is of a suitable size for the fabric, your design and the thread.

Thread quality: invest in high-quality embroidery thread. Lower quality threads can be more prone to breaking or shredding. Ensure the thread is not old or has been stored in damp conditions, as this can weaken it.

Thread path: ensure the thread is correctly threaded through the machine, following the manufacturer's guidelines. Incorrect threading can cause unnecessary tension on the thread and cause it to break.
Thread tension: adjust the tension settings. If the tension is too high, it can cause the thread to break.
Machine speed: if you're running your machine at a very high speed, try slowing it down, especially for designs with intricate details or many jumps.
Maintenance: regularly clean the machine, especially around the bobbin case and tension discs, to remove lint, dust and thread fragments that could be causing issues.
Bobbin: ensure that the bobbin thread is smoothly wound and that the bobbin case is free from any damages or lint.
Stabiliser: using the wrong type or weight of stabiliser can lead to tension issues, which might cause thread breaks.
Design issues: if you're using a digitised design, ensure that it's well-digitised. Poor-quality designs can have too many stitches or too dense areas, leading to thread breaks.

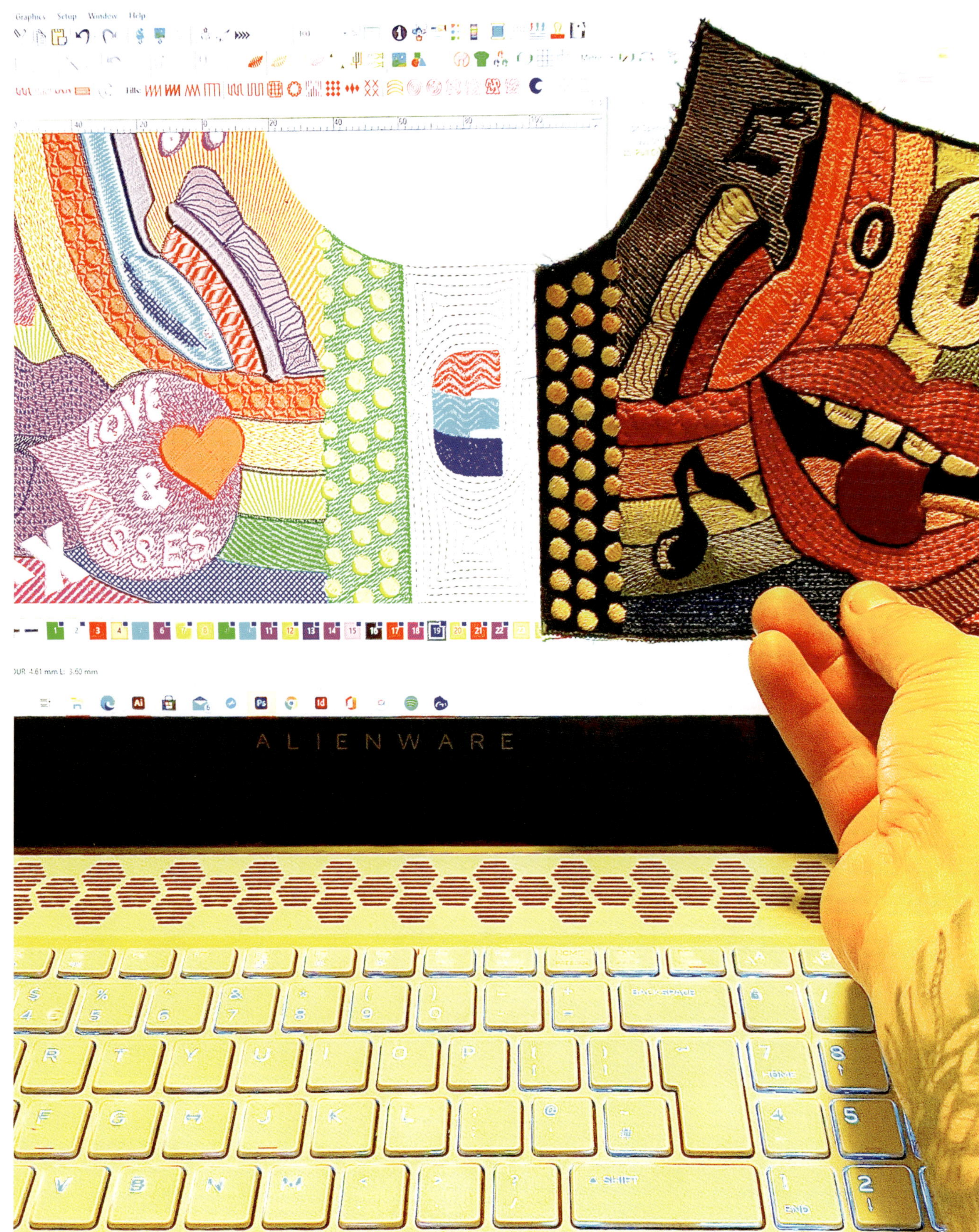
Graphics Setup Window Help
LOVE
&
ALIENWARE
BACKSPACE
SHIFT

CHAPTER 2

GETTING STARTED: FUNDAMENTALS YOU NEED TO KNOW BEFORE YOU BEGIN

Digitising for embroidery is the process of creating a digital embroidery file that can be read and interpreted by an embroidery machine.

UNDERSTANDING THE DIGITISING PROCESS

There is a big difference between commercial and creative digitising. Commercial digitising is aimed at creating embroidery that can be produced over and over again, exactly the same and as cost-effectively as possible. This type of embroidery is commonly found as logos on sports and designer tops, school uniform badges, patches and more. To keep costs low and production speed as fast as possible, often the stitch fill types and colours are reduced, thus reducing the amount of machine travel, needle changes and slow production speed needed for the more complex fill types. Tatami and satin fills are the two most common stitch fill types seen in commercial digital embroidery, with tatami a very stable fill able to cover large surface areas, and satin stitch able to give a more luxurious, shiny finish – perfect for borders, edges, flower stems text and more. The image here shows a typical embroidered sports badge with reduced colours and stitch types. Reducing the colours can make a difference to costs, but mass production industrial machines are often multi-head, multi-needled, which can mean little difference in costs between a 4-colour image and a 9-colour image, for example. How a digitised graphic is created can be very different for an image prepared for mass production (with efficiency in mind), and one that is prepared for a one-off piece (with design detailing in mind). This chapter will cover key fundamentals that are applicable to both commercial and creative outputs.

Typical embroidered sporting logos with very limited stitch fills and colours.

OPPOSITE: Right-hand embroidered yoke panel of a jacket held against the left-hand yoke digitised panel on the screen.

OVERVIEW OF THE DIGITISING PROCESS

Digitising for embroidery is the process of creating a digital embroidery file that can be read and interpreted by an embroidery machine. Here are the basic steps involved in digitising for embroidery.

Stage 1: Design creation
The first step is to create the design that will be embroidered, either by traditional hand methods such as sketching, painting, drawing, collage, photography, using computer software such as Adobe Photoshop, Illustrator or CorelDRAW or using the latest AI technologies. How you come up with the design is up to you, allowing you a lot of freedom to be creative and experimental. My go-to method is collage working at 100 per cent scale, mixing drawings, photographs and printouts.

Stage 2: Design conversion
After creating your design, it needs to be converted into a digital format, such as a vector file. This will allow the digitiser (you) to manipulate the design and create the stitch commands necessary for the embroidery machine to create the design. *Please note*: this stage is optional and depends on whether or not you are planning to auto or manually digitise your work into stitches. If you are intending to auto digitise (if your software has this feature), then cleaning the image in CAD software and converting into a vector form is recommended. If manually digitising, then you can skip this stage and import a photograph of your artwork directly into your digitising software.

Stage 3: Digitising software
Whether you carried out stage 2 or not, you will need to import your artwork into your digitising software. The software allows the digitiser to set stitch parameters such as stitch type, stitch direction, density and more. You design the embroidery stitches!

Stage 4: Stitching commands
The digitising software creates stitch commands based on the design and stitch parameters that you have assigned. These

A panda design being virtually stitched out on the computer screen.

commands tell the embroidery machine what type of stitch to use, where to start and stop stitching, sequence order, colour selection and other details. The transfer of information from the computer to the machine can be done by a cable, USB device or on newer machines wi-fi or Bluetooth (please refer to your machine's instruction manual).

Stage 5: Testing and refinement

After creating the digitised embroidery file and uploading it to your machine, you are ready to begin embroidering (also known as 'stitch-out'). *Before you attempt your final embroidery on your chosen fabric, it is recommended that you produce a test piece first* to ensure that the stitched design matches the original design and that the stitch parameters are correct. This also enable you to review your colour selection, thread type and stabiliser choice. If necessary, make changes based on the quality of the stitch-out.

For large designs, you may wish to stitch out a small section only in order to gauge how the design responds to the fabric and the quality of the design. Your software may have a virtual visualisation feature that allows you to see the whole design stitched out on your computer screen. This feature is useful for checking sequencing and identifying unwanted shapes, misalignment and so on. The virtual visualisation will stitch out the design exactly as your embroidery machine would, but on your computer screen, thus saving resources, time and lowering costs. Although this is a great time saver, it cannot show you how the fabric will behave when embroidered.

Stage 6: Exporting

Once your digitised embroidery file is refined and finalised, it is exported once again and stitched out on your final fabric choice. The format you export your file in depends on your machine type. Common formats include DST, PES and JEF (please refer to your machine's instruction manual). Most digitising software programs can export for a variety of machine models, but it is worth double-checking before investing in a software program.

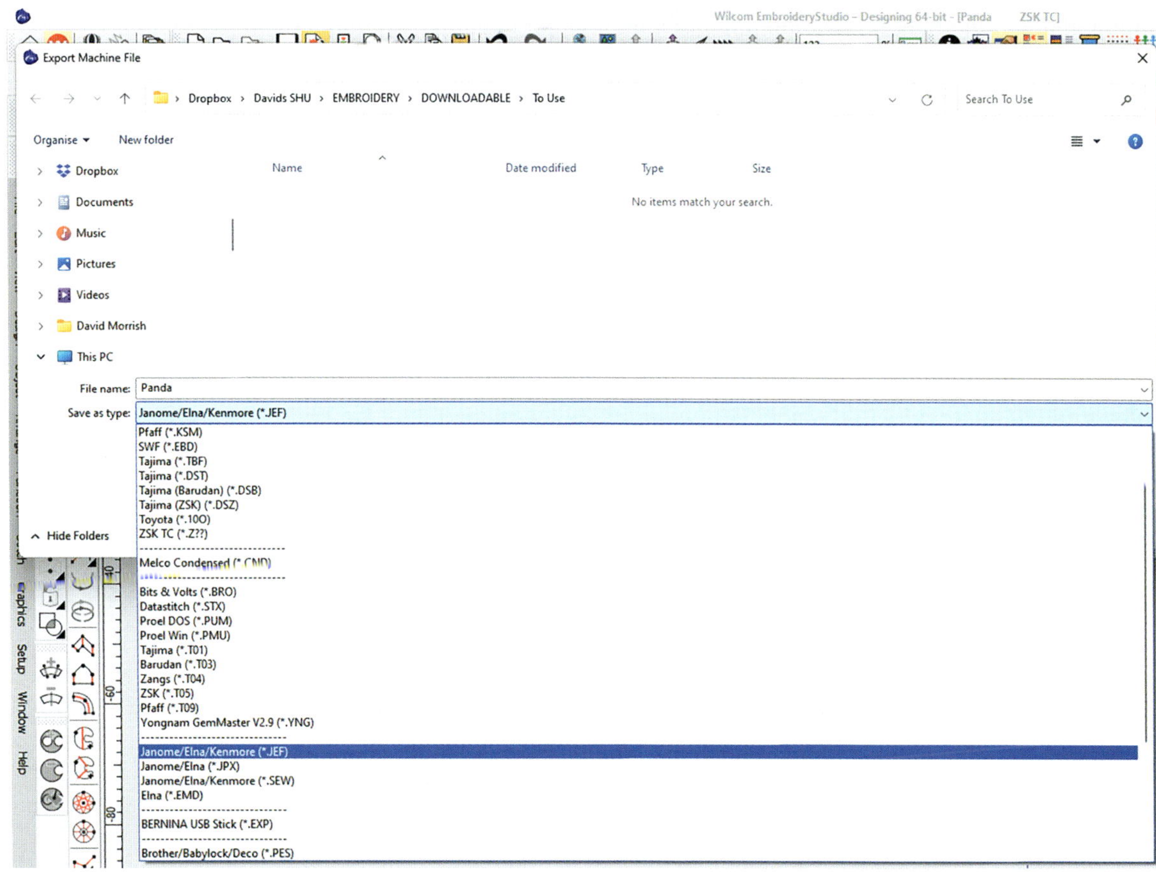

Screenshot of the file export menu on Wilcom software.

Process of Digitising your Artwork

Once you have created your artwork and uploaded it to your computer, you have a few choices on how you are going to digitise your image. This flow chart shows the different approaches between digitising for commercial outcome and digitising for a one-off creative outcome.

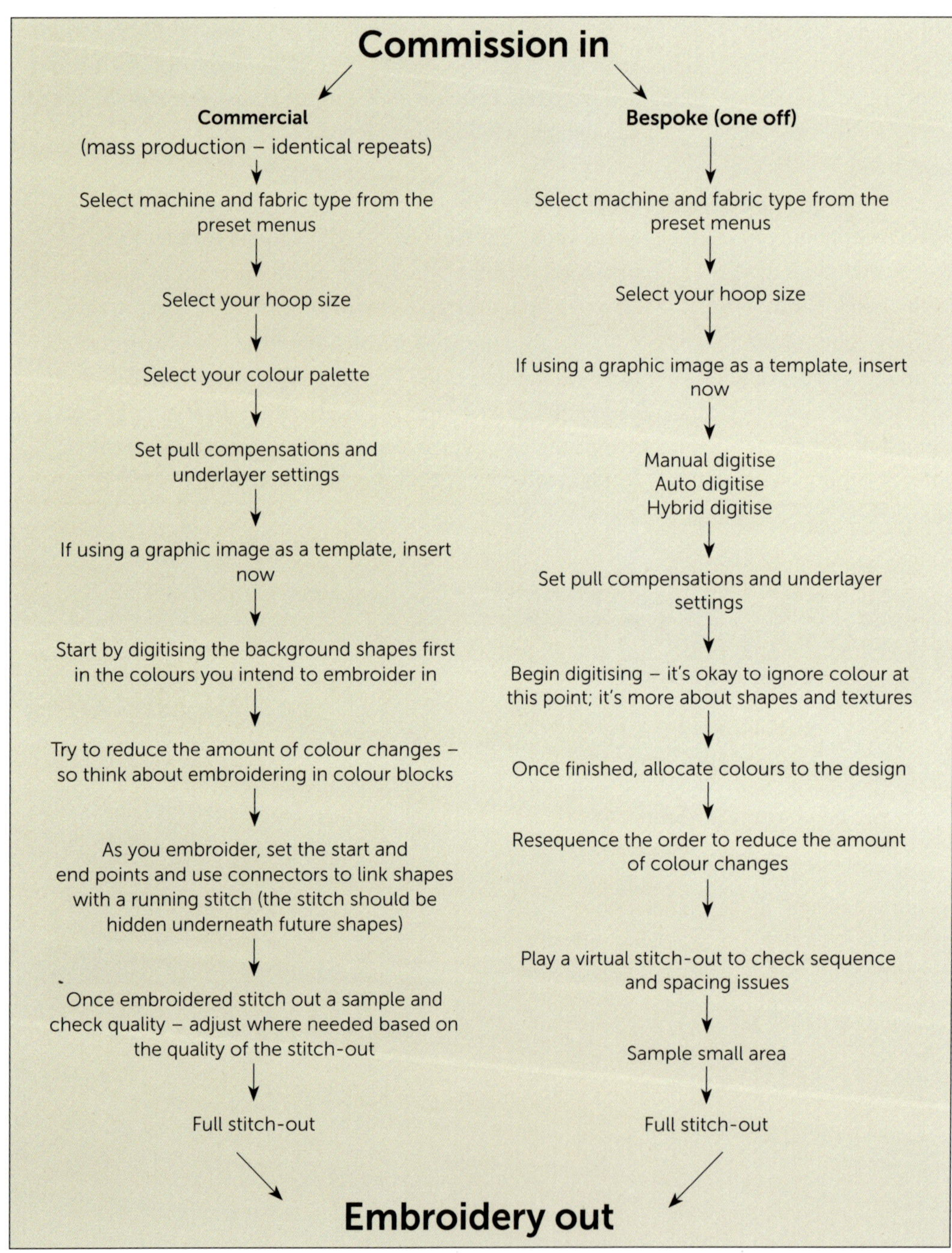

Digitising flow chart, showing the difference between commercial and one-off digitising.

KEY FUNDAMENTALS YOU NEED TO KNOW

Hooping Methods

Digital embroidery hooping methods refer to the techniques used to secure the fabric and backing materials in (or to) the embroidery hoop before it is placed in the embroidery machine. Hooping is an important part of the process, which can directly affect the quality of the design. If the fabric is too loose it will enable the fabric to move, thus causing misalignment and distortion. If the fabric is stretched too much, then the embroidered outcome can gather in on itself when removed from the hoop as the fabric returns to its natural state of tension, thus causing unwanted fluting around the embroidery. Ideally, you need to achieve a drum-tight tension, somewhere in between the two extremes. Stretchy fabrics are hard to gauge, and you need to produce some test samples before your final project in order to

Fluting caused by overstretching the fabric in the hoop, often seen around the edge of the design or in between shapes.

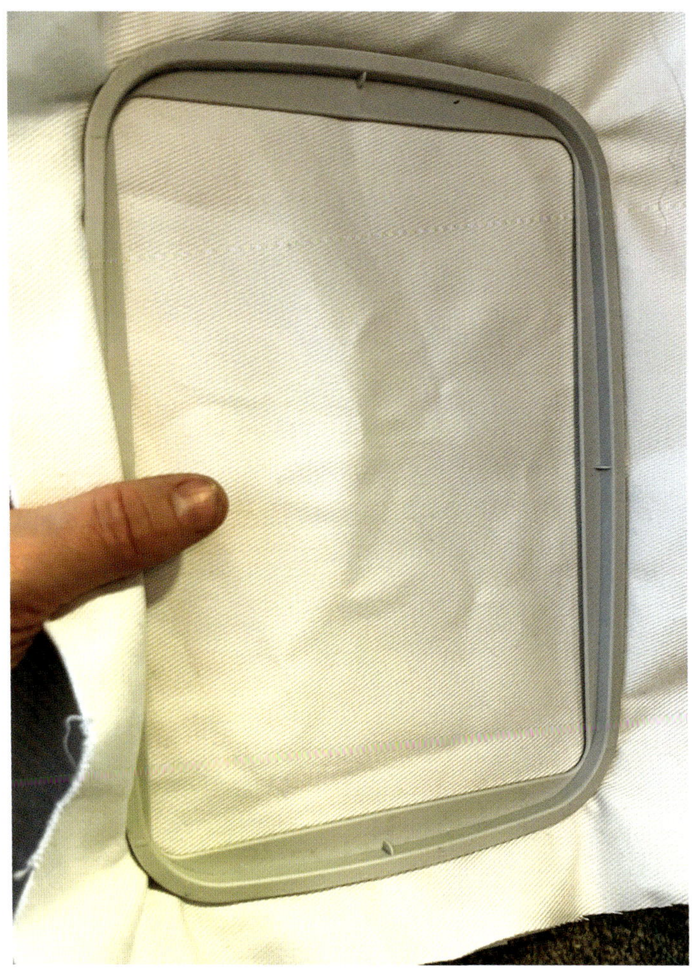

Hooped canvas fabric, which is too loose in the frame.

A drum-tight hooped fabric in a frame.

achieve the most suitable hooping stretch for the fabric type. Selecting the most appropriate hooping method for the fabric is important as some fabrics are prone to surface damage, which can be caused by the embroidery hoop.

Common hooping methods

Standard Hooping (sandwiching): this method involves placing the fabric and backing material in the embroidery hoop and tightening the hoop to secure them. The fabric should be taut, but not overly stretched, ensuring that it remains stable during the embroidery process. The hoop is then attached to the embroidery machine for stitching. Be careful with fabrics that could be damaged if trapped and fabrics that are too bulky, as this makes hooping more problematic.

Floating Method: in the floating method, the fabric is not secured directly in the embroidery hoop. Instead, a layer of stabiliser is hooped tightly, and the fabric is placed on top of it. The fabric is then fixed using temporary adhesive, pins or basting threads. This method is useful for delicate fabrics or materials that may be difficult to hoop directly. Using a stabiliser with an adhesive layer makes this method a lot easier, as the fabric secures itself to the backing without the need for pins or other securing methods.

It's important to follow the instructions provided by the embroidery machine manufacturer and consider the fabric type, design complexity and desired outcome when choosing the hooping method. Proper hooping ensures that the fabric remains stable and flat, resulting in accurate and high-quality embroidery.

Lightly spray the stabiliser with a temporary adhesive before placing the fabric on top. This helps keep the fabric in position while you're securing it in the hoop.

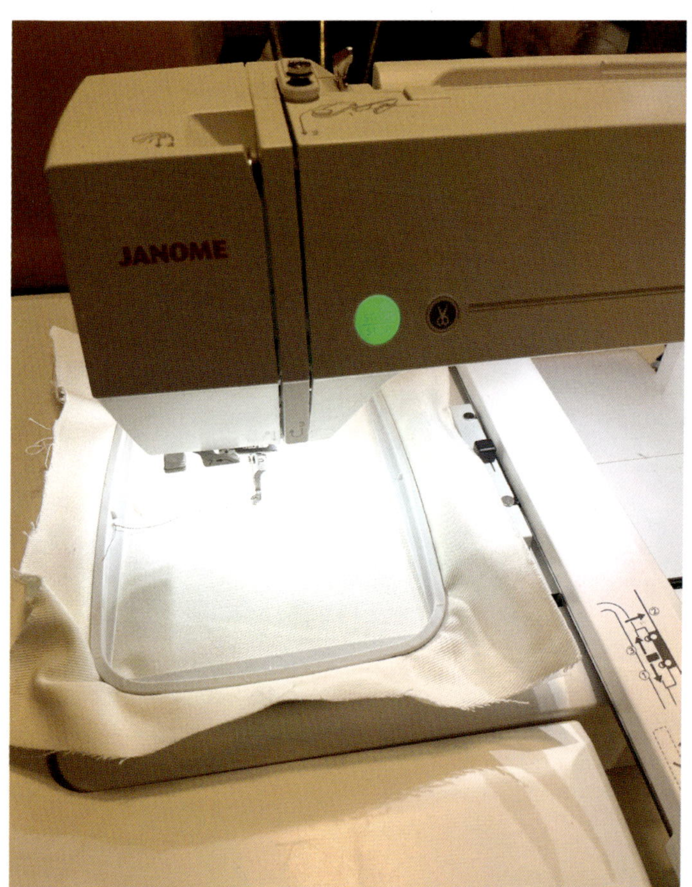

Hooped fabric in a frame, attached to an embroidery machine.

Denim jacket being embroidered using the floating method.

Underlays and Fill Types

When you watch an embroidery machine in action, you will notice it embroiders one shape at a time, using only one needle at a time (even if you are using a multi-needle machine, only one needle is embroidering at any given time). The machine will then move to a new location and begin embroidering the next shape. An image is a series of shapes, with each shape containing form, colour and texture. The digitiser (you) is responsible for designing the shapes, selecting the fills (texture), colours and instructing the machine on what order to embroider the shapes in.

Underlays

As the machine embroiders a shape, you will notice it does it in two stages.

The first stage is the creation of the underlayer. This layer adds structure and stability to the fabric, it is a vital layer that often gets overlooked or underutilised and can make a big difference to the quality of the outcome. (If we were building a house, the underlayer would be the foundation, often unseen, but vital to supporting the weight of the building.) If a fabric distorts too much by the embroidery, you may be tempted to add more stabiliser to strengthen it before attempting again; this can work in some cases, but there is a risk the cloth will become too thick and heavy, causing it to become rigid like cardboard and lose its hanging qualities. However, experimenting with the underlayer settings – type, angle, spacing and stitch length – can prevent the need for additional stabiliser and potentially reduce bulk and costs. Underlays also create a base for the decorative stitches to sit on top of and can prevent them sinking too much into the fabric.

As best practice, it is always worth creating samples on the actual fabric, with your intended stabiliser(s) to best

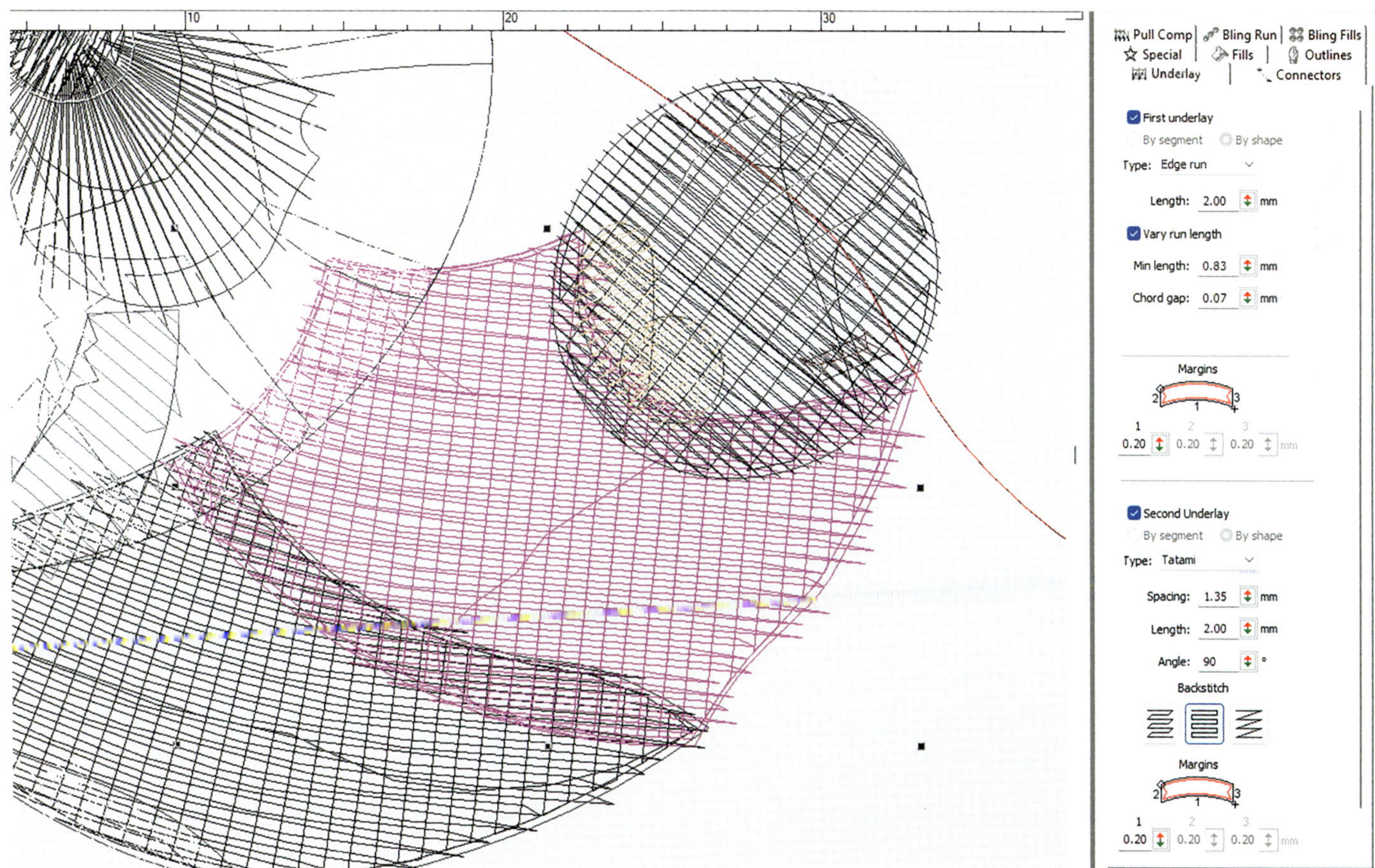

A highlighted shape's underlayer and underlayer settings.

evaluate the quality of the embroidery outcome before deciding if you need to change the underlayer settings or not.

You have three main options when it comes to your underlayer (when using Wilcom E4.5 software): no underlayer, only one underlayer or two underlayers. The types of underlayers available are:

Edge run: a single line of stitching around the outside edge of your shape.

Centre stitch: a single line of stitching through the centre of your shape.

Zigzag: mainly used with satin fills, this underlayer creates zigzag stitches covering the complete area of your shape.

Tatami: creates a net type underlayer, ideal for tatami and textured fills.

Double tatami: as above, but provides more stability.

My preferred underlayer settings differ depending on whether I am using tatami or satin fills.

For tatami fills: edge run and tatami

For satin fills: centre stitch and zigzag

To increase stability of the fabric, reduce the stitch size and spacing.

Avoid going under 1mm spacing and stitch size. There is a common misconception that increasing the spacing and stitch size will make the fabric more stable, when in fact it is the opposite.

Always test your fabric as some embroider better with no underlayer. Fabrics to be careful of include leathers and skins, delicates, loose weave fabric, PVC and stretch fabrics. The more stable, woven fabrics of a medium to heavy weight – for example, cotton, canvas, calico, denim and even wools – are generally a good, reliable choice for embroidering on.

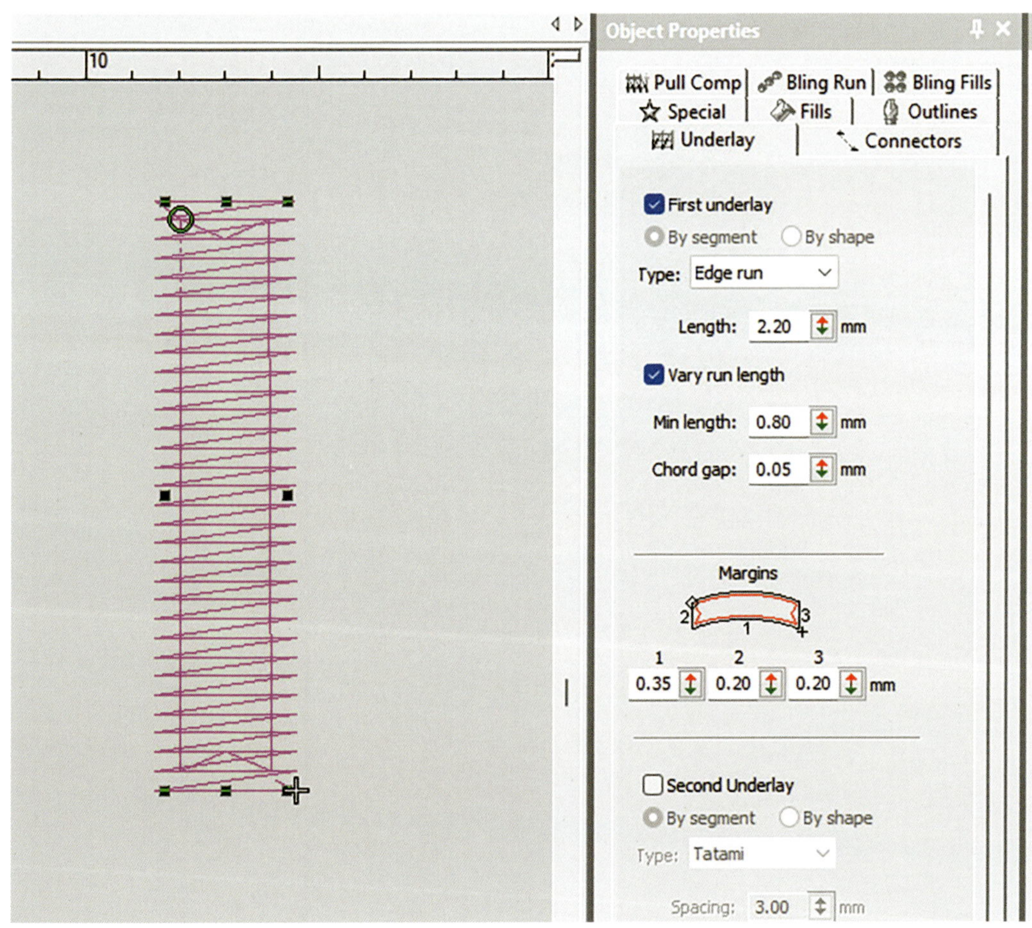

Underlayer with edge run applied.

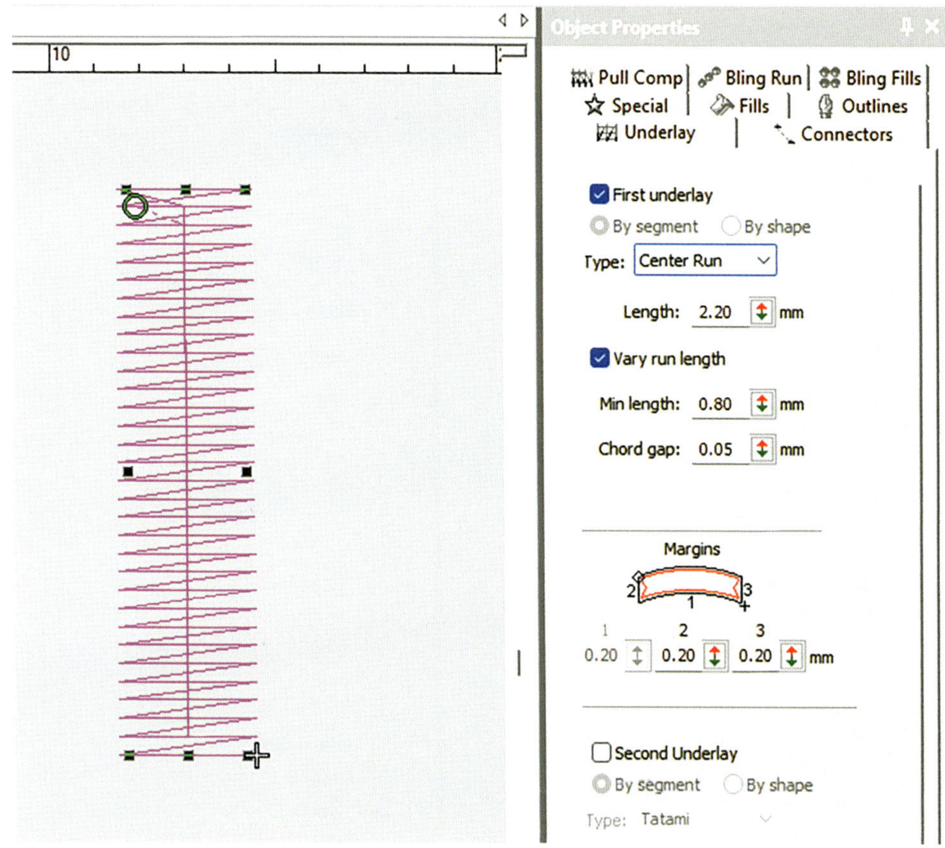

Underlayer with centre run stitch applied.

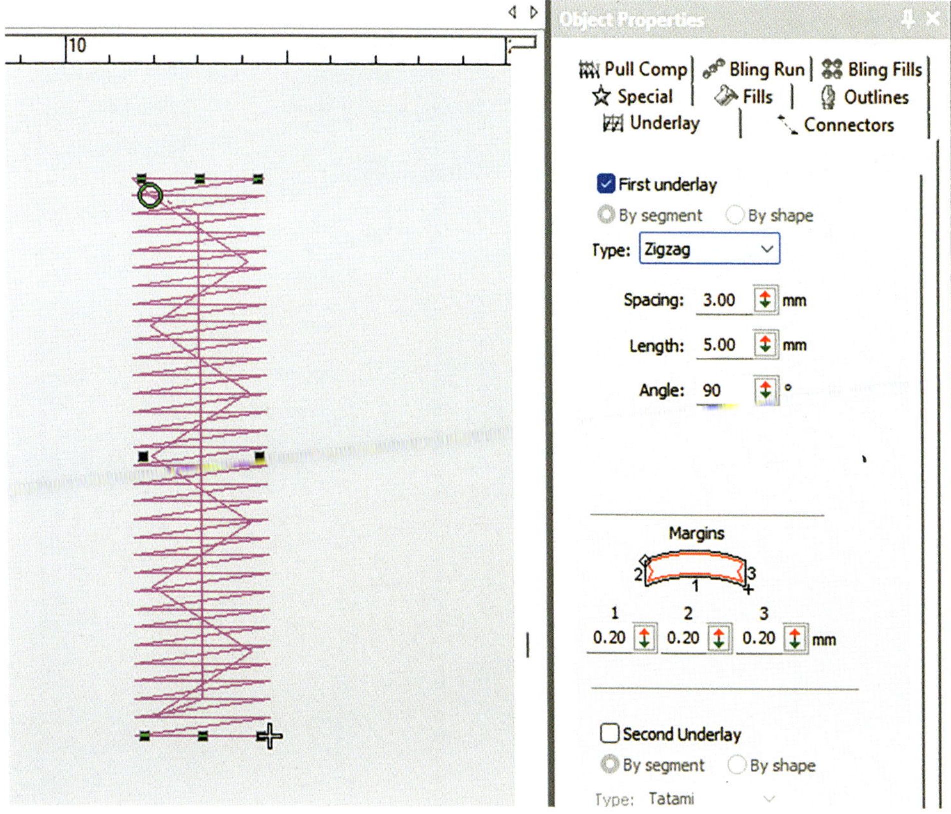

Underlayer with zigzag stitch applied.

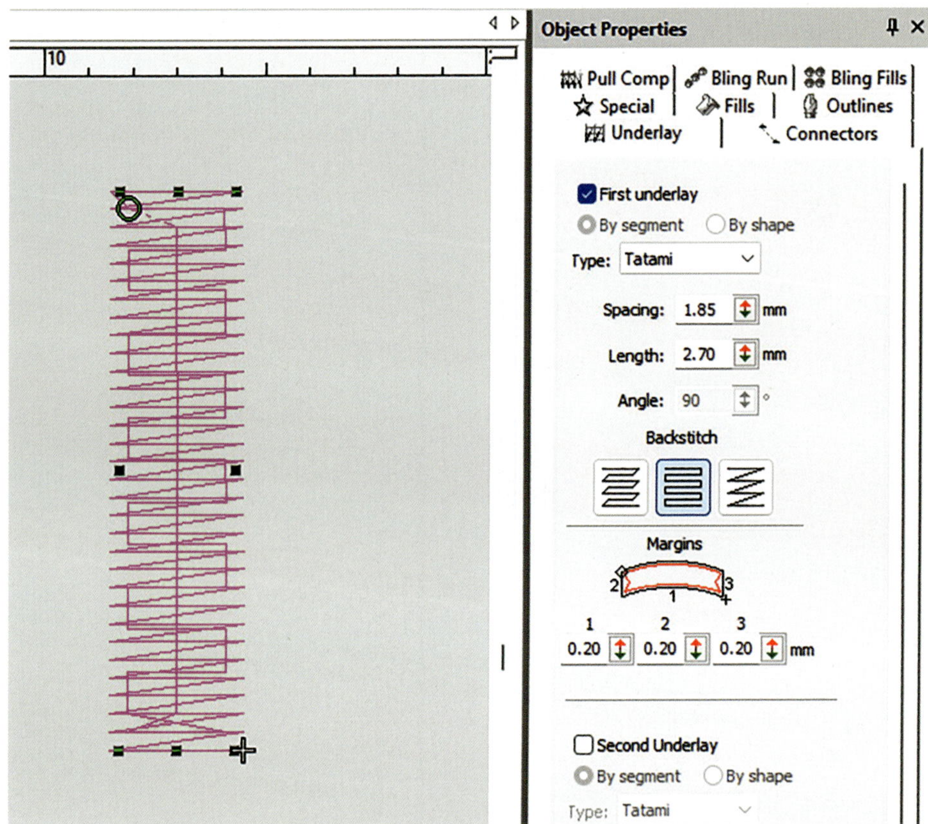

Underlayer with tatami stitch applied.

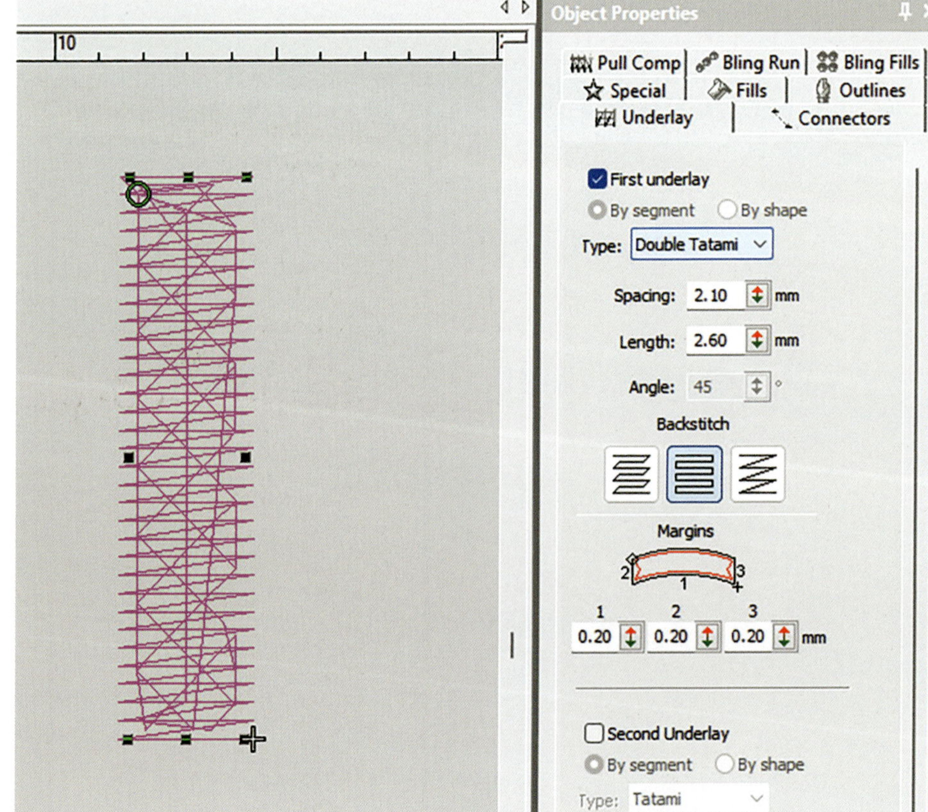

Underlayer with double tatami stitch applied.

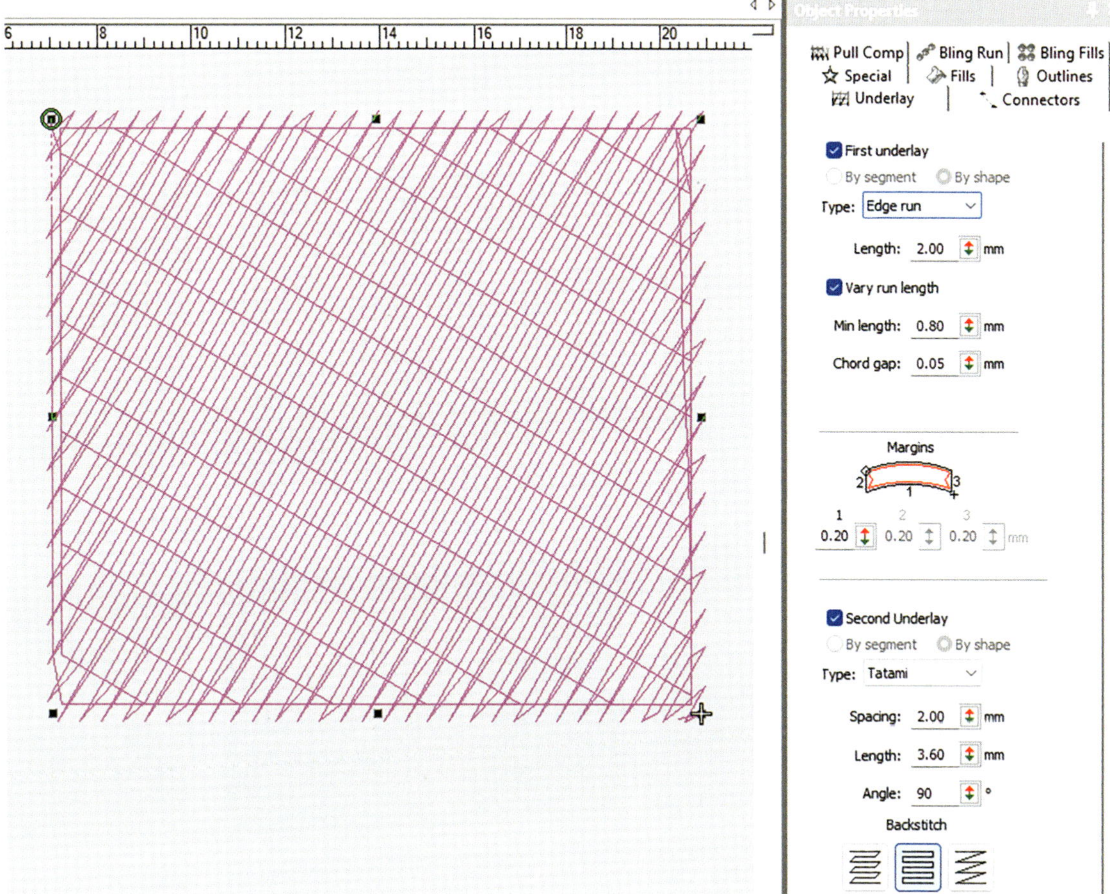

My go-to settings for tatami shapes.

Tatami underlayer with edge stitched - stitched out on cotton fabric.

FILLS

The second stage of embroidering a shape is the creation of a top decorative layer (often referred to as a 'fill'); this is the layer you visibly see when looking at the embroidery. This layer hides an underlayer if the shape has been assigned one. Some fills such as maze, contour and motif do not have an underlayer by default. When you start experimenting with gradients and layering, then turning off the underlayer can help to enhance the fill effect. Overleaf is a selection of fill types using the Wilcom E4.5 software.

OUTLINES

Generally, shapes can be filled or outlined. If an outline is assigned to a shape, only the edge will be stitched, leaving the internal area empty. Types of outline stitches include running, triple, zigzag and motif. Adding an outline over a filled shape can be used to create finer details and borders.

Variety of applied fills.

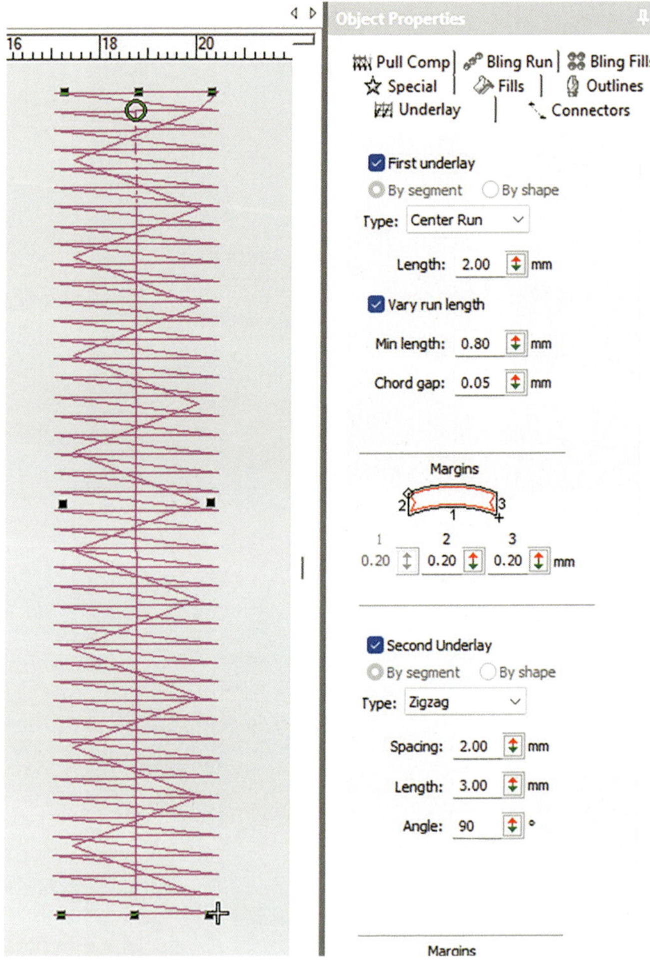

My go-to settings for satin shapes.

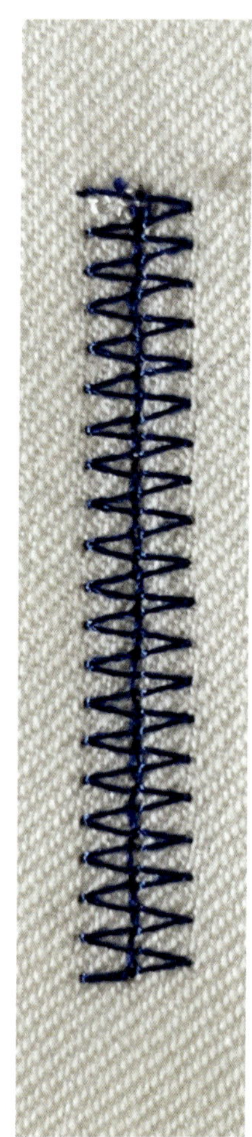

Satin underlayer stitched out.

PULL COMPENSATION

Pull compensation refers to the process of adjusting the stitching in an embroidery design to compensate for fabric distortion caused by the addition of embroidery threads being added to the fabric.

Applying pull compensation is necessary because the fabric can be pulled in different directions by the stitching, which can cause the design to be misaligned or distorted. As stitches are added into the cloth, the top thread pushes through the weave, interacts with the bobbin thread and then pulls up through the cloth. This process is repeated many times, often causing the cloth to contract (shrink) on its warp and/or weft. The amount the cloth shrinks depends on the thread thickness, stitch density, stitch type, needle selection, fabric properties and stabiliser(s) used. Because of the number of variables that are in play, it is important to create test samples prior to starting your final stitch-out.

By adjusting the stitching (Pull Compensation setting) at the digitising stage, the embroidery machine can compensate for this, producing a cleaner, neater outcome.

If you are using a fabric type for the first time and you are not sure how it will behave when embroidered on, it is worth creating pull compensation test samples. Save these in your archives to refer to in the future.

How to Create a Pull Compensation Test Sample

Follow these steps to work out the pull compensation you need to allocate to your design. To do this, I generally only create tatami and satin test swatches.

1. Hoop the fabric and stabiliser(s) you are planning to use for your project.
2. Digitise a square using the following settings:
   Size: 4cm × 4cm
   Decorative fill: Tatami

Embroidered art piece labelled with stitch types used.

Stitch angle: 45 degrees
Underlayer 1: Edge stitch
Underlayer 2: Tatami – borderline backstitch 90 degrees
Stitch Density: 0.40mm
Pull Compensation: 20mm (default setting using Wilcom Software)

3. Digitise a vertical rectangle using the following settings:

   Size: 0.5cm × 4cm
   Decorative fill: satin
   Underlayer 1: zigzag
   Underlayer 2: none
   Stitch Density: 0.36mm
   Pull Compensation: 20 (default)

4. Embroider on your chosen fabric (stitch-out) and review the outcome.

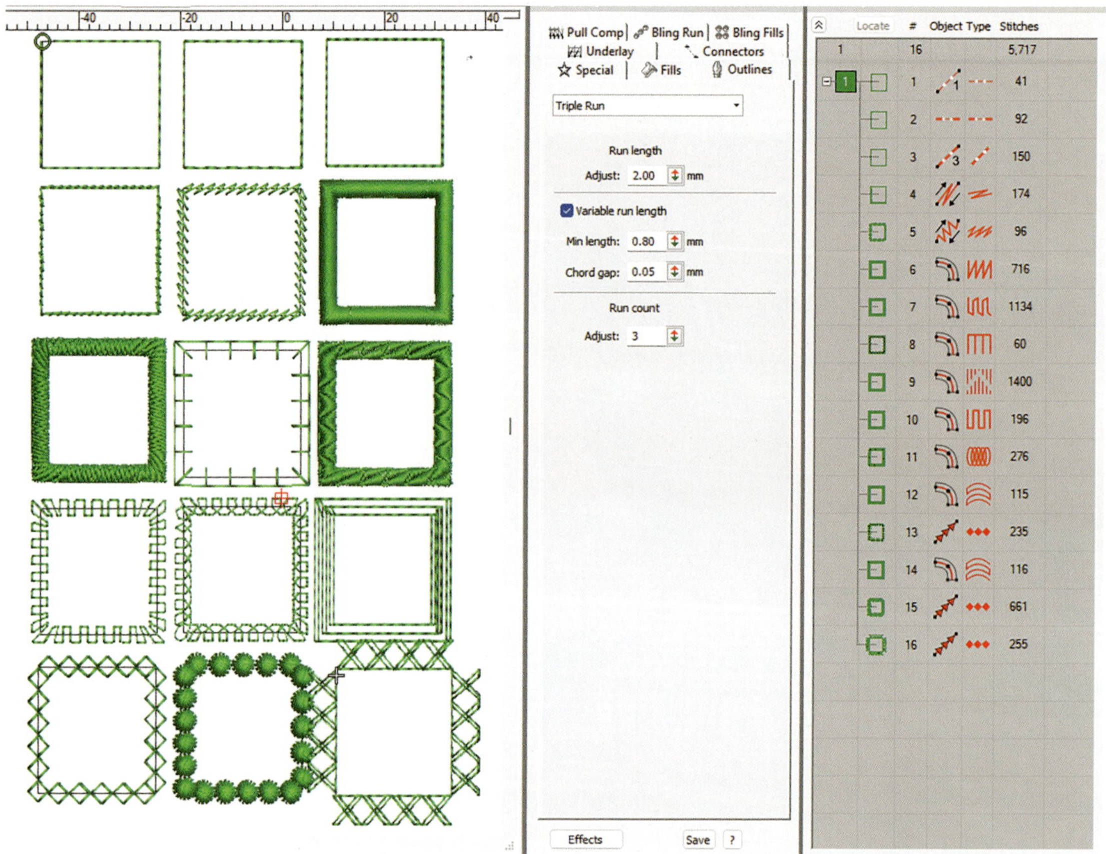

#	Stitches
1	5,717
1	41
2	92
3	150
4	174
5	96
6	716
7	1134
8	60
9	1400
10	196
11	276
12	115
13	235
14	116
15	661
16	255

The different outlines applied to the same shape.

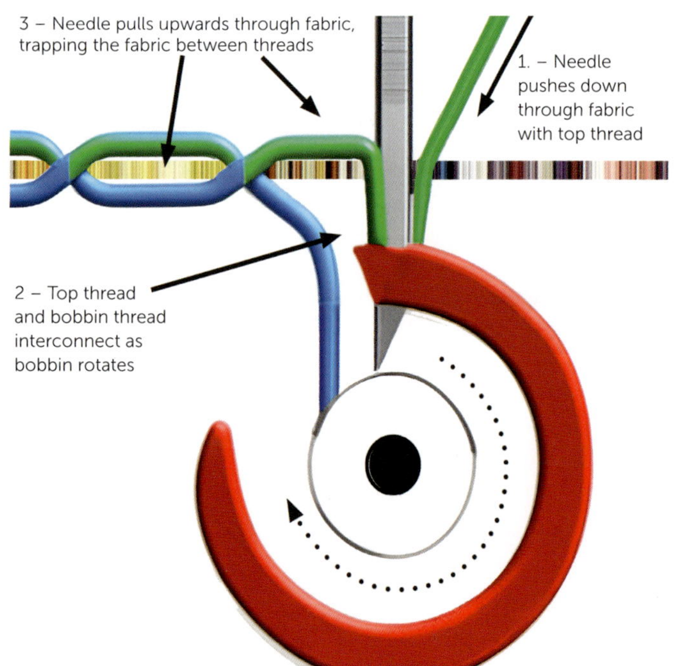

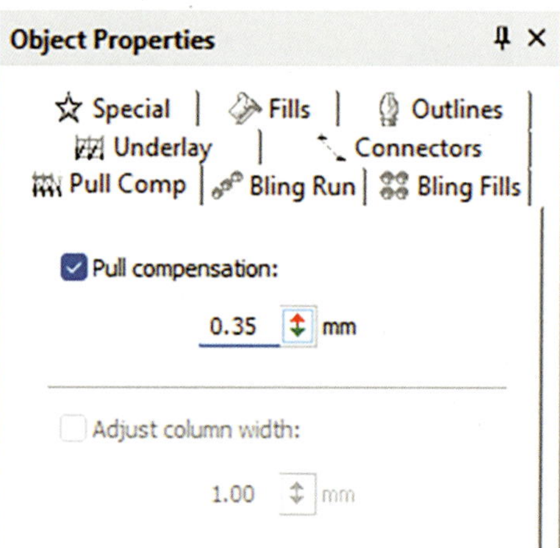

Adjusting pull compensation settings on Wilcom software.

Image showing visible gaps appearing between shapes; increasing the pull compensation could solve this issue.

What you are looking for

Tatami Square

For the tatami square you may notice the edge stitching underlayer becoming visible, telling me the decorative layer (top layer) has distorted the fabric when applied. The gap between the visible edge stitched underlayer and the decorative layer gives you an idea of how much the decorative layer has distorted the fabric (both on its vertical and horizontal directions).

If you measure this gap in millimetres and then add this distance to the pull compensation default setting, it should correct the issue. Embroider the sample again to check and amend if necessary.

Note: When you alter the pull compensation for a shape, it will change appearance on your screen, and may no longer look correct; however, when you embroider the shape on the fabric it should appear correct. For this

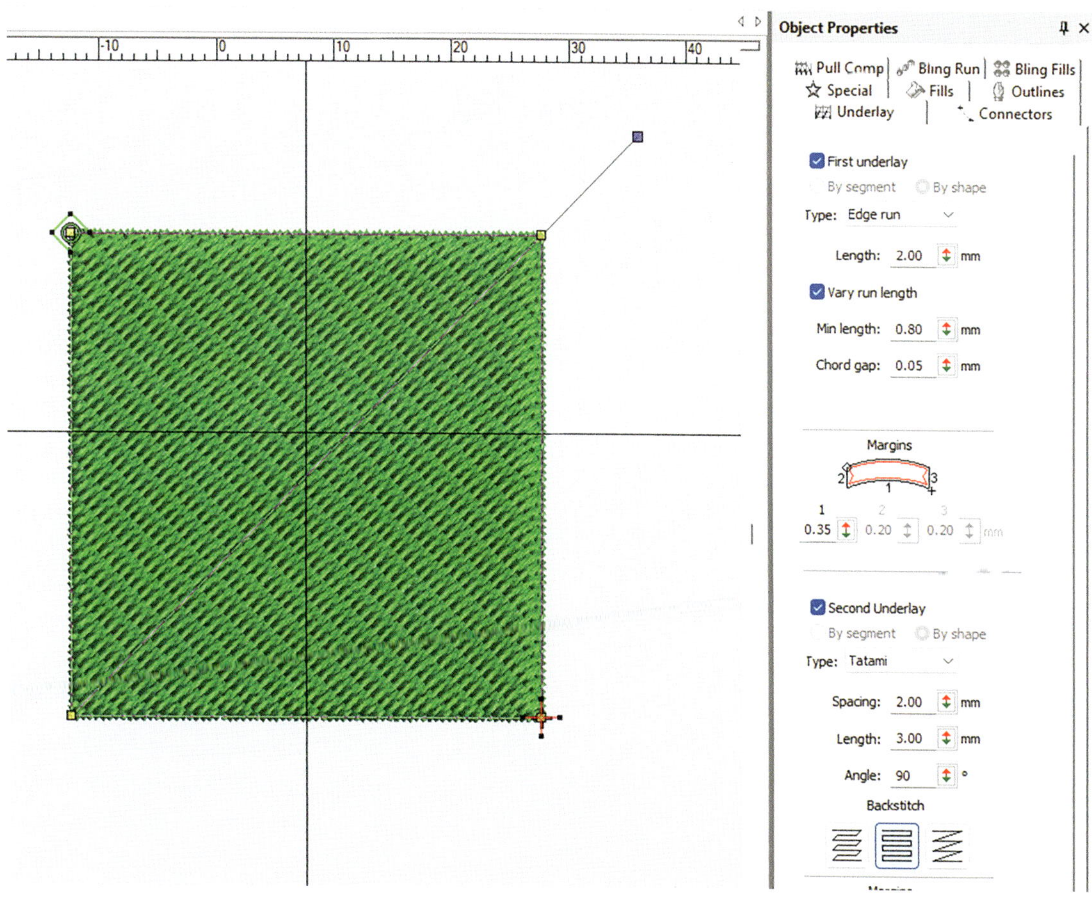

Tatami square and underlayer settings for a pull compensation test sample on a cotton fabric.

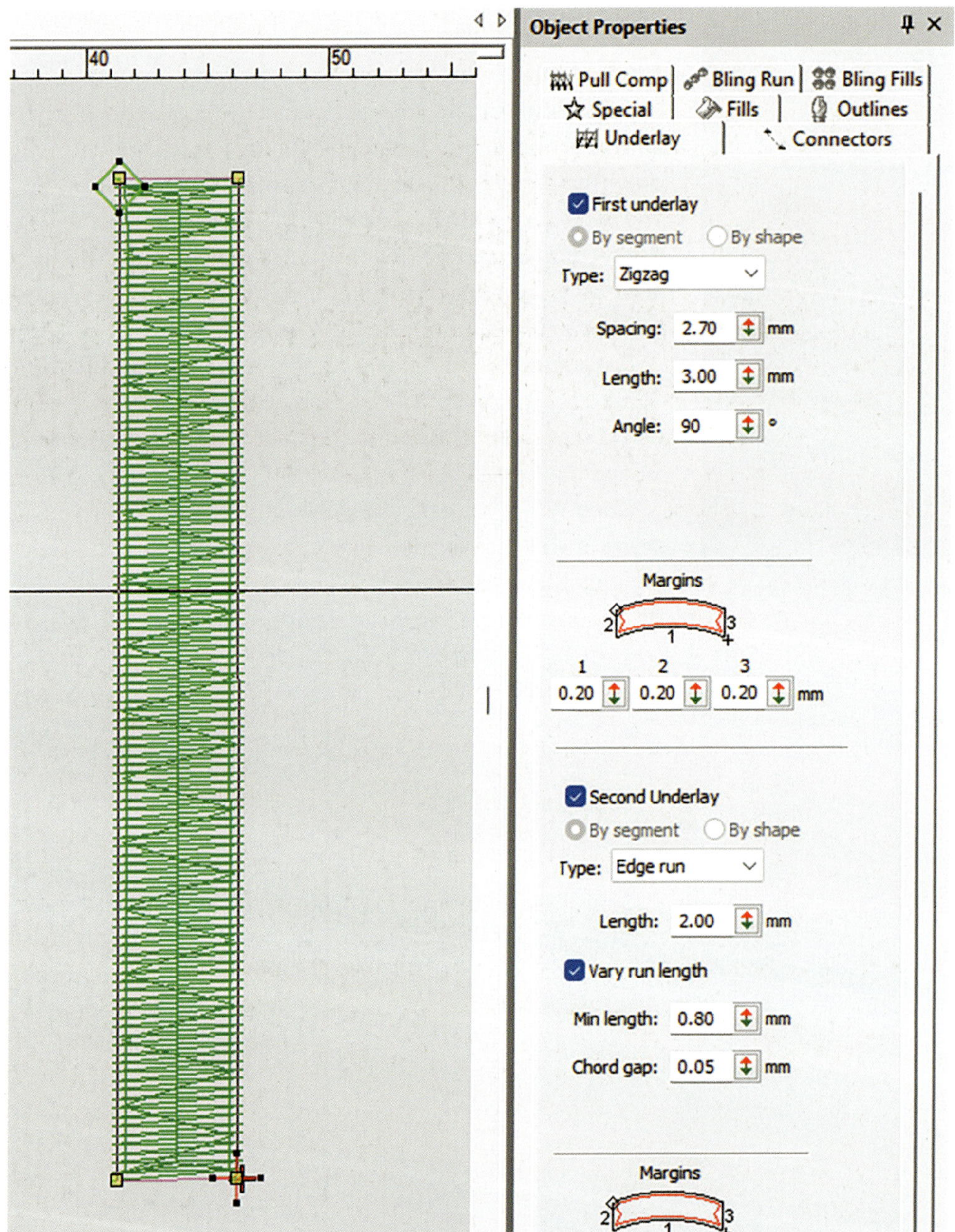

Satin rectangle and underlayer settings for a pull compensation test on a cotton fabric.

reason, I often apply the pull compensation settings after I have digitised my artwork (unless I already know the settings for the fabric and stabilisers I have selected). For this fabric and stabiliser, I have applied a pull of 0.20mm.

Satin Rectangle

For the satin rectangle, you are looking to see if the vertical line is still vertical, if the zigzag underlayer is visible or not and if there is any distortion to the shape or surrounding fabric. What you may see is some of the zigzag stitching appearing from underneath, or the vertical line becoming slanted (like the Leaning Tower of Pisa). Increasing the pull compensation should correct this, hiding the zigzag stitching and straightening the rectangle.

To save time, I often embroider x5 vertical rectangles all with satin stitch, next to each other, but assign a

Visible edge stitching underlayer after the decorative top layer has been embroidered.

A correctly digitised tatami square, with no underlayer visible.

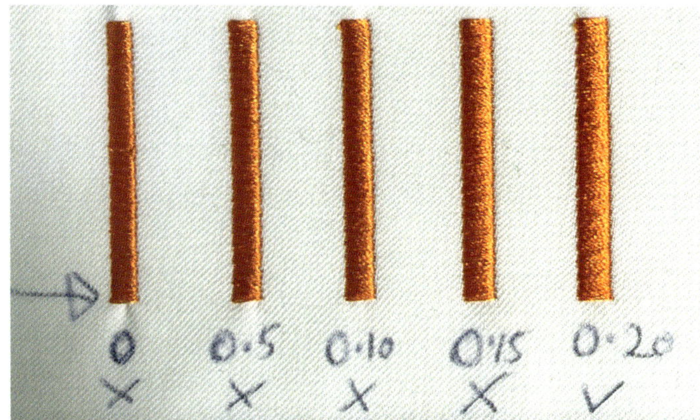

Pull compensation test sample, for five vertical rectangles all with different pull compensation settings applied.

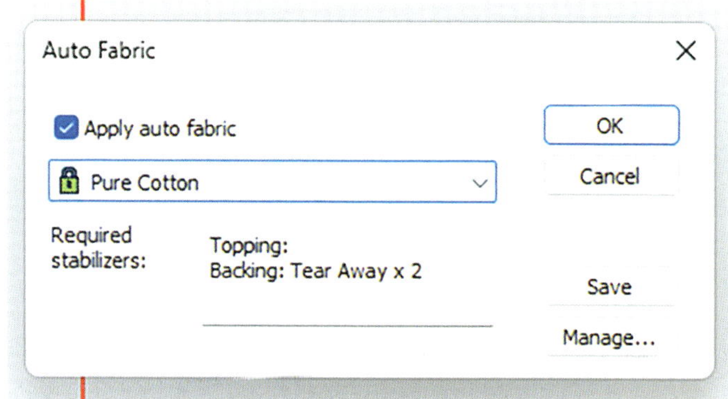

Auto Fabric window types on the Wilcom Software.

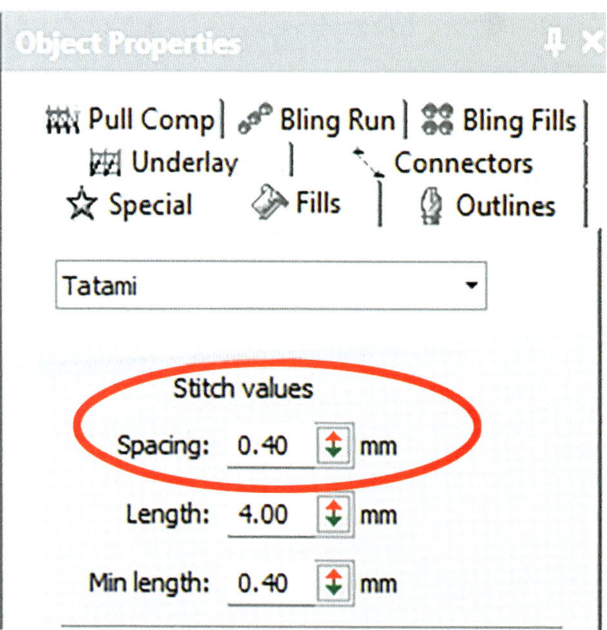

Screenshot showing the stitch spacing settings for a shape.

different pull compensation setting to each one. I will then embroider this in one go and choose the rectangle that appears to be the most accurate when stitched out.

Based on the sample, the best pull compensation setting for this fabric and stabiliser selection, is 0.20mm. The others (0, 0.5, 0.10) show fabric distortion around the ends, whilst 0.15 feels more raised than 0.20mm. Once you know your pull compensation settings for tatami and satin stitches, you can apply these to all the other shapes in your artwork.

Note: I often give program fills (Wilcom terminology for the more textured fill types) the same setting as the tatami fill; however, depending on the density of the program fill, it may cause more distortion than a tatami fill and therefore I would increase the pull compensation even more to be safe. You can always create a pull compensation test swatch with your intended program fill if you are not confident.

Remember that all fabric types distort by different amounts. Stabilisers and underlayers help to stabilise the fabric to prevent or reduce distortion; however, it is always recommended to carry out a pull compensation test swatch if you are using a new fabric or different stabiliser(s) for the first time. Some software programs allow you to select the fabric type from a preset selection menu, which automatically adjusts the pull compensation settings for you (as well as telling you which stabilisers to use).

Save and label your test samples to create your own pull compensation library, you can refer to this in the future which can save you time.

STITCH DENSITY

Stitch density refers to the *spacing* given to stitches within a shape. Using a polyester 40 thread as an example, if we allocate a stitch density setting of 0.40mm to a digitised shape, the threads will sit flush to each other. If we increase the stitch density setting, gaps will begin to appear between the stitches. As a preference, if I want a clean, gap-free embroidered shape, I allocate a stitch density of 0.38mm for a poly 40 thread. Some fabrics such as lightweight delicates and skins such as leather and suede cannot accommodate a lot of densely filled shapes without severe distortion occurring. Experimenting with the stitch density can result in some interesting effects, especially when you start to layer shapes, remove the underlayers and experiment with stitch fill types, direction and gradients. The image of the dog shows how layering and manipulating the stitch densities of shapes can be used effectively to create a sense of depth, texture and intrigue.

LAYERING

To create interesting effects, layering shapes and altering the shapes fill settings, it is possible to give a sense of depth, texture, form and motion to your artwork. The two images, the Old English Sheepdog and the self-portrait use a variety of layers to create a sense depth and texture and the use of layering and fill angles, to create form, shadows and highlights, seen in the face and folds of the waistcoat.

Four tatami squares with different stitch spacings applied.

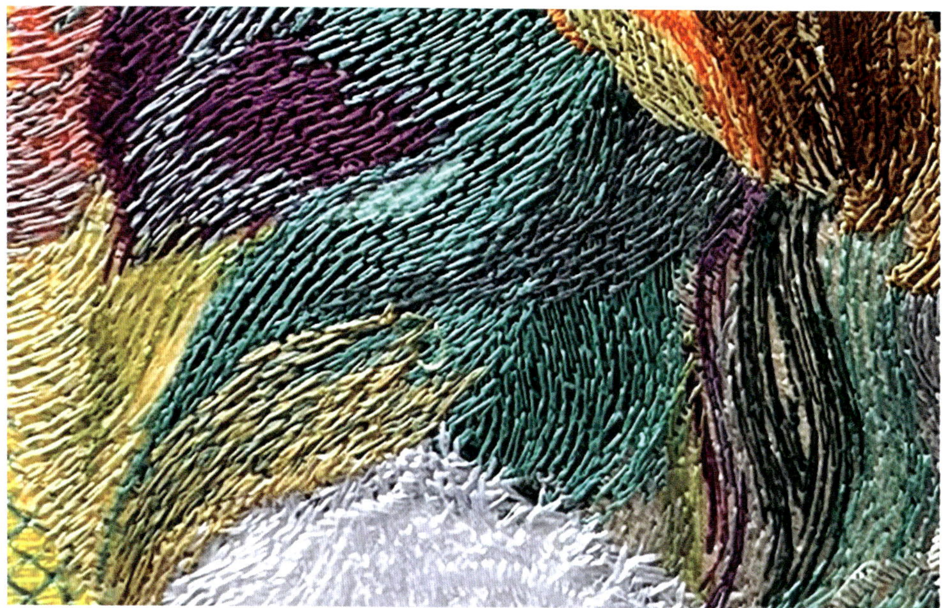

Close-up of an embroidery with various stitch spacings applied.

An embroidered Old English Sheepdog with various layers of different density fills.

SPECIAL EFFECTS

Depending on your software program, you may have options to apply special effects to a fill. These effects can give your design an extra quality adding further texture, intrigue, a sense of movement or even a hand-stitched look. On the Wilcom software these include:

Hand stitch: to give your filled shape a more natural hand-stitched look.

Jagged edge: to give a softer look to a shape's edge.

Accordion: varies the stitch density of the fill within a shape to create a sense of form.

Stamp: stamp an image into a fill as if stamped.

Florentine: adds curves to the fill, helping to create a sense of movement and form.

Radial: adds a central focal point to a shape with the stitches radiating from this point.

Self-portrait to show layering, creating form, shadows and highlights.

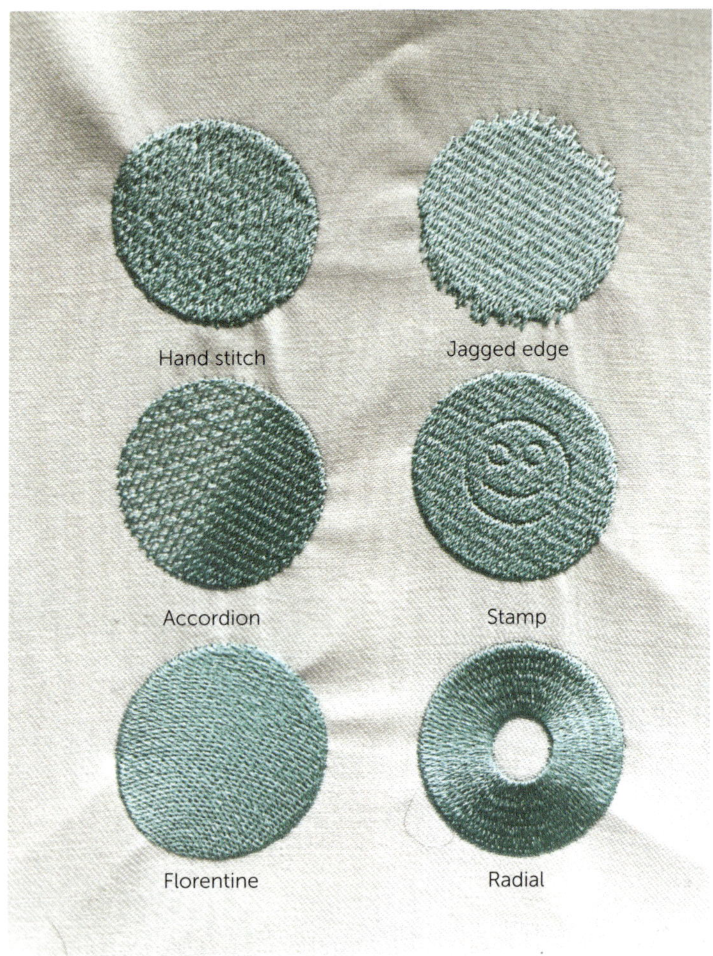

Special effects applied to circles.

An artwork with lots of fills and effects.

THREAD TENSIONS

Thread tension plays a crucial role in ensuring the quality of your embroidery. Both the upper (top) and bobbin (bottom) thread tensions need to be correctly adjusted to achieve a balanced stitch.

The upper thread tension is typically adjusted based on the thread type and fabric being used. If the tension is too tight, the thread may break, pull the fabric, cause puckering, or the bobbin thread may appear on the top side of the fabric. If the upper thread is too loose, the thread may loop on the surface of the fabric.

The bobbin tension, on the other hand, is usually set to a standard tension that works with a wide range of materials and should be adjusted less frequently. It's often fine-tuned when using very thick or thin threads.

Generally, you adjust the upper tension when you see issues with the stitch quality on the top side of the fabric, and the bobbin tension when issues appear on the underside. It's essential to perform a test run on a scrap piece of the same fabric to get these settings right before proceeding with your main project. Remember, achieving the right tension balance is key to preventing problems like fabric puckering or distorted stitches.

Black upper thread tension dials on a multi-needle industrial machine.

Tension settings on a domestic embroidery machine.

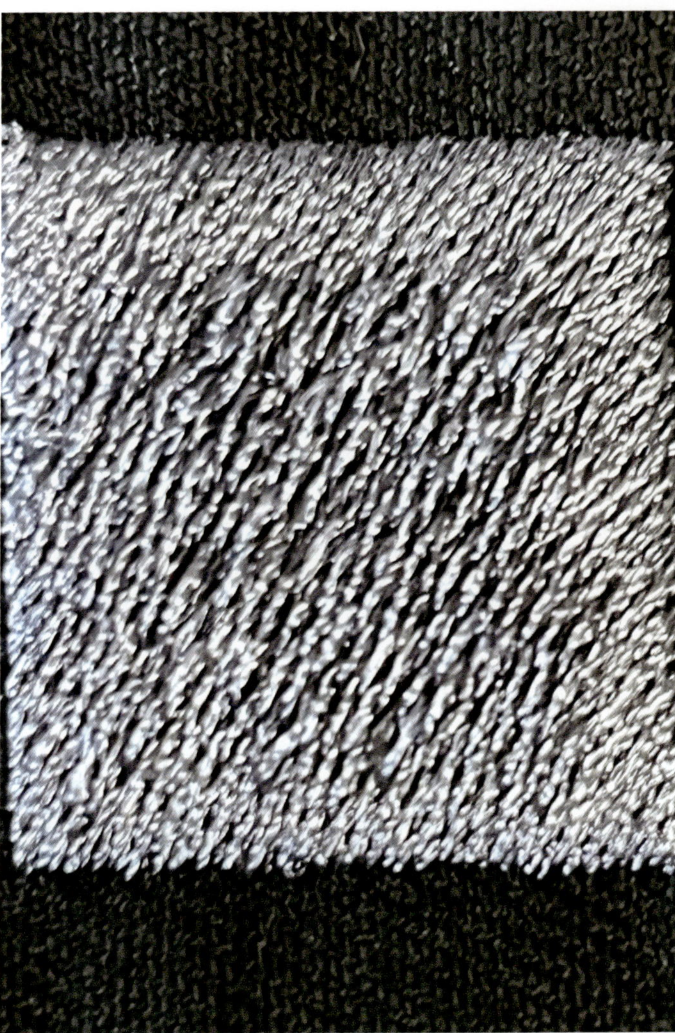

Looping threads on the top side of fabric caused by the top tension being too loose (visible here in the centre of the square).

Two bobbin cases showing the tension adjustment screws; (left) domestic machine and (right) industrial machine.

UPPER THREAD ADJUSTMENTS

Tighten: if looping is happening, or threads look too loose on top side of fabric.

Loosen: if the thread keeps breaking or the bobbin thread shows through on the top side of the fabric.

CASE STUDY: PETE TARRANT, DIGITEK

Pete Tarrant has over 30 years' experience in the design/textile industry as a successful freelance consultant working with industry leaders such as Wilcom and Midwest Europe, Stocks ZSK and fashion brands such as Ted Baker. Pete is the founder of Digitek, a company providing embroidery, software training, supply, installation and maintenance of embroidery machines. Pete uses his knowledge as a subject matter expert working with Falmouth University and Arts University Bournemouth, the Royal College of Art and Birmingham City University, as a visiting lecturer. Pete was the lead digital embroiderer who worked with the Royal School of Needlework on King Charles III's Anointing Screen for the Coronation in 2023. Pete also works with artist Helen Amy Murray and various other interior design companies in London, using his vast experience and knowledge to create wonderful and inspiring pieces of art.

Pete Tarrant sitting on an extremely large bespoke embroidery machine, creating the anointment screen for King Charles III's coronation.

OVERVIEW

As we reach the conclusion of this chapter, it is my hope that you are now armed with the fundamental knowledge necessary to embark on your first – or next – embroidery endeavour. Embroidery involves a dynamic set of variables, all of which may shift based on the specific requirements of your project. Embrace the process, knowing that perfection may not be achieved on the initial attempt (or ever, in some cases). Sampling your design is a critical step, providing a clear gauge of your starting point. This insight will guide you in making informed adjustments, whether that's switching needles, trying a different thread type, tweaking the tension, or experimenting with stabiliser options. And so on. There is no universal solution in embroidery; every project is unique. However, as you accumulate experience, the intricacies of material and method selection will become clearer. With time, you'll find that the necessity for adjustments diminishes as your choices become more precise and your techniques more refined.

'Embrace the process, knowing that perfection may not be achieved on the initial attempt (or ever in some cases).'

TROUBLESHOOTING

Question 1: Why isn't my design aligning properly on the fabric?

Design alignment issues can be a challenge, especially when working on multi-part designs or re-hooping projects. Here's a breakdown of potential causes and solutions in order of priority:
Machine movement: ensure there's nothing obstructing the movement of the hoop and arm, like excess fabric, other objects, or you! I have often leant too far forwards to watch the machine needle do its job and unwittingly pushed my body on the near edge of the hoop. Ensure the machine is on a stable surface; any unnecessary movement can cause misalignment.
Hooping technique: ensure the fabric is hooped correctly and tautly. Slack or improperly hooped fabric can lead to alignment issues. Make use of hooping aids or templates to ensure consistent placement.
Stabilisers: use the correct type and weight of stabiliser for your fabric. If the fabric moves because the stabiliser isn't providing enough support, alignment issues can occur.
Design digitisation: If you're working with a multi-part design, ensure that the design parts align correctly in your digitising software. Make use of alignment stitches or registration marks to aid in aligning multi-part designs.
Fabric type: stretchy or unstable fabrics can distort during embroidery. Using the right stabiliser and hooping technique is essential for these fabrics.
Re-hooping: if you're re-hooping for larger designs, mark the centre or corners of the design on the fabric with a water-soluble marker or chalk. This can aid in aligning the next part of the design. Consider using positioning tools or cameras, available in some advanced embroidery machines, to help with precise alignment.
Thread nesting: ensure there's no thread nesting underneath the hoop. This can elevate the hoop slightly and cause alignment issues.
Design transfer: make sure the design has been transferred to the machine without any errors or corruptions.
Machine calibration: some advanced machines have calibration settings. If your machine has been bumped or moved recently, you might need to recalibrate it.
Software updates: ensure your machine's firmware and any software you're using are up to date. Software glitches can sometimes cause alignment issues.

Question 2: How can I reduce the amount of puckering my embroidery is causing to the fabric?

Fabric puckering after embroidery is a common challenge and can be very annoying, it's the biggest battle I have when embroidering. There are several effective solutions to minimise or prevent it, but bear in mind that for some fabrics and designs it might not be possible to eliminate it totally. I would recommend looking at the following elements to help improve your work if you are having issues with puckering.
Proper stabilisation: use the right type and weight of stabiliser for your fabric. A cut-away stabiliser is generally better for stretchy fabrics, while a tear-away stabiliser works well for more stable fabrics. Sometimes, using two layers of stabiliser can be beneficial, especially for designs with high stitch density. You may need to produce several test samples in order to identify the most suitable stabiliser(s) for your project.
Underlayers: check the underlayer settings on your digital file to see if they are being effective; try reducing the stitch length, spacing and angle in order to set a more solid structure for your decorative level to sit on top of.

Appropriate hooping technique: ensure the fabric is hooped correctly – it should be taut but not overstretched. Think of it like a drum skin; it should not have wrinkles or be too loose.
Correct thread tension: incorrect thread tension on the embroidery machine can cause puckering. Both the top and bobbin tensions should be properly adjusted for the type of fabric and thread being used.
Design density: high-density designs can pull on the fabric and cause puckering. Reducing the density or choosing designs that are appropriate for the fabric type can help.
Fabric choice: some fabrics are more prone to puckering than others. Lightweight and stretchy fabrics are more susceptible. Using a more stable fabric or applying a fusible interfacing can reduce this risk.
Reducing embroidery speed: slowing down the embroidery machine can sometimes help in reducing puckering, as it allows more accurate stitch placement.
Post-embroidery pressing: sometimes gently pressing the embroidered area with an iron (use a pressing cloth to protect the embroidery) can smooth out minor puckers. Be careful with the heat and pressure, especially on delicate fabrics.
Use of sprays or adhesives: temporary adhesives can help to keep the fabric stable during the embroidery process. But use them sparingly as they can gum up needles and other machine parts.

in the
details
Textures
Colour
Composition
Repeat patterns
Using my
embroidery.
SEB ALI

CHAPTER 3

ARTWORK AND SUBJECT MATTER

Don't let the physical size of your hoop frame hinder your creativity.

INITIAL ARTWORK

Any artwork can be used as a starting point for your project. I have started with images of graffiti on walls, tattoos on arms, doodles on scraps of paper, old family photographs, baby scans and even an original painting on a canvas. At this point you can be as expressive and experimental as you like, until you are at a point where you feel you have enough to move into digitising and creating stitches.

Collage

My go-to method when creating a design is to work 100 per cent scale using a collage technique. This allows me to focus on scale and composition, moving elements (photocopies, sketches, photos and so on) around the area until I am happy with the look. I utilise tracing paper a lot as it allows me to duplicate details quickly, whilst the transparency of the paper allows me to still view the composition as it evolves.

Collage and design board for a section of a larger piece in a defined shape using tracing paper to show the design idea.

OPPOSITE: The author creating a design using mixed media.

Foam Mount Board

Foam mount board is a wonderful solid material to use as a base in which to add your cut outs, tracing paper, fabrics and other reference source materials as you create your collage. For the back tattoo design (below), I worked full scale using an outline of the human torso (my back). The surrounding area I used to store images and fabric samples for reference, whilst within the outline I used several layers of tracing paper, photocopies and hand-rendered sketching in order to finalise the composition. The great thing about working like this is the flexibly you have to move the elements and replace as you go along, without having to start from scratch. As a physical object you can lean the board against a wall and stand back to get a realistic idea of how it would look. Working to 100 per cent gives a good sense of the outcome without you having to imagine it scaled up or down.

As I sample areas of the design, I use the mount board to add notes on stitch fills, colour codes, thread types, stitch count and so on. The mount board becomes a master blueprint for the final design.

Once I am happy with my design concept, I lay it on the floor and take a photograph standing directly above with my camera level. This turns the physical object into a digital version, which I can then either prepare for digitising by taking into a CAD software program, or upload directly into the embroidery software to digitise (*see* Chapter 4).

Collage back tattoo design on foam mount board at 100 per cent scale to gauge scale and composition.

Taking a photo of my artwork from directly above with the best lighting possible.

SOFTWARE PROGRAMS TO HELP 'SIMPLIFY' YOUR ARTWORK

There are several CAD programs that can help you clean up images before you use them for digitising and turning the image into embroidery. This is more important for auto digitising than manual digitising. The following programs offer various tools to enhance contrast, remove noise and clarify the details of your design.

Adobe Photoshop: advanced features for image clean-up, including background removal, colour correction, colour change and image editing. The beta versions have built-in AI features.

Adobe Illustrator: capable of vector tracing to turn images into clean, scalable vector files.

GIMP (GNU Image Manipulation Program): a free alternative to Photoshop with many similar image-editing capabilities.

CorelDRAW: offers vector and raster editing tools, good for preparing images for digitising and currently comes with Wilcom as a joint package.

Inkscape: a vector graphics editor that can convert raster images to vector format.

Paint.NET: a user-friendly image editor with basic tools for image clean-up.

Canva: an easy-to-use online tool with basic editing options such as background removal.

Pixlr: provides a set of intuitive image-editing tools in a cloud-based app.

Affinity Photo 2: professional photo-editing software with comprehensive clean-up tools.

Photopea: an online editor that can handle various formats and offers Photoshop-like features.

Remember to check the compatibility of the file formats these programs can produce with your auto digitising software and your computer to ensure they can all work together. There's no point using a software to simplify your artwork if your digitiser cannot read it.

SMART DEVICE APPS TO HELP CLEAN UP YOUR ARTWORK

With mobile devices such as smart phones and tablets a popular choice for taking photos and editing them, there has been a surge of art-based applications (apps) on the market,

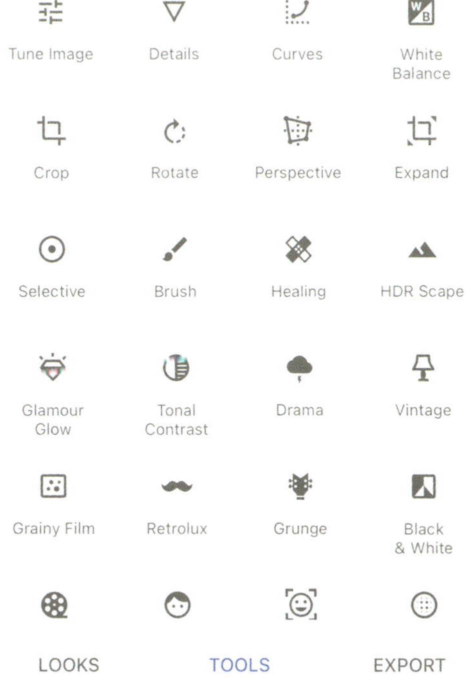

Snapseed menu with manipulation options.

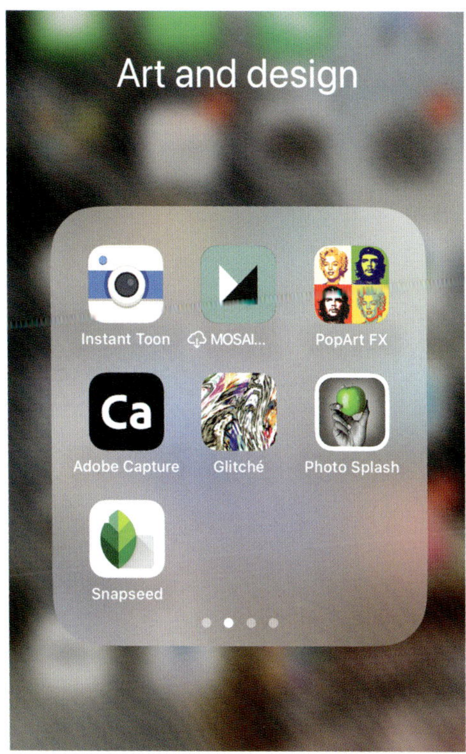

Useful art and design manipulation apps.

giving you a multitude of manipulation options. These are the apps I use on my iPhone which have served me well.

Snapseed *(my go-to app once I have taken a photo)*
Snapseed is a mobile photo-editing application developed by Google that provides a wide range of filter effects and default settings for editing images on the go. It's known for its user-friendly interface and the ability to handle various adjustments such as tuning an image, applying filters and cropping, which can be particularly handy for quick touch-ups and straightforward image clean-ups for auto-digitising purposes.

Insta Toon *(my go-to for turning a complex image into a simplified, stylised version)*
Insta Toon transforms photos into cartoon-style images. It uses filters and digital effects to give photographs a hand-drawn or animated look. While this type of app is more for artistic transformation rather than cleaning up images for digitising purposes, creative uses could include stylising a photo to simplify it before attempting to auto-digitise for embroidery, depending on the desired outcome. However, for standard digitising processes, more conventional image-editing tools that focus on clarity, contrast and detail preservation are typically recommended.

Adobe Capture *(compatible with Adobe Photoshop and Illustrator programs)*
A versatile mobile app that allows users to turn images into various creative assets, including vector graphics, colour palettes, patterns and custom brushes. It's particularly useful for digitising because it can convert photos into vector shapes, which can then be refined and used in other Adobe software such as Adobe Illustrator or Photoshop.

The process involves capturing an image with your device and using the app's features to isolate and refine the design into a cleaner, more digitise-friendly format. For embroidery digitising, the shapes and lines can be smoothed out and simplified, making it easier for auto-digitising software to accurately interpret the design for stitching. Adobe Capture is an excellent tool for designers looking to quickly create and use elements from the world around them in their digital artwork.

(Left) Original photograph of the author and (right) after Insta Toon filter applied.

Adobe Capture colour palette feature used on a pattern headboard to extract colours.

Procreate *(a powerful app available on the iPad Pro)*
Procreate is a designer favourite! It is an intuitive digital illustration app designed for creatives, offering a suite of advanced features such as a high-resolution canvas, over 130 brushes, advanced layering system, real-time collaboration and the ability to animate and export in various formats, all optimised for iPad and Apple Pencil; easy to use and very intuitive. If you have an Ipad Pro, then this is a must-have program!

Keep searching and testing applications available for your device, as new ones appear all the time. A good app can save you a lot of time when it comes to preparing your image for digitising.

GARMENTS: DESIGNING 3D

Designing for a 3D object, such as an all-over embroidered garment, is a bit more challenging, but very rewarding when you finally see the result. I again apply the above methods as if working 2D, but the initial design and composition is carried out on the 3D object and not a flat sheet of mount board.

Here is my guide to working on a garment (with an all-over embroidery design).

Stage 1: Place the garment on a mannequin or a person.

Stage 2: Two options:
Option A: If the garment is a prototype (toile) and you can write directly onto it, then use a combination of pencils, felt pens and collage images pinned in place in order to design your composition.

Option B: If the garment cannot be damaged, then use paper to create a top layer over the area that is intended to be embroidered. I then use pencils and felt pens to sketch a rough design on the paper. Working this way, if you are not happy with the design element, you can either replace the paper or place another piece over the top and redraw.

Stage 3: Once you are happy with your design, you need to get it flat so you can take a photo from above. If you chose option A, you may be able to lay the garment flat on the floor, or you may need to transfer the design on the pattern paper piece; alternatively, you can unpick the toile and lay it flat.

Option B is easier; simply remove the paper and lay it flat.

Stage 4: upload your photograph to your digitising software and begin digitising.

Calico toile being worn, with a floral design drawn on the cloth with felt pens.

Paper pinned to a garment whilst on a mannequin, with the design drawn on with felt pens.

ARTIFICIAL INTELLIGENCE (AI)

Love it or hate it, AI is changing the landscape of how we design and work. With lots of programs and apps on the market, incorporating AI into your creative practice can have its advantages such as:

- Helping to generate visual concepts if you are having a creative block or struggling to get started.
- Generating variations of your initial design idea within seconds based on your text input and suggestions.
- Enabling you to visualise your embroidery concepts on garments, items or in environments.
- Replacing areas of your design with something else, quickly, and seamlessly.

AI tools are being built into popular CAD programs such as Adobe Photoshop and Illustrator, and with lots of AI smart device apps available, there is a lot of choice on which ones suit you, your style of work and which you find easiest to use.

The following AI apps are my favourites (at time of writing).

PhotoRoom

This is one of my favourite apps. PhotoRoom stands out as an indispensable tool, providing seamless photo-editing capabilities and background removal that is perfect for crafting product images for e-commerce, designing impactful marketing materials, or prepping visuals for graphic design projects. It proves especially invaluable for embroiderers preparing artwork for auto digitising, delivering crisp, clean images devoid of distractions. The app's AI-enhanced features not only simplify the creation of high-contrast designs essential for accurate digitisation, but also offer the flexibility to conjure up alternative backgrounds with ease. Whether you're using preset options or AI-powered text-to-image prompts, PhotoRoom's precision in altering backgrounds is so impressive, it promises to pass even the most scrutinising eye.

Midjouney Discord

Midjourney is an AI-powered program that revolutionises the creative process. It interprets textual descriptions to generate stunning visual concepts and artwork. Featuring a user-friendly interface, it provides tools for real-time iteration and customisation, enabling artists and designers to explore a vast landscape of styles and ideas. Text input

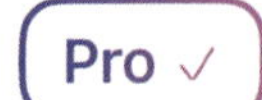

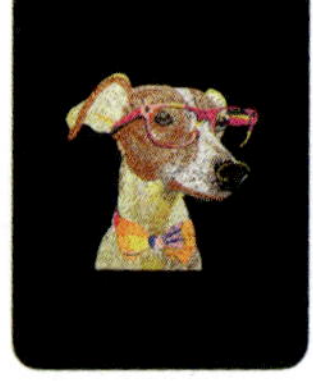

An embroidered dog, uploaded through app and AI backgrounds applied.

Midjourney used to create art deco embroidered designs.

is translated by AI algorithms to create four outcomes, which you can upscale, or select the one you like to produce variations based on your selection. This program enables you to choose specific areas to replace, making it more suitable to your intended aim.

Wonder

Wonder is a text to image AI app available on smart devices. This app has many preset styles to select from, including Hyper Realistic, Pen and Ink, Tattoo, Vice, Oil Painting, Polaroid, Neo, Origami, Graffiti, CGI, Comic Book, Pop Art and many more. Once you have added your text prompt, you can select a preset from the menu, click on the Create button and within 10 seconds you will have two visual suggestions. If you don't like them, you can ask it to create again, amend your text or try another preset! It's a fun and intuitive app.

The following image uses the text 'Embroidered baby dragon holding a cake' with a selected style filter applied.

DALL•E

DALL•E is an AI-powered program by OpenAI that generates original images from textual descriptions. Embedded in the ChatGPT AI program, this package is a powerful must-have for any creative. DALL•E combines elements of machine learning with natural language processing to create diverse, high-quality visuals. Capable of producing artwork, realistic photos and complex compositions, DALL•E enables users to bring their imaginative concepts to life with just a few keystrokes, bridging the gap between words and visual art in a seamless and innovative way.

AI is an ever-evolving tool that is highly relevant today. Discussions about its role in design, education, and everyday life are ongoing in academic and creative spheres. Some speculate that AI might overshadow human creativity, but I view it as the latest technological advancement at a designer's disposal. Choosing to use it is a personal decision, yet understanding its potential is crucial. This book includes AI to show how it can integrate with your craftsmanship, enhancing your design process while maintaining your unique style and identity. I encourage you to explore AI's possibilities to see how it can serve your specific creative needs.

In summary, the initial phase of design in digital embroidery allows for unbridled creativity; let your imagination guide you in crafting an original concept. Once you are happy with your design, you need to create a digital version which you can upload to your embroidery software; this can be as easy as taking a photo with your phone camera. In the next chapter we will look at the vital stage in the process, designing the stitches or better known as 'digitising'.

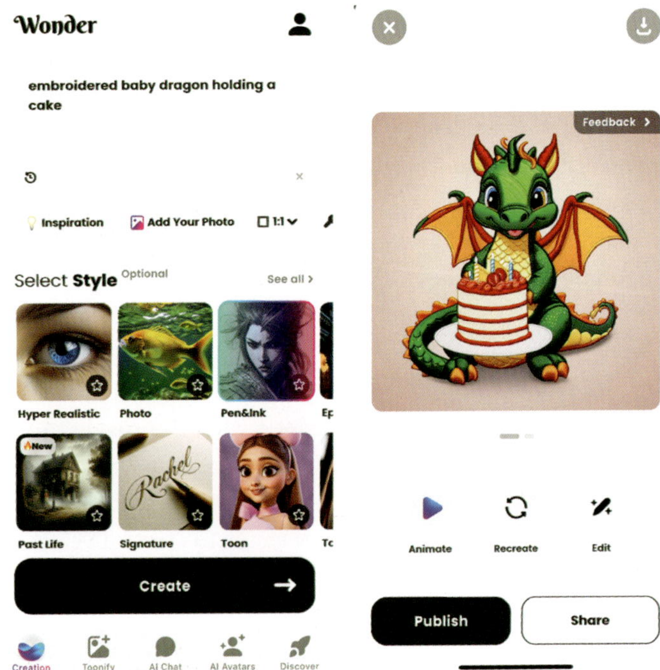

(Left) Text prompt and chosen filter (Right) AI created outcome.

DA You

Create an image of an embroidered baby dragon holding a cake

Here's the image of an embroidered baby dragon holding a cake. I hope you like how it turned out!

Dragon outcome and text prompt using ChatGPT-4.

CASE STUDY: HAWTHORNE & HEANEY

Based in the heart of London just off Regent Street, Hawthorne & Heaney is a team of embroiderers offering beautiful bespoke embroidery, logos and live events. Hawthorn & Heaney offers a range of hand and machine embroidery, providing custom designs for a variety of applications, from fashion and textiles to interiors and performance. Some high-profile jobs include work for Hakkasan in Mayfair, Damien Hirst, FKA Twigs and Jason Momoa. If you're interested in professional embroidery digitising services, Hawthorn & Heaney is known for craftsmanship and attention to detail. They can take artwork and prepare it for digitising, ensuring that the final embroidered product is of high quality. H&H also has a sister embroidery company called London Embroidery School.

A digital goldwork interpretation by Hawthorn & Heaney. (Photo: H&H)

TROUBLESHOOTING

Question 1: I can't afford to invest in expensive CAD software programs, on top of the digitising software and equipment. Is there a way I can clean up images without having to use CAD software?

Computer-Aided Design (CAD) software can be expensive and often requires a significant amount of time to learn. If you're looking for more cost-effective alternatives, there are free software options available online. Also, some digitising programs include built-in CAD features, like Wilcom's inclusion of CorelDRAW.

But you don't have to limit yourself to traditional software. Many mobile apps can edit and prepare images for digitising, and these can be free or much cheaper than full CAD packages. I've recommended some useful apps for image editing above.

Personally, I prefer manual digitising over automatic because it saves me the step of editing my artwork. I import a photograph of my artwork into my digitising software, resize it to the actual scale I want, lock it in place, and then digitise it by hand using the tools available. This way, I don't need to use a separate CAD program to clean up the image before digitising.

One other solution is to outsource your work to a third party and ask them to 'vectorise' it for you.

Question 2: My artwork is larger than my embroidery hoop area; is this going to be an issue?

If you want to embroider a large design that doesn't fit in your machine's hoop, don't worry – it's still doable, though a bit more complex. Chapter 7 explains the solution to this problem. The initial steps, for digitising, stay the same. After digitising, you'll divide your large design into smaller sections that will fit within your hoop. Save and export each section as a separate file to your machine. Then you embroider the design piece by piece, starting with the first section, then the second, third, and so on, making sure each part lines up perfectly with the others, like assembling a jigsaw puzzle. The trickiest part is aligning the sections correctly, as any misalignment will be noticeable and can ruin your work.

STARTING POINT
ALIENWARE
Effects
Save
18°C Mostly cloudy

CHAPTER 4

DIGITISING 101

The digitising stage is the most important stage in the process; spend quality time to ensure your outputs are the best than can possibly be.

Digitising in embroidery is the art of converting your designs into formats that embroidery machines can interpret and stitch. It's akin to instructing your machine on how to 'paint with threads' in order to create exquisite, tactile art. The market offers various digitising software options, each featuring a core set of tools alongside unique enhancements. The choice is personal, aligning with what fits your needs. Every software can adapt designs for different machine types, so your decision ultimately hinges on finding the right fit for your budget and creative aspirations. For this book I will be referring to the Wilcom E4.5 software program.

METHODS OF DIGITISING YOUR ARTWORK

There are three options when it comes to digitising, and which one you select depends on the original artwork, what you are trying to achieve and look you are after. The three options are: auto digitising, manual digitising and hybrid digitising. We will have a closer look at all three options so you can better understand the specifics of each.

AUTO DIGITISING

An auto-digitising option may be available in your software program. In Wilcom software this is referred to as *Smart Design* and can be found in the menu options. This feature enables the artist to convert graphic designs into stitch patterns that can be sewn onto fabric by an embroidery machine. The tool automates the process of digitising, which is the process of creating a stitch file that an embroidery machine can read and interpret.

The auto-digitising tool works by analysing the graphic design image and identifying its different shapes and colours. It then assigns stitches to each shape based on predefined settings (often tatami and satin fills only). The tool adjusts the shapes' stitch density and direction to ensure that the design looks good and is easy to sew.

One of the advantages of an auto-digitising tool is that it saves time and effort compared to manual digitising. However, auto-digitising tools are not perfect and may not always produce the desired results. The tool may struggle to accurately represent complex designs or designs with intricate details. The stitch file generated by the tool may also require additional tweaking to ensure that the design sews correctly. Resequencing may also

OPPOSITE: The author tracing a design from laptop to acetate grid using a Sharpie pen.

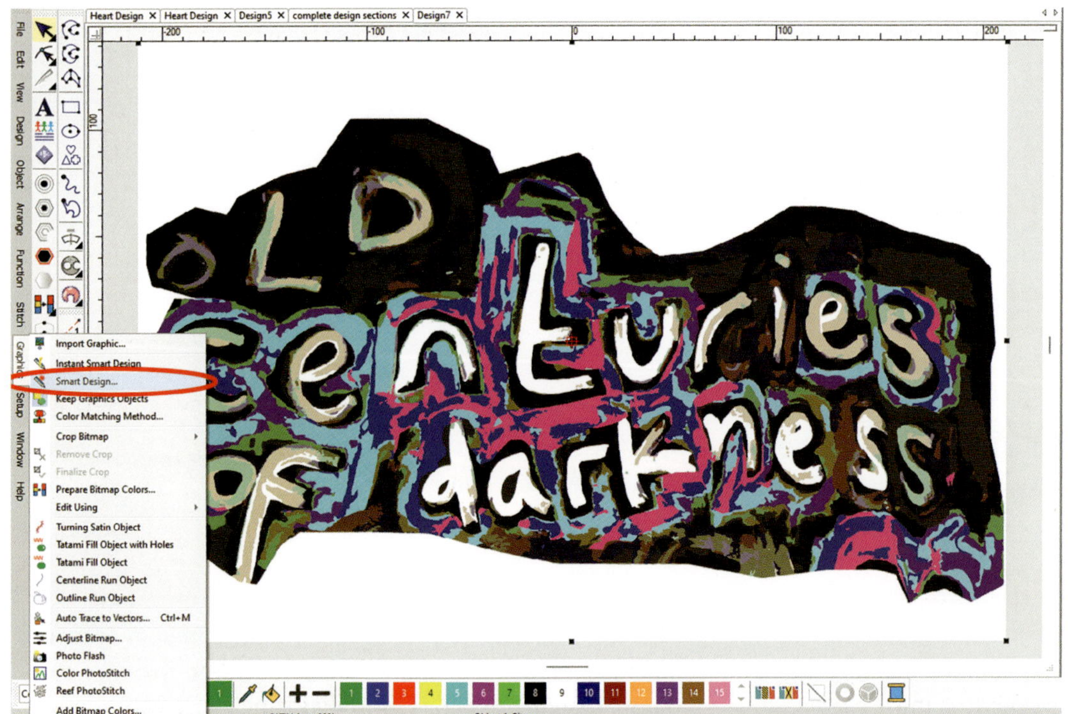

Smart Design (Auto Digitising) selection in the menu options bar on Wilcom software.

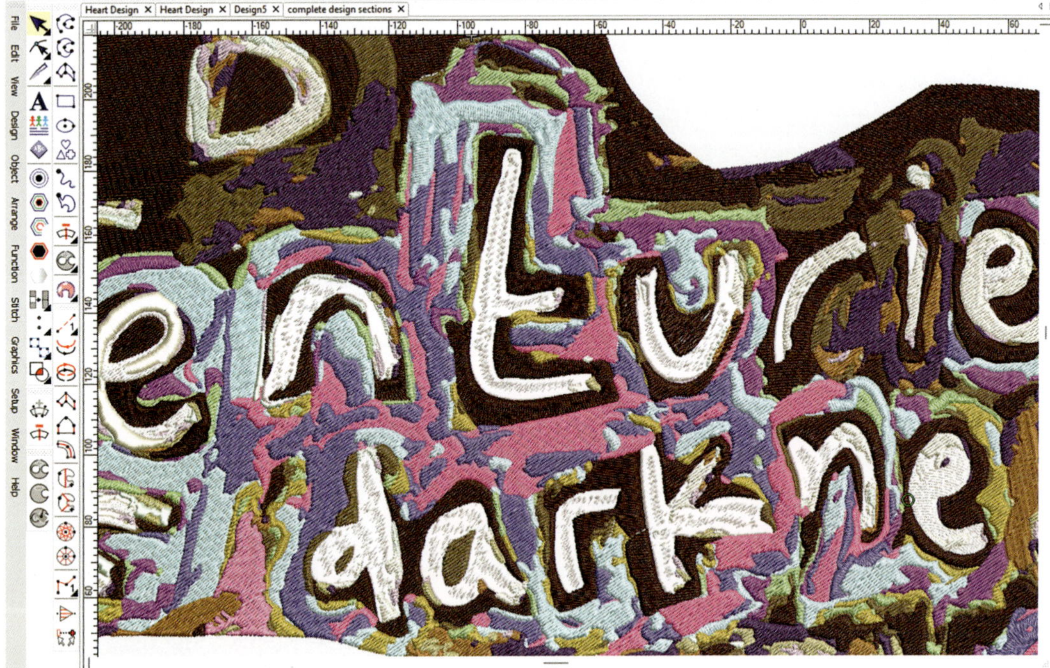

An image that has been auto digitised only, with many individual shapes.

be required. The creative aspect that a designer brings to the table is lost when auto digitising, with the outcomes often feeling flat, safe and underwhelming. However, auto digitising can be good when it comes to simple logos and images.

Tip: Very simple designs that are clean (vector-based, cartoon type images are perfect) can be auto digitised with outcomes that may require minor tweaking only; however, complex images, lots of shadow and shade, lots of colours and tones, when digitised will often produce outcomes that appear very 'bitty' with many shapes, lots of small impractical stitches and lots of colour changes.

MANUAL DIGITISING

Manual digitising is the process of creating a stitch file for digital embroidery by manually assigning stitches to each shape in a design. This process is typically done by a skilled operator using specialised software that allows them to create and edit stitches at a granular level.

The process of manual digitising involves several steps. First, the operator imports the design into the digitising software and traces each shape in the design using a tool called a digitising tablet (mouse or laptop work pad). The operator then assigns stitch types and parameters to each shape, such as stitch length, density and direction.

Manual digitising requires a high degree of skill and experience. Some may argue that it is an art form in its own right. How well an image is digitised will directly affect the outcome quality. The operator must have a deep understanding of the embroidery machine and the characteristics of different fabrics in order to create a stitch file that produces a high-quality result. They must also be able to interpret and recreate the design accurately, paying close attention to details such as shading and texture.

One of the advantages of manual digitising is that it allows for a high degree of control and customisation. The operator can tweak the stitch file to create a specific look or texture, such as a raised or textured effect. Manual digitising also allows for greater precision and accuracy than auto digitising tools, as the operator can adjust stitches at a granular level.

However, manual digitising is a time-consuming and labour-intensive process. It can take several hours or even days to manually digitise a complex design, and the operator must be able to maintain focus and concentration throughout the process.

'Manual digitising is an art form in its own right.'

HYBRID DIGITISING

Hybrid digitising is a term I use to describe a mix of auto and manual digitising. Hybrid digitising can create some interesting visual effects, particularly if you are after a tactile, natural or oil painting type of feel. The second image

A manually digitised design only, with a cleaner, more accurate feel.

A hybrid design, auto digitised first and then worked into manually.

on the previous page shows this technique applied to a baby scan image, where the auto digitising was used first on the complete image and remains visible around the outer areas, whilst the baby itself was worked into manually to create a more solid block fill, with a texture fill applied in order to stand out and contrast.

Artwork Decision

Once you have created your original artwork for your design (in whatever format and medium), you have two options available to you.

You can recreate your artwork into a digital format by taking a photograph of it – upload or open your photograph in a CAD software program and convert your initial design into a vector image, breaking it down into distinct colour areas and eliminating fine details that cannot be replicated by stitches.

Alternatively, you can upload the photograph of your artwork straight into the embroidery software program and either auto, manually or hybrid digitise it.

As the artist, you must also consider the type of fabric and the interplay of thread types, as these factors influence the final appearance and texture of the embroidered piece. By carefully preparing artwork for digitising, you are setting the foundation for a seamless transition from art to tactile embroidery, ensuring that the end product retains the charm and intent of the original design.

DIGITISING FLOW CHART: Commercial vs Bespoke Projects

You may find yourself working on a project where the outcome is intended to be repeated (commercial), for example, logos or badges on garments, or you may be asked to create a one-of-a-kind (bespoke) piece of art to be mounted on a wall. The process I adopt differs between commercial and bespoke. The following flow chart shows the differences and works for me. Over time and with increased experience, you will find your own way of working that suits your style and preferences.

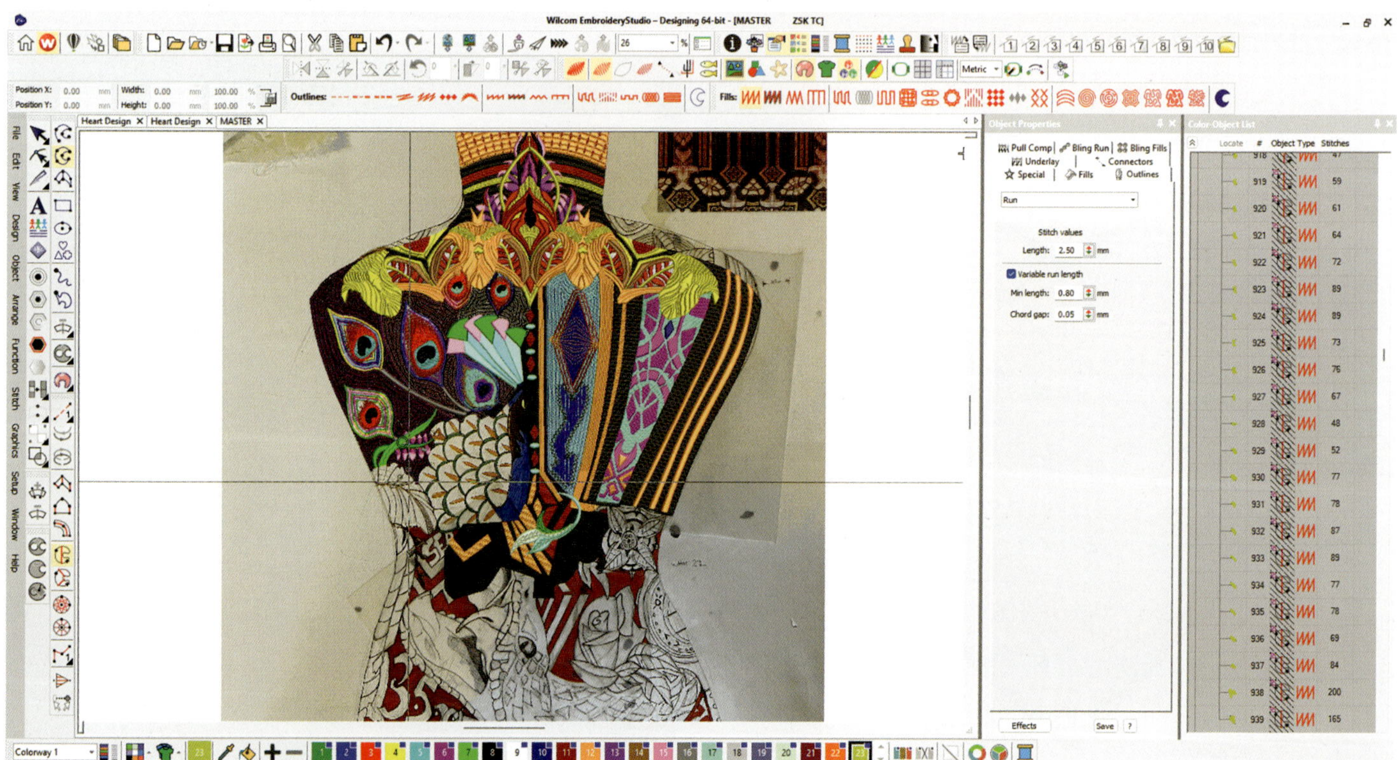

Back tattoo collage used as a template which has been digitised manually over the top.

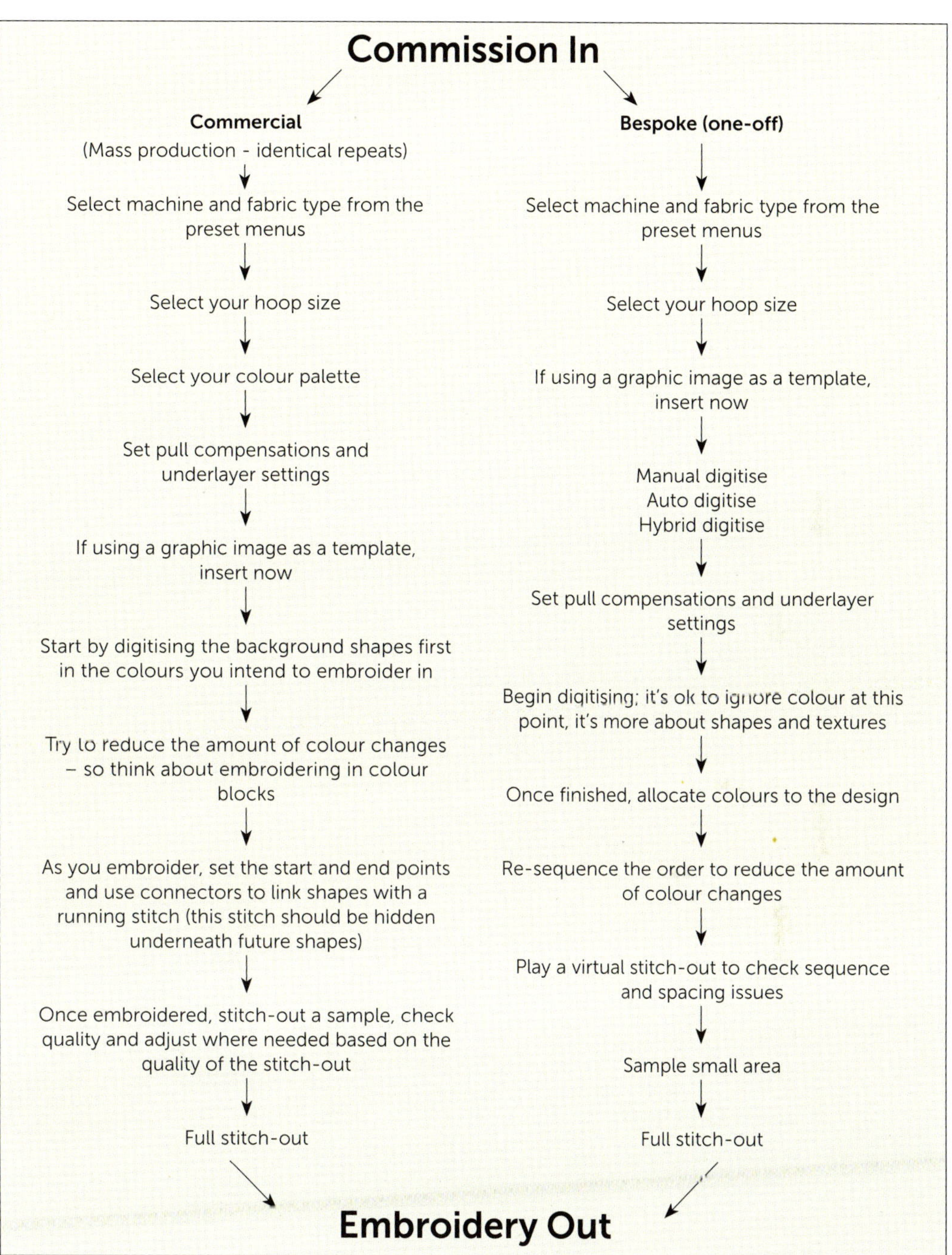

Digitising flow chart, showing the difference between commercial and one-off digitising.

KEY DIGITISING TOOLS TO GET YOU GOING

Digitising software programs have different tools and features. These are a few of the tools using the Wilcom E4.5 program, that will help you get going. Once you build up your confidence, have a look at online tutorials for advance tools and techniques. Software programs have similar tools, interfaces and features, so whichever you pick, you will soon get used to its nuances and be able to produce embroidery ready to go in no time. I often fluctuate between Wilcom E4.5 and Janome Artistic Digitiser as both have features the other doesn't, and collectively it gives me more options to apply to my work.

Key digitising tools for the Wilcom Software to get you started:

- Digitise closed shape
- Digitise open shape
- Selection tools
- Reshape
- Knife (cut objects)
- Add holes

Digitise Closed Shape

Using this tool alone can help you create an array of shapes. It is simply a case of clicking the mouse button where you wish to start your shape and continue clicking to create the outline of your shape, with each click creating a node. Left click will create an angle node and right clicking will create a curve node. When you are ready, press the return (Enter) key on your keyboard and the start and end points will join together, creating a solid shape, and a fill will be applied. You can tweak your shape by using the *Reshape* tool and moving, adding, deleting, or converting nodes (from curve to angle or vice versa) or you can change the fill type, angle, stitch density, underlayers and more. Remember, if you produce a second shape, it will be stacked on top of the previous shape, and this should appear in your *Color-Object List* window. By clicking and dragging a shape's icon in the objects window and moving it up or down in order you can send shapes behind or in front of other objects. This is known as sequencing. For the Wilcom software, the top shape in the layers window will be the shape that is embroidered first, followed by the second icon and so forth.

Digitise Closed Shape icon.

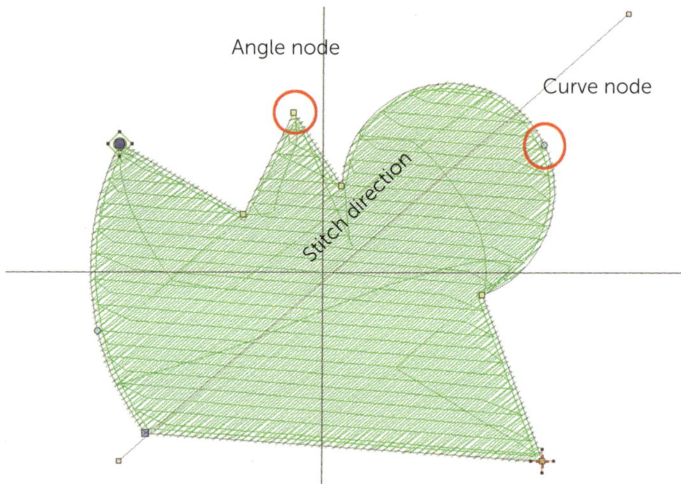

Angle and curve nodes.

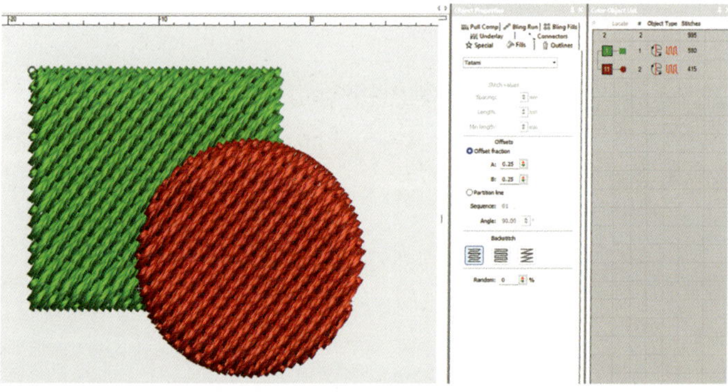

Two shapes and their icons in the *Color Object List* (layers/sequence) window.

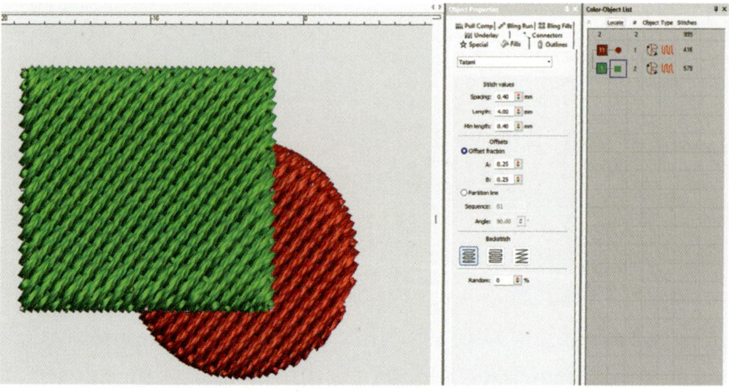

Two shapes and their icons in the *Color Objects List* window re-sequenced.

Digitise Open Shape

The open shape tool operates with a straightforward click-to-create mechanism, akin to the closed shape tool. Begin by clicking to start and continue to click to form your desired shape. Unlike the closed shape tool, hitting the Enter button on your keyboard at the end doesn't close the loop; it produces an open line. This line is fully customisable using the reshape tool – you can alter run types, introduce motifs, modify stitch lengths, or adjust nodes, transforming them from sharp angles to smooth curves. This feature is useful for adding intricate details to your design, where even a simple running stitch can dramatically enhance the overall effect.

Select Objects (Black Arrow)

The *select objects* tool enables you to select a shape with a single click. Once selected, you can press and hold the mouse button to drag the shape to a preferred location. For duplication, simply use the edit function to copy and paste, which adds a new layer icon at the bottom of your *Color-Object List* window. When a shape is selected, handles will appear around its perimeter, allowing you to easily adjust its size and orientation by clicking and dragging them to your desired dimensions and angle. If you click on a blank area of the canvas and drag over the shapes, it will select multiple shapes with the square or rectangular marquee, enabling you to edit several shapes at the same time. *Note*: It will only select complete shapes within the marquee, so if you let go of the marquee partially over a shape, it will not select it.

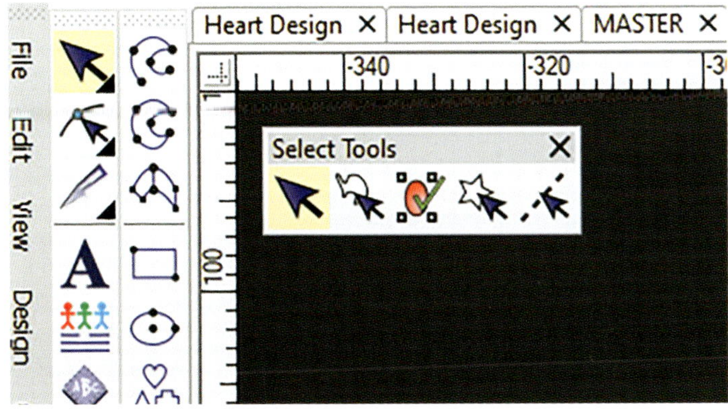

Select Tools icons.

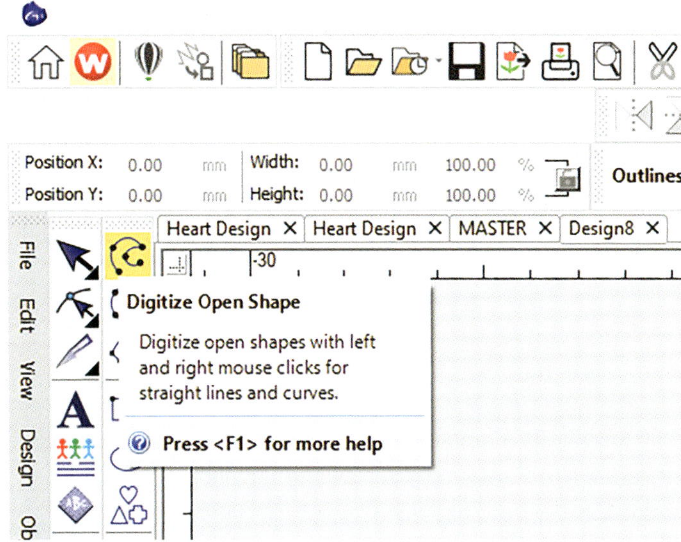

Digitise open shape tool icon.

Digitise Open Shape used to create detailing on a dog design.

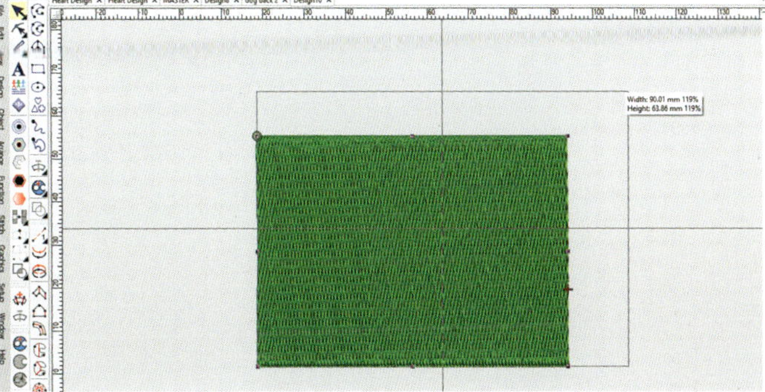

Shape being scaled up using the black arrow selection tool.

Freehand Selection Tool

The freehand selection tool removes the square marquee you see with the black arrow selection tool and allows you to draw a freehand marquee of any shape. Again, the same rule applies where a shape needs to be fully inside the marquee in order to be selected. This tool is very useful when working on designs with lots of small shapes and detailed areas.

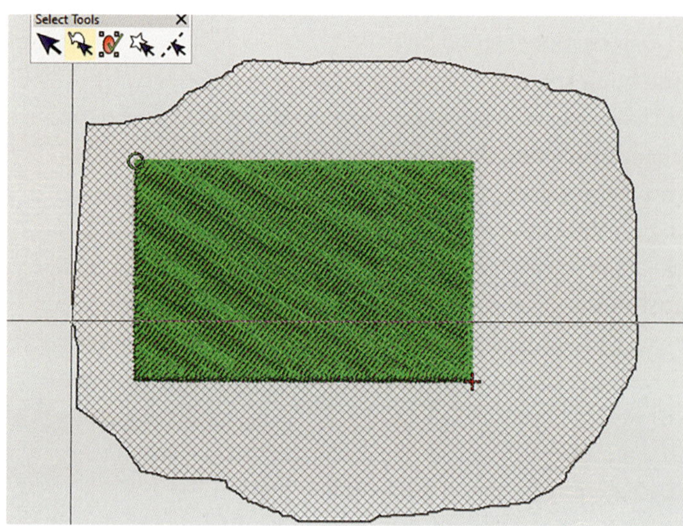

Shape being selected using the freehand selection tool.

Reshape Tool

The reshape tool is vital for fine-tuning your design. While previous tools allow for basic adjustments like resizing, recolouring, changing stitch fills, rotating and moving shapes, they don't provide the functionality to reshape or alter a shape's structure or modify the stitch fill angle. With the reshape tool, clicking on a shape reveals all its nodes and the stitch angle adjustment line, complete with terminal end nodes. You can manipulate the shape's nodes to change the form, transforming points into curves or angles with a simple click. To introduce a new node, click on the shape's outline; to remove one, select it and hit the delete key. Adjusting the stitch angle is just as intuitive – click on an end node of the angle line and drag to set a new angle, refining the direction of the stitch for the shape.

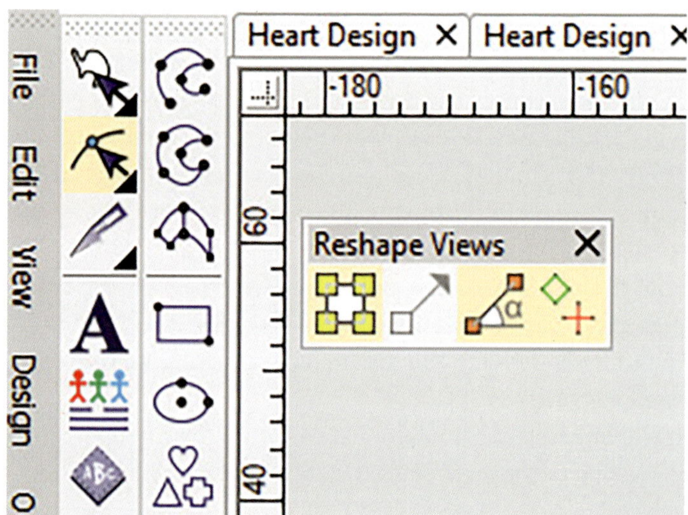

Reshape tool icons.

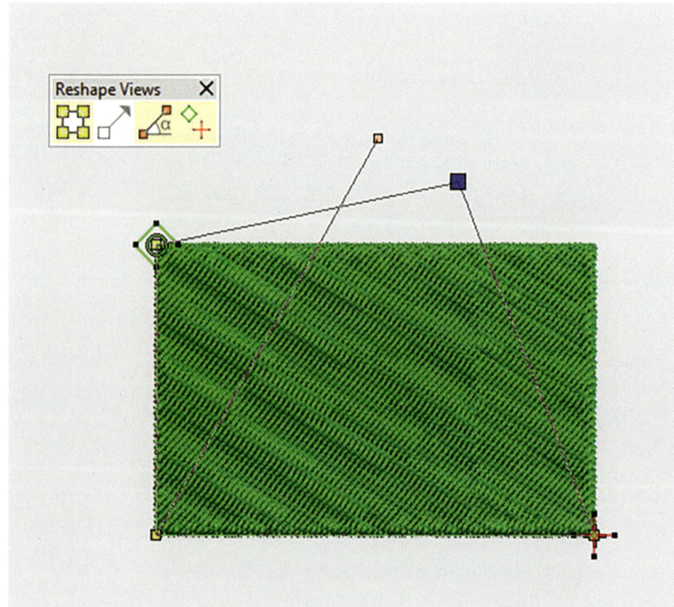

Reshape tool being used on a shape revealing its nodes and angle line.

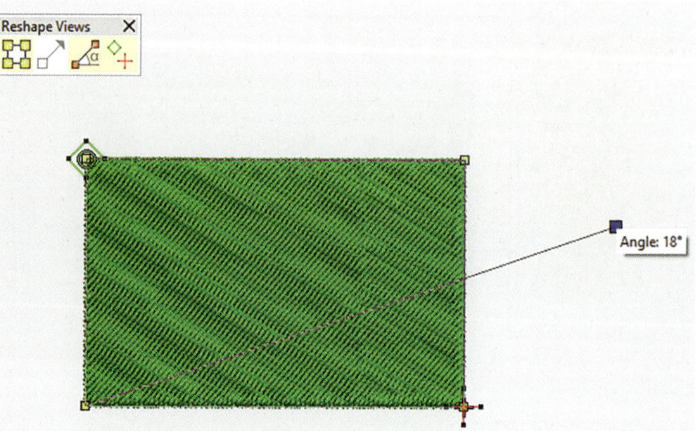

Reshape tool re-angling the stitch fill.

Knife

The knife (cutting tool) is an invaluable asset in my toolkit. After selecting a shape, activating this tool allows you to split the shape, effectively dividing it into distinct segments, which will appear as individual elements within the layers window. Visually, the change might not be immediately apparent, but this operation provides the flexibility to modify each resulting shape separately, offering the opportunity to assign varied colours, stitch fills and stitch angles. To utilise the cut tool, simply select your shape with a selection tool, click cut tool icon, click outside your shape to start the cut line and drag across to set the cut line. If you click within the shape's boundary, it creates a node – left click for an angle or right click for a curve – giving you precise control over the cut line path. Completing the action by pressing the return key will finalise the cutting of the shape. Notice in the *Color-Object List* window the new individual shapes have appeared and your once-larger shape icon has reduced to reflect its new shape.

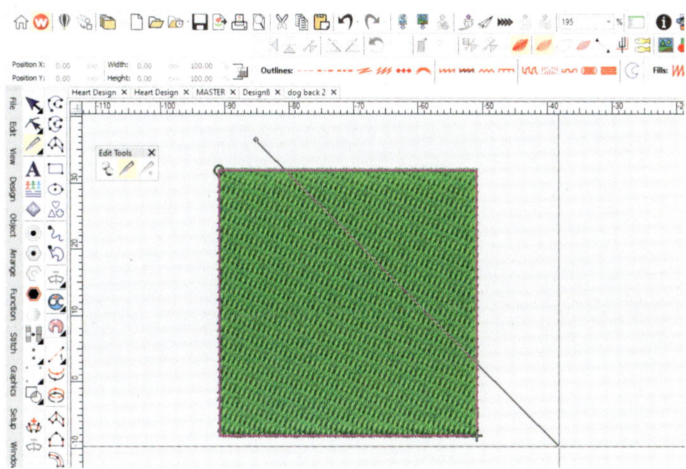

Cut tool used to split up a square tatami shape.

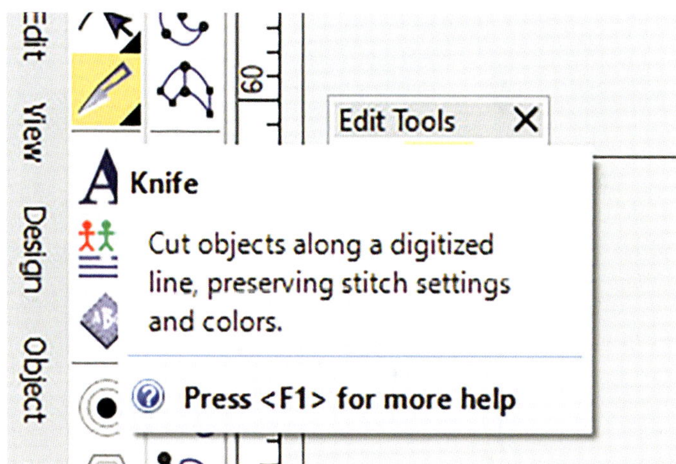

Cut tool icon.

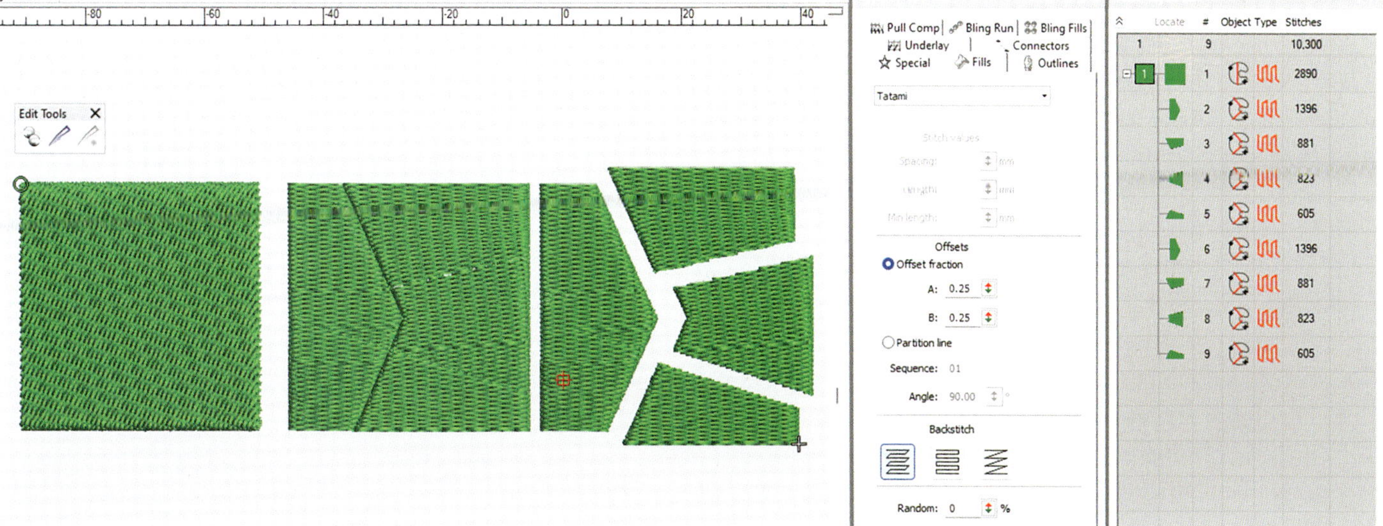

Tatami shape prior to cut, cut and split apart.

Add Holes

This tool does what its name suggests – it creates holes within shapes. To use, firstly create your shape and ensure it is selected. Click on the *Add Holes* tool icon and you will be prompted to draw the hole shape within the shape; this can be any shape. Once you have drawn the hole, click return and a hole will appear.

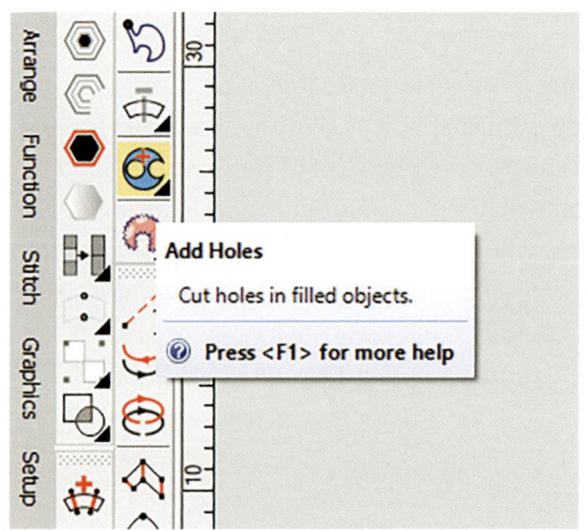

Add Holes tool icon.

Tatami square with hole.

Sequencing

Sequencing refers to the order in which the machine stitches the design, and it plays a crucial role in achieving a smooth, even finish. Proper sequencing ensures that the machine stitches each section of the design in the correct order, avoiding overlaps, skipped stitches and thread breaks. This not only improves the overall appearance of the design, but also reduces the risk of errors or damage to the fabric. Without proper sequencing, the embroidery design may be uneven, incomplete or even unusable. For commercial digitising, careful sequencing can reduce production time as the machine will stitch in the most economical order, thus saving time by omitting unnecessary machine movement and colour changes. For creative (one-off) digitising, sequencing is less important, but it is still worth reordering to avoid too many thread trims, thus impacting overall quality.

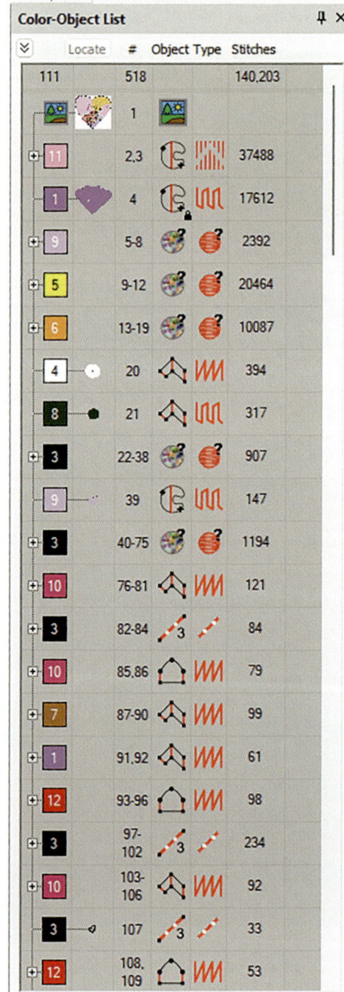

Color Objects List (sequencing) window and object shapes.

Remove Overlaps

This feature may not be a tool in the traditional sense, but it's incredibly handy and can save you a lot of time. If you select multiple shapes and then choose *'Remove Overlaps'* from the menu, the feature will eliminate any parts of the shapes that are hidden beneath others. By removing these hidden sections, you reduce the number of stitches needed for your design, which in turn decreases the overall thickness.

Start and End Point

In embroidery, the 'start point' and 'end point' of a shape determine where the embroidery machine begins and ends stitching a particular shape. In Wilcom embroidery software, these points are marked by a green square for the 'start point' and a red cross for the 'end point'. Adjusting the start and end points is crucial because it can improve the stitch quality and increase the efficiency of the embroidery process. By placing the 'end point' of one shape close to the 'start point' of the next shape, you minimise the movement of the machine between stitching different shapes and possibly eliminate thread cutting, both of which saves time.

Stitch Player

The *Stitch Player* is an essential feature of Wilcom software that can save you both time and expense. It simulates your design being stitched out by an embroidery machine. As it shows the stitching process step by step, you can spot and fix any problems before you start embroidering on fabric. The control panel lets you adjust the speed, move to specific sections, and pause the playback. It's crucial to avoid stitching errors like misplaced shapes, incorrect stitch angles, or poor fill choices. A frequent issue I notice is overlapping objects that should be removed. Always use the *Stitch Player* after finishing your design for a final quality check to avoid these mistakes.

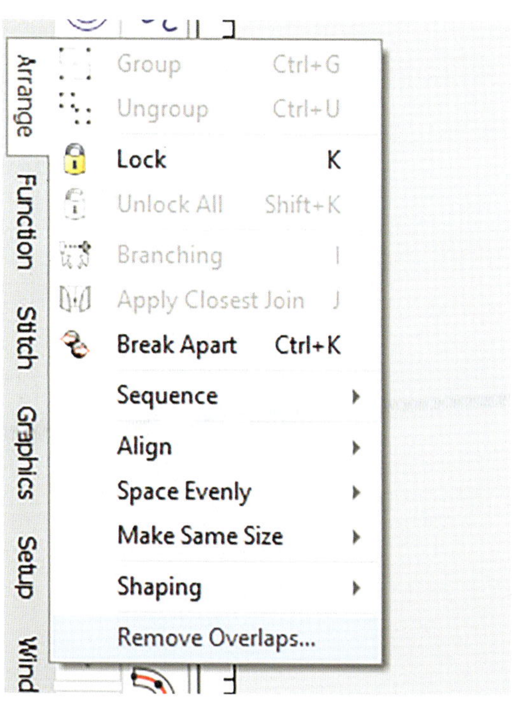

Remove Overlaps in the menu bar.

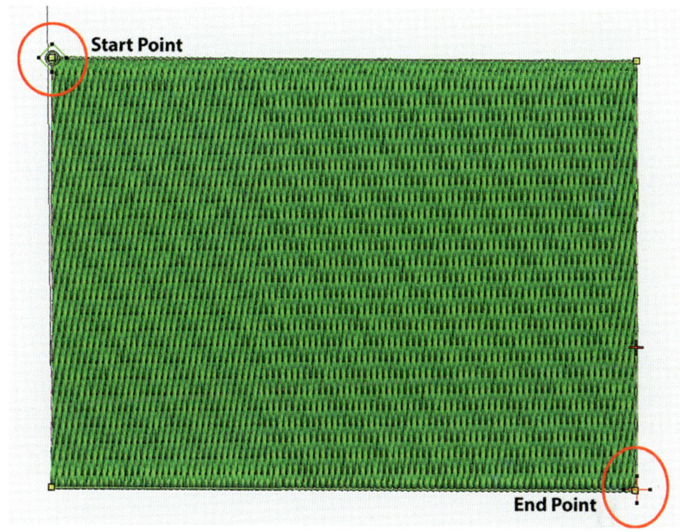

Shapes showing a start and end point.

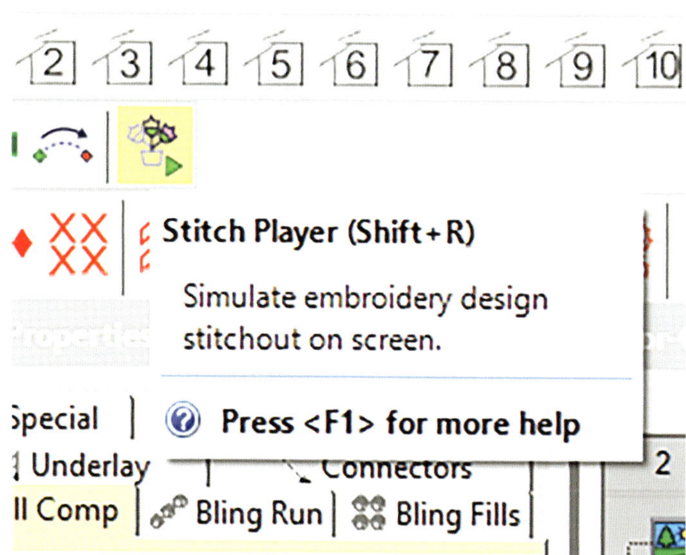

Stitch Player tool, useful for seeing a virtual stitch-out of your design.

Exporting

After finishing the digitising process, the next step is to export the file in a format that your embroidery machine can read. The method you use to transfer the digitised file to your machine varies based on the machine's features. You might use wi-fi, a direct cable connection, a USB flash drive, or an SD card to transfer the file. Refer to your machine's user manual on transfer method and required file format.

Common export options include:

- Tajima .DST
- Janome .JEF
- Brother .PES

OVERVIEW

As we move forward to the next chapter, we'll guide you through a straightforward project. This project is designed to give you practical experience and help you become more acquainted with how the software operates, as well as the tools and processes involved in using it. With each step you take in using the software, you'll find your comfort level increasing which, in turn, will boost your confidence. Remember, proficiency comes with practice, and as you grow more familiar with the software's environment, you'll find your ability to utilise its capabilities improving steadily. So, stay curious, keep experimenting, and watch as your confidence in digital design blossoms.

CASE STUDY: LISS COOKE – HAND & LOCK

Senior Digital Embroidery Designer and Production Coordinator.

Born in the picturesque county of Staffordshire, Liss embarked on her academic journey studying Textile Design at Birmingham City University. This foundation led her to pursue further mastery with an MA from Nottingham Trent University. Her early professional experiences saw her leading as the Head of Embroidery at the renowned Mary Katrantzou. In 2020, Liss found her new home at Hand & Lock, fuelled by a fervent passion for redefining the boundaries of contemporary digital embroidery. Her mission? To broaden the horizons of what's achievable in digital embroidery and elevate the offerings to clients. With a rich background that includes roles as a swatch designer and lecturer, Liss boasts an extensive grasp of both textile theory and hands-on practice. Her knack for weaving embroideries with vibrant textures and depth is only paralleled by her ability to illuminate the art's potential to those she collaborates with. Currently, Liss steers the helm of in-house bespoke digital embroidery design and production at Hand & Lock. Her prowess extends to orchestrating large-scale, off-site digital projects. One of her most notable contributions has been forging a groundbreaking alliance with Coloreel, a trailblazer in innovative embroidery technology.

Liss Cooke – Head of Digital Embroidery Production at Hand & Lock.

TROUBLESHOOTING

Question 1: I am trying to auto digitise, and the outcome is not good enough?

Auto digitising often requires adjustments; it's rare to use the feature and not make any changes before stitching out the design. You have three choices to improve the result:

1. Use graphic design software to clean up your original image. The clearer and simpler the image, like a cartoon, the better it will be for automatic digitising.
2. Use a combination method where you start with automatic digitising, then refine the results with the available editing tools.
3. Skip automatic digitising and do it manually from the beginning, using your original image as a guide that stays in place (locked) while you work.

Question 2: My embroidery machine cannot read my exported file?

If your embroidery machine isn't recognising your design, here are a few things to check:

1. Refer to your machine's user manual to make sure you're saving the file in the format it requires.
2. Look for any parts of your design that are outside the embroidery area, which might make the machine think the design is too large. Remove any unwanted elements that are beyond the hoop's boundaries.
3. Check your hoop's orientation. Some machines work only with the hoop in a specific position, like horizontal or vertical. For example, my Janome machines need the hoop to be vertical, while my HappyJapan machine requires it to be horizontal. The machines won't read the file if the hoop is not oriented correctly.
4. You might need to set a starting point in your digitising software. There should be an option to select where the embroidery starts and ends. If not, a workaround is to digitise a small circle, give it a fill and place it at the beginning of your embroidery sequence. Position this circle in the centre of the hoop area. When you start embroidering, just skip this first shape so it doesn't get stitched.
5. Check your USB device or cable; over time this can be corrupt or damaged.

BIG FLEX

CHAPTER 5

YOUR FIRST PROJECTS

Learn through errors; these are opportunities you were not expecting!

Now you have everything you need and understand the fundamentals, you are ready to put them into practice. This chapter will lead you through two basic projects, introducing you systematically to the process of digital embroidery whilst building your confidence to enable you to apply the new skills to your own project work.

PROJECT ONE: DIGITISING A SIMPLE GRAPHIC USING KEY SOFTWARE TOOLS AND STITCHES, EMBROIDERED ON A FABRIC USING THE TRAPPED HOOPING METHOD AND CUT-AWAY STABILISER

One very common application of digital embroidery, which you can see all around us, is in the visible branding of garments or accessories for business identification. Many uniforms or sporting goods have embroidered emblems applied directly, often consisting of an image and text.

Once digitised and a final sample is approved, the production of this type of embroidery is often quick and replicated by the hundreds or thousands. Stitch count for this type of project will usually be under 10,000 stitches and consist of limited colours and basic fill types only, in order to keep costs low and profit margins high. The graphic we are going to use for this project is a good example of a business logo that could be embroidered on merchandise.

Business logo for the brand, Ria Belle, which we will digitise.

OPPOSITE: The author embroidering outside in public with machine, laptop and threads.

For upcoming projects, I'll be using Wilcom software to show the digitising process. There are other software options you could use, and many of them have similar features. With some patience and practice, you can transfer the techniques I demonstrate to whichever software you prefer.

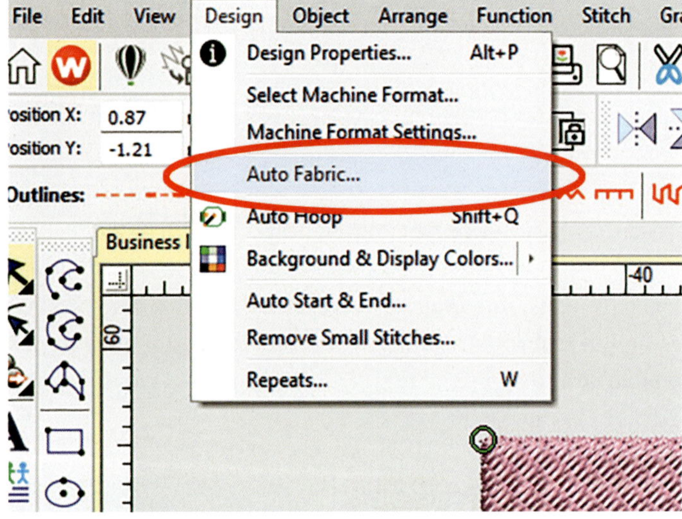

Auto fabric preset settings in Wilcom digitising software.

Step One

Open a *new file* and select the *Auto Fabric* and *Machine Format* from the menu options. Ensure the settings match your machine and the fabric type you intend to embroider on.

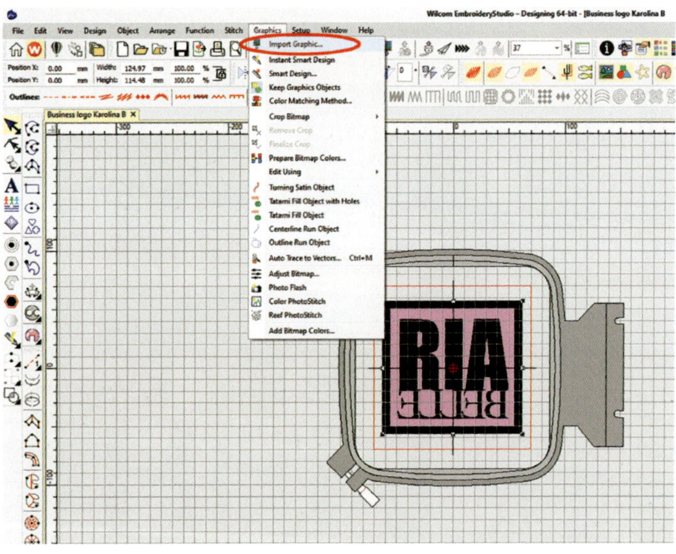
Imported graphic and hoop visualisation.

Step Two

Import your graphic, amend the size to suit your intended purpose and ensure an appropriately sized hoop is selected.

This graphic consists of both shapes and text, made up of two colours. It is essentially a pink square with a black border, consisting of two types of text font in the centre, sitting within the border frame.

Decision Time

Decide on whether you would like to digitise manually or try the automatic digitising option (should your software have this feature). For very simple graphics such as this one, auto features could work well and save you a lot of time. For this project we will attempt both methods and compare the outputs.

ATTEMPT 1: AUTO DIGITISING

Step Three

Ensure your graphic is selected and click on the appropriate auto-digitising icon or setting. For Wilcom, this is called *Instant Smart Design.*

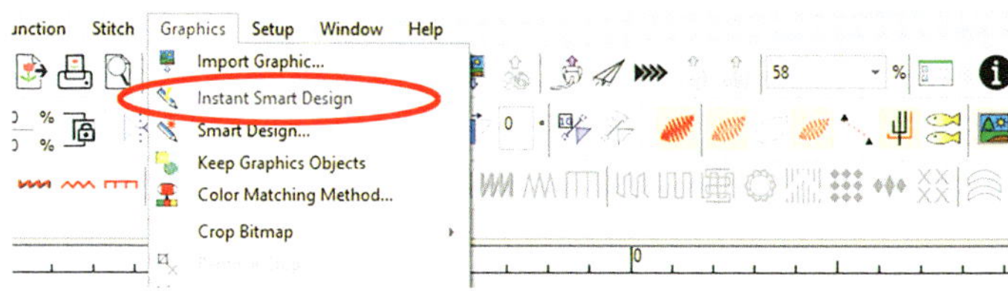

Instant smart design selection from menu allows the computer to digitise the design for you.

Step Four

Analyse the outcome – is it what you are after? Does it need more work to refine or correct?

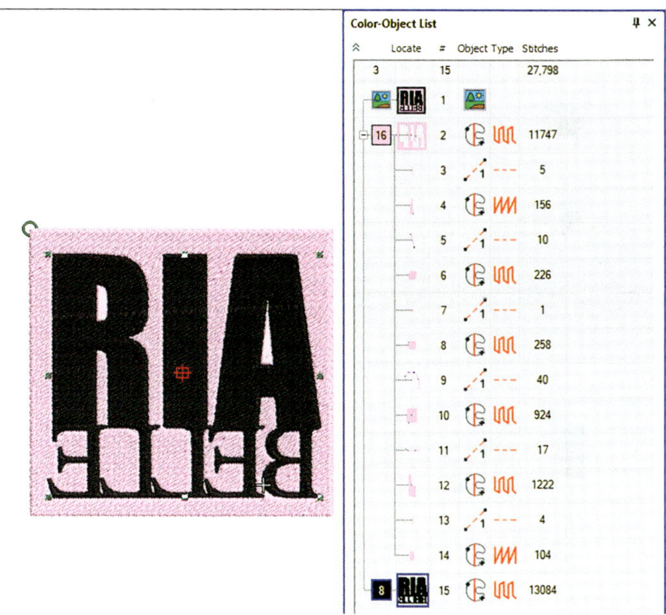

Instant smart design result applied to the graphic logo.

Analysing the Outcome

Looking at the outcome, we can see that the border is missing, and the text and pink background are in the tatami stitch type with the centre of the letter A in a satin fill. The sequence looks in a good logical order. The background has been cut away under the text, which reduces any bulking issues. My only concern would be any visible gaps appearing between the text and background. You could spend a little time to correct all these issues if you deemed it worthwhile. With larger, more complex pieces, auto digitising first and working manually into the outcome can generate some interesting and very exciting results.

ATTEMPT 2: MANUAL DIGITISING

With simple designs it can be easier and quicker to manually digitise. Let's try digitising the logo manually.

Step One

Repeat Step One as above.

Rectangle tool selected.

Step Two

Select the rectangle shape tool (The *Digitise Closed Shape* feature will work equally well) and draw around the pink square. Change the stitch fill to suit your requirements.

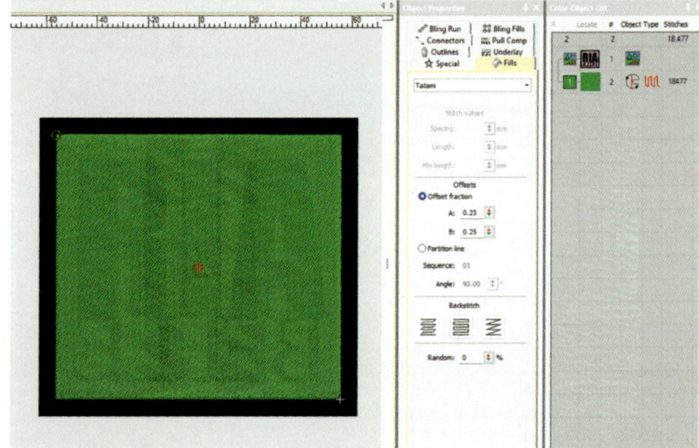

Digitised square with a tatami fill.

You should have a new symbol appear in the sequence window. When I digitise an image, I visualise it as a set of layers and starting from the background layer working towards the top layers makes things easier.

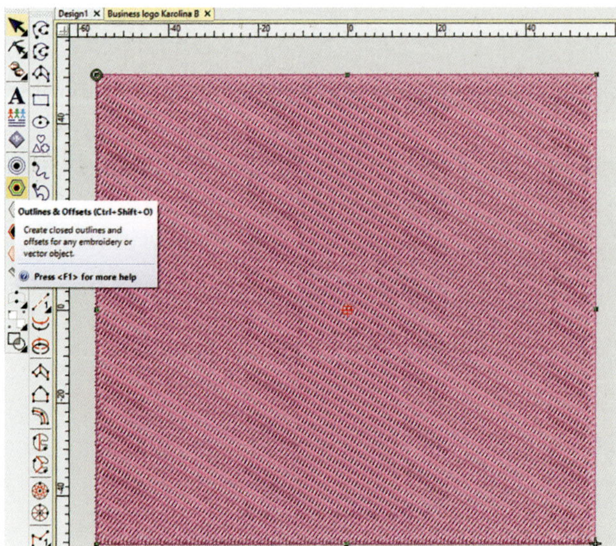

Pink square and *Outlines & Offsets* tool selected.

Step Three

Ensure the square is selected and click on a colour palette at the bottom of the screen to change to pink. Click on the *Outline and Offset* tool.

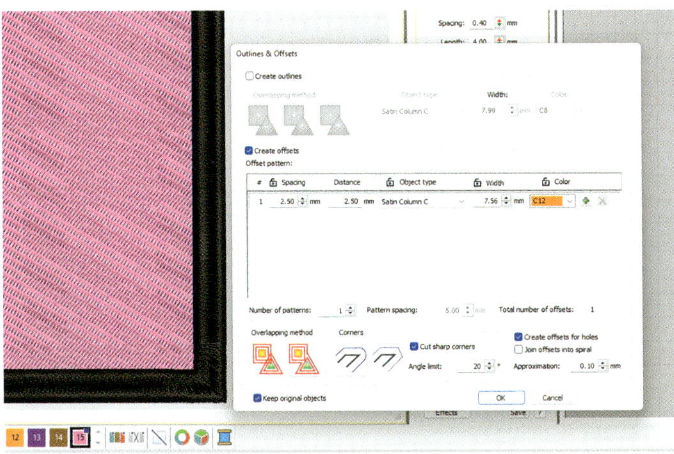

Outlines & Offsets options box and changed border.

Step Four

Experiment with the settings to create a border that you are happy with. Ensure there is a slight overlap of about 0.2mm to avoid gaps appearing.

Here I have selected the satin fill, 7.56mm width, square corners. Altering the spacing setting changes the distance the border sits around the edge of the square (it creates a gap or increases the overlap).

Step Five

The text consists of two different fonts, so we will need to digitise them individually. Using the *Type* feature, I look for a font as similar as possible to the original graphic and experiment with sizing and spacing to best match.

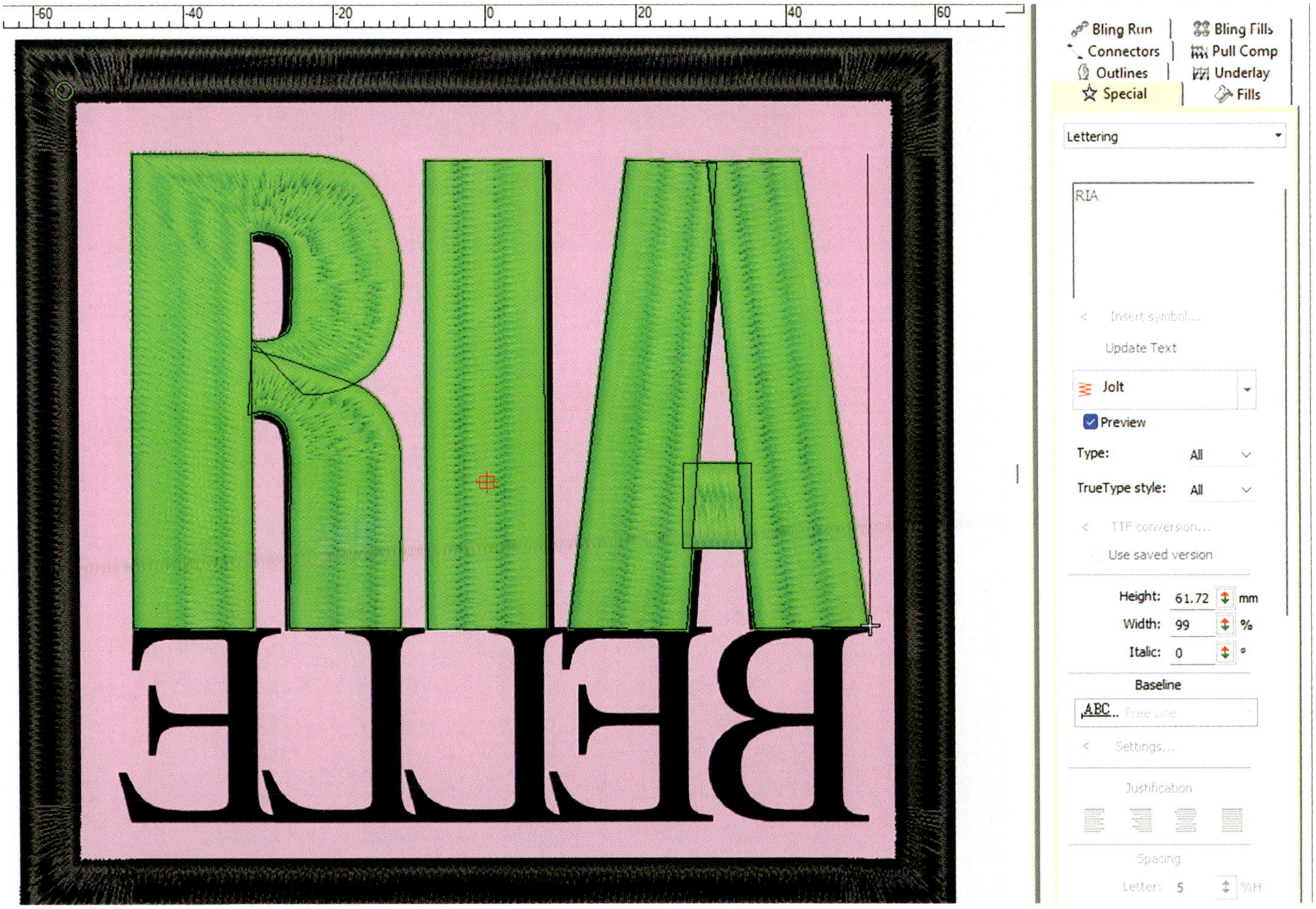

Font applied to part of the graphic.

I repeat this again for the second set of text and then flip it horizontally.

Applied and flipped text.

You may be lucky and find the perfect font to match your logo; however, if the text has been altered or is unique, then the best you can do is find the nearest font, break it into its individual components and use the reshape tools to alter the areas that do not match the artwork. If there are no type fonts that are remotely similar, then I would use the *Digitise Closed Shape* tool and treat the text as a normal image object, tracing around the edge and closing to apply a fill.

Step Six

Change the font colour to black. Hide the artwork so you just see your new digitised graphic. We are nearly ready to embroider; however, there are a few things we need to look at first:

1. The sequence
2. Stitch direction
3. Start and end points
4. Underlay
5. Pull compensation

I prefer to look at these settings together, shape by shape. Starting with the top shape in the sequence window (which should be my background pink square in this case), I hide all the other shapes, then change and amend the settings, before moving on to the next shape.

Let's look at this, starting with the pink background square.

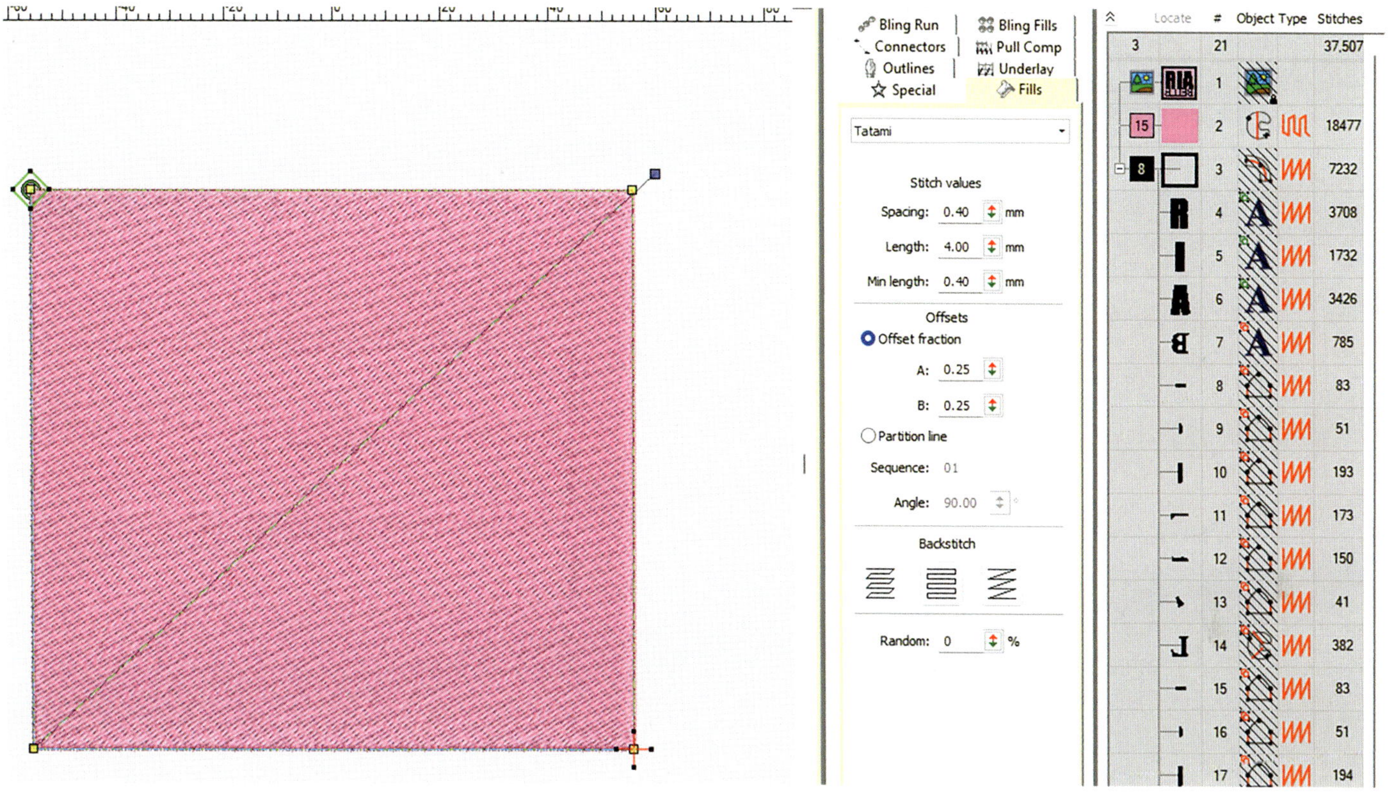

Pink square shape visible only with all the other layers hidden.

I have chosen a stitch angle of 45 degrees, with the start and end points in opposite corners (Green Square, entry, red cross, exit). By choosing opposite corners it allows for continuous stitching without the machine stopping and joining midway through, thus reducing the risk of a visible join line. The default fill settings will result in a solid fill; however, if you increase and decrease this it will alter the visual affect. Increasing the spacing creates a mesh appearance, which is a fantastic technique to create a sense of depth to an artwork, especially if used as layers.

Next, we will look at the pull compensation

The pull compensation by default will be based on what fabric type you have selected at the beginning. In this case it was 0.20mm. You can do a test sample and if a gap appears between this shape and the border, then one method of rectifying is to increase the pull compensation. From experience I prefer a 0.35–0.40mm pull compensation for non-satin fill types, but the resulting sample will determine if this needs increasing or decreasing (*see* Pull Compensation, Chapter 2).

Pull compensation options.

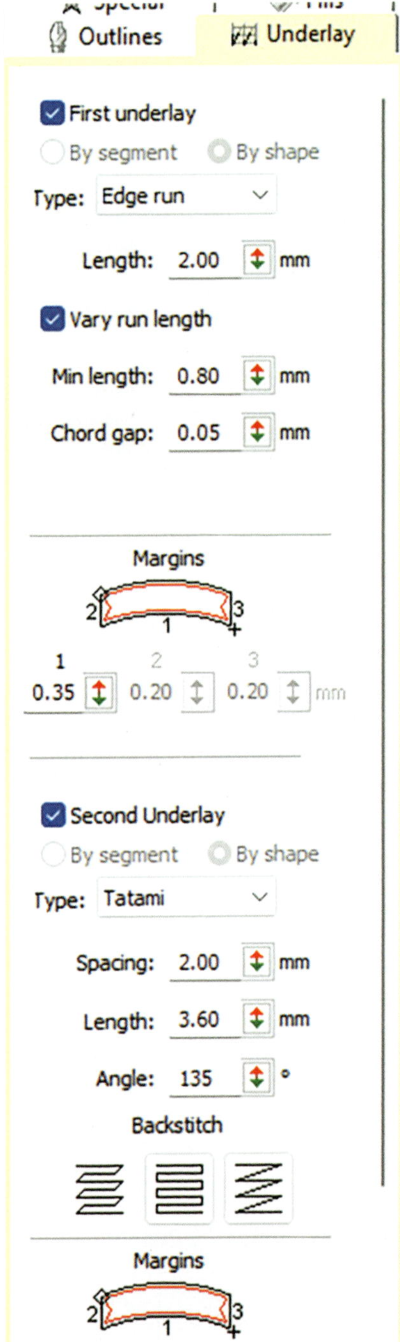

Underlayer settings window.

Finally, let's check the underlay

The underlayer is very important and must not be undervalued. It can have a massive impact on the quality of the outcome and prevent fabric distortion. Your software program will have defined default settings; it's worth becoming familiar with these and don't be scared to change them.

It consists of two underlayers, firstly an edge run. This will produce a running stich around the edge of the shape – useful when doing appliqué!

Secondly, a tatami underlayer, with a set spacing, stitch length, stitch angle and back stitch option. You can choose to have 0, 1, or 2 underlayers per shape. These settings will need changing based on the fabric you are stitching on and your design.

For this shape and assuming the fabric is something stable such as a medium-weight cotton, I will keep the first setting activated and its current setting, as well as the second underlayer and type. However, I prefer to alter the angle, backstitch type, the spacing and length.

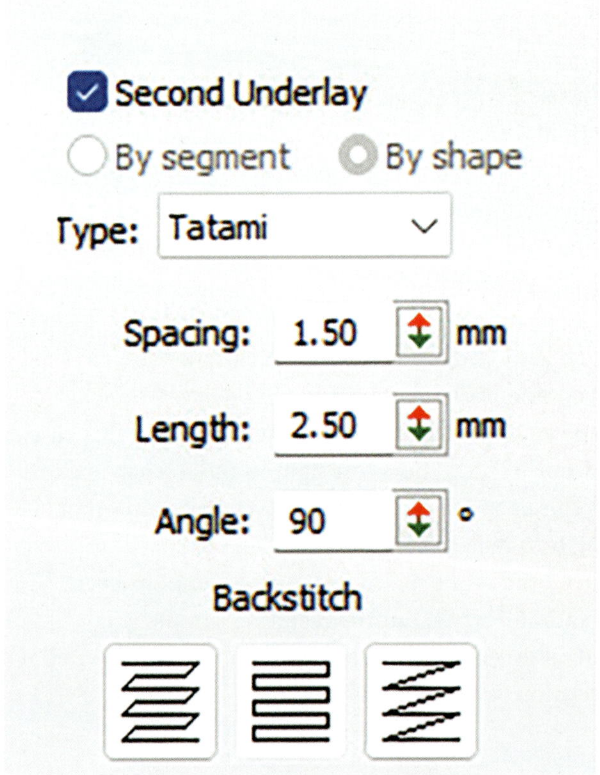

Applied new underlayer settings for the second underlayer option.

I find having an angle of 90 degrees and the square backstitch option (middle of the three bottom icons) produces a better-quality finish. The spacing and stitch length I reduce for small shapes and keep to the default for larger shapes. For fabrics that easily distort, I use smaller settings. (Please refer to the underlayer section in Chapter 2 for more information about underlayers.)

Step Seven

Repeat for the remaining shapes. For shapes that sit on top of other shapes, there is no need for an underlayer as the fabric has already been stabilised from previous shapes. If turning the underlayer off makes the shape appear a little transparent, then I would increase the layer fill density to compensate and reduce the risk of the underlayer showing through the top layer.

RESULT

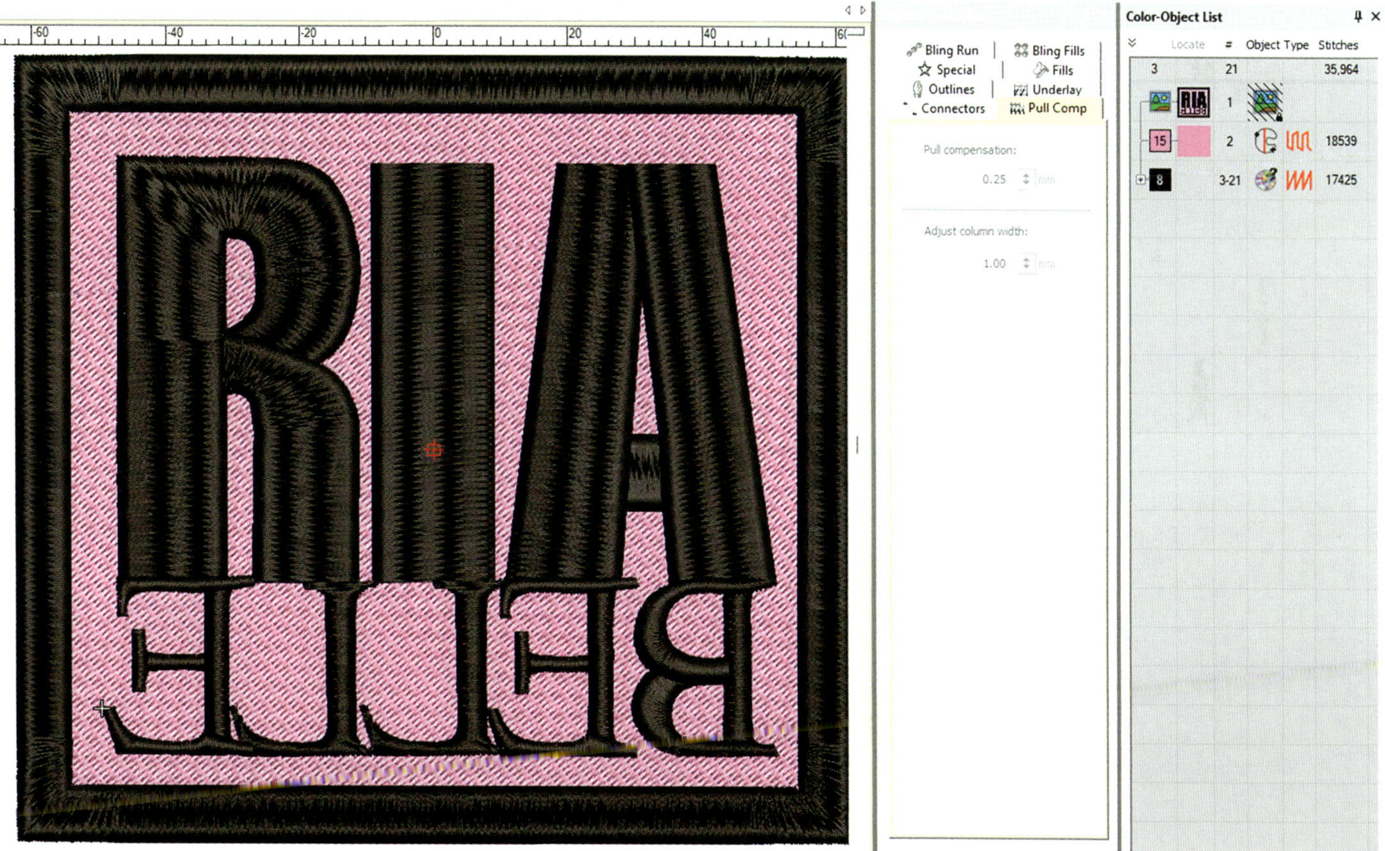

Final manually digitised logo and *Colour Object* List window.

You will notice that the background shape in the *Color-Object List* window is solid (no gaps), which is not what we saw in the auto digitised version. There is a feature on the Wilcom software program called *Remove Overlaps* (*see* Chapter 4). If I select the text layer and select the *Remove Overlaps* feature, it will remove the stitches underneath the text, leaving some for overlapping based on settings. The benefit of doing this is that it removes the possibility of bulk and over-thickening of the embroidery. A disadvantage is that it could affect the visual appearance of the background stitch fill, and there is a chance of gaps appearing between the text and background. I use both methods, depending on the fabric and the design. In this case, I would be tempted to keep the background solid as above. I will review this choice based on the outcome of the sample.

The outcome when *Remove Overlaps* has been applied.

You can see the differences in the sequence order and visual impact between the letter 'L's. Let's hide the black text and select the *reshape* tool to see how we can rectify this.

Looking at the background in this way, we can now see a couple of potential issues. Firstly, the end point (red cross) has moved to midway on the right-hand side. Moving this back to the bottom right corner may rectify this. Secondly, there are very small gap areas visible at the ends of the letters that could also affect the visual outcome. In this case, I would relocate the red cross and refill the small areas.

We can see the areas between the two letter 'L's has been rectified. If we choose this method, then we need to make sure the underlayers for the text objects are reinstated.

At this stage I would be happy to sample this graphic. Once embroidered, I would review the quality of the lettering and decide if I need to change anything. Until the file has been sampled, you can never 100 per cent know how it will turn out.

EMBROIDERING (STITCH-OUT)

Step One

Select your fabric, stabiliser backing and the hoop you intend to use. Here I have a 140 × 140mm hoop, medium-weight cotton twill fabric and two sheets of cut-away medium-weight backing.

Frame, fabric and backings required for stitch-out.

Hooped fabric and backing stabilisers secured in a frame.

For this embroidery I will use a *trapping* hooping technique where the backing layers and fabric are trapped together in between the frame's inner and outer hoops. The tension is important; it cannot be too loose or too tight as this can cause issues when embroidering, particularly distortions when the hoop is removed. You are looking for a tension like that you see on a drum.

Step Two

Once you are happy, attach the hoop to your machine, upload your file and thread the machine with the first colour. Please refer to your machine's instruction manual on how to do this, as all machines differ.

Based on your machine type, you may be able to see a digital display of your design along with its properties.

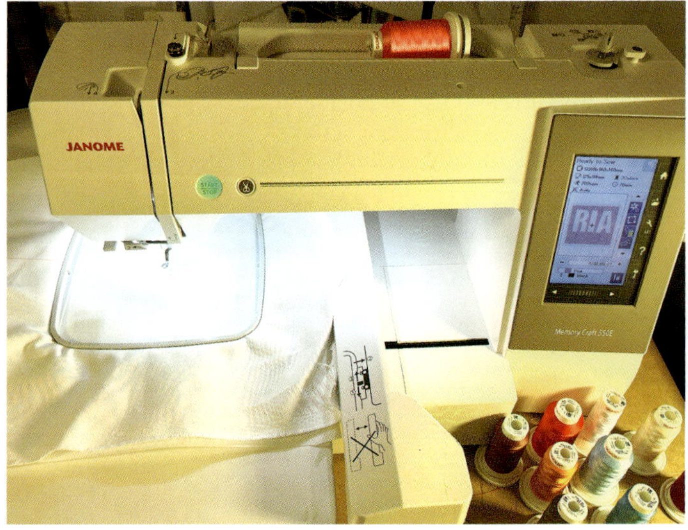

Embroidery machine ready to stitch out design.

From my display it confirms the hoop size selected (140 × 140mm), embroidery size (125 × 114mm), the speed the machine will embroider at (700spm), tension settings (auto), how many colours (2) and an estimate on how long it will take to embroider (70 mins). This display also allows me to rotate the design, apply basting stitches, fast forward or rewind stitches. It is worth spending time getting to know your machine and what options are available to you, as this can inform your creative thinking.

My embroidery machine's digital display with key information.

As the machine embroiders, keep an eye on it as they can be temperamental. It's worth stopping the machine as soon as anything doesn't look correct or sound right. By watching closely, you can determine if the digital file needs amending. Areas to focus on are the sequence, any gaps, areas of considerable overstitching thus increasing the risk of bulk, and any signs of distortion.

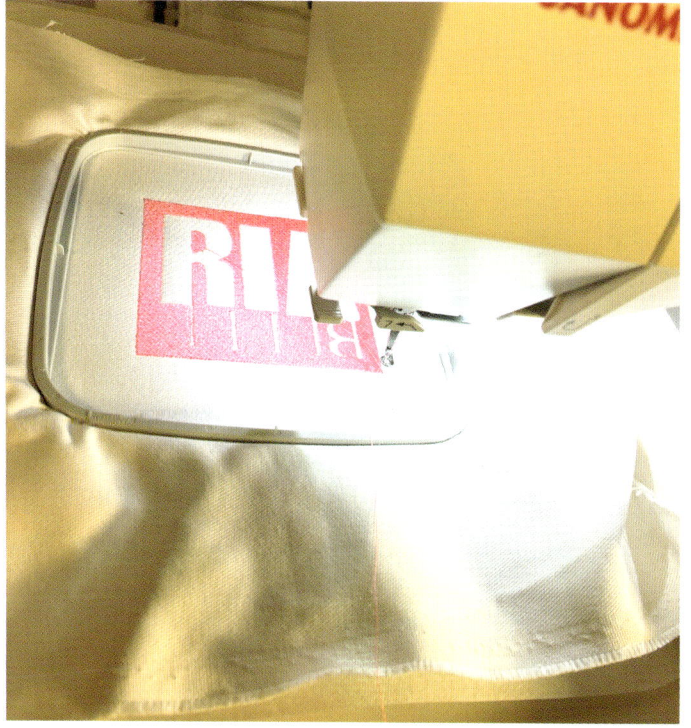

Stitch-out in progress.

Step Three

Once the embroidery is complete, turn the fabric over and cut away any trailing threads. With scissors (or snips) cut away the backing as near to the embroidery as possible. Be careful not to cut any stitches!

Cut-away stabiliser being removed from around the edge.

Stitch-out sample ready for review and improvements.

Step Four

Iron your embroidery on a medium setting. If it's too hot you risk the danger of melting or causing a shine on the threads. I also fold the embroidery to determine if it is too thick or not. For art pieces where the outcome is to be displayed only, I would opt for a heavyweight backing to give it stability. For garments, medium-weight backing is my normal go-to, unless the garment is lightweight or stretchy, then I may need to be more selective on the backing (*see* Chapter 1, Stabilisers). Several samples may need to be created to work out the best backing combination and machine settings for your project. Unfortunately, there is no one-size-fits-all for this aspect of the process.

Testing the thickness by folding in half.

Logo on a garment in styled shoot.

PROJECT TWO: HAND-RENDERED IMAGE WITH TEXT EMBROIDERED ON A SWEATSHIRT USING THE FLOATING HOOPING METHOD

For this project, I will be using one of my client commissions and taking you through the complete process, from hand-rendered sketch through to embroidering on a sweatshirt. My client in this case is Kim-Joy, a very talented baker who made the finals of *The Great British Bake Off* in 2018 and has since published several recipe books and collaborated with leading brands. Kim's style I would describe as quirky, playful, positive and joyful with a particular passion for baking, cute creatures and cats. Involving my client in the design process (co-designing) helps to build a stronger emotional connection between the client and the product, helping to reinforce that feeling of specialness whilst also reducing the risk the client won't like the outcome at the end.

For this project, I was asked to create a cartoon cat to be embroidered on a sweatshirt as a giveaway prize in the build-up to the launch of her cat-themed recipe book.

The author holding up a copy of Kim-Joy's cat recipe cookbook.

Step One

Create your artwork.

Here I have used A3 paper, a pencil and felt pens. This is a rough sketch of the design complete with notes, colours and stitch suggestions. As it is going to be symmetrical, I have only coloured one side. The sketch is not neat and tidy as you may expect, but it is enough to give me an idea of shapes, scale, proportion and colour. When I digitise, I continue designing and refining the concept. The tendency is to recreate the drawing exactly, but you need to use the sketch as a template and allow it to evolve through the digitising process. Trust your creative judgement and instincts.

Hand rendered design drawing of a cat for Kim-Joy.

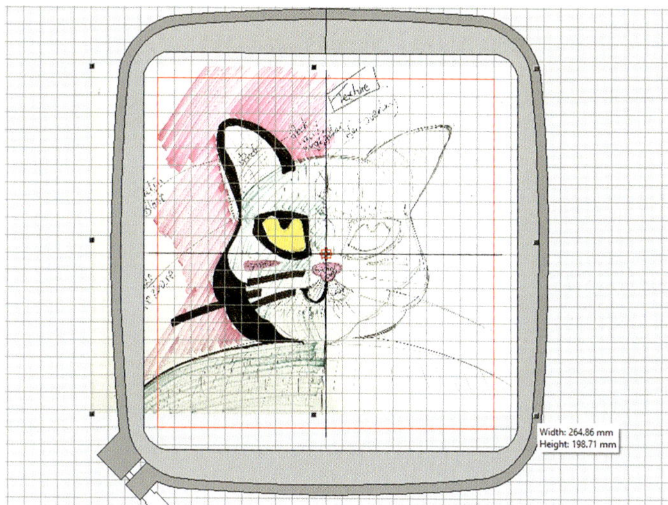

Design imported in the Wilcom software and shown with a virtual hoop to get an idea of scale.

Step Two

Open your digitising software program and create a new file, import your graphic and rescale to your intended size (once again I am using Wilcom digitising software).

I have chosen the Janome SQ (200 × 200mm) hoop for this project. You will be limited to the hoops available for your machine, so pick the one that is most suitable for your vision.

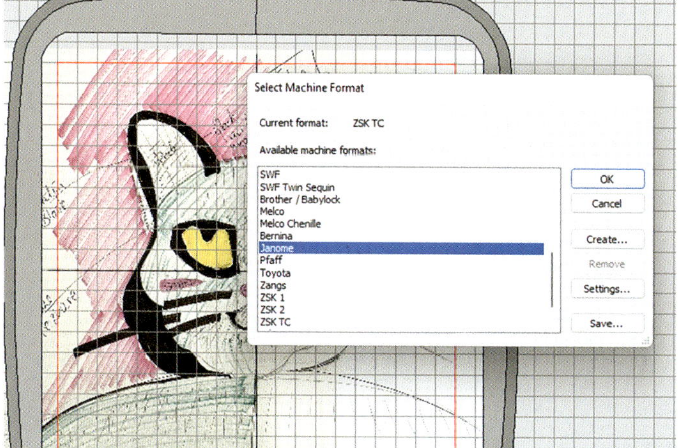

Machine selection options.

Step Three

Select your machine from the menu (if this is available to you). I will be using a Janome MC 550e machine.

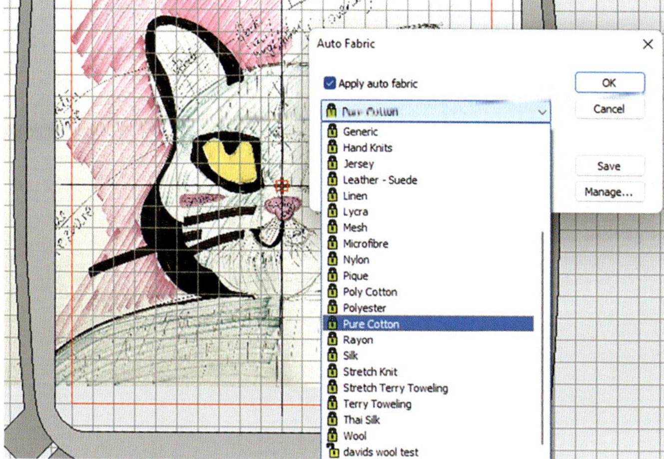

Fabric selection options.

Step Four

Select your fabric type from the menu (if this is available to you). I will be embroidering on a cotton sweatshirt. By selecting the fabric type, it will adjust the pull compensation and underlayer settings to suit. (I take these with a pinch of salt and prefer to sample my design on a fabric similar to my final fabric, making setting adjustments in order to refine.)

Step Five

Select your image and lock it in place. This will prevent you accidently moving it. You should see a padlock or other icon telling you the layer is now locked.

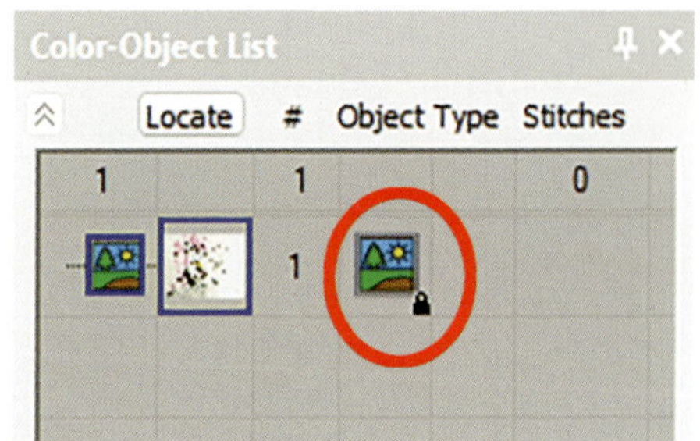

Colour Object list showing the design layer is locked in place.

Step Six

Trace the outline of the cat's head and shoulders using the *Digitise Closed Shape* tool. You only need to trace half the image as we are going to reflect this to ensure both sides are the same. To make life easier you may want to use guidelines to help identify the centre line (vertical) or ensure the bottom of the image is aligned (horizontal).

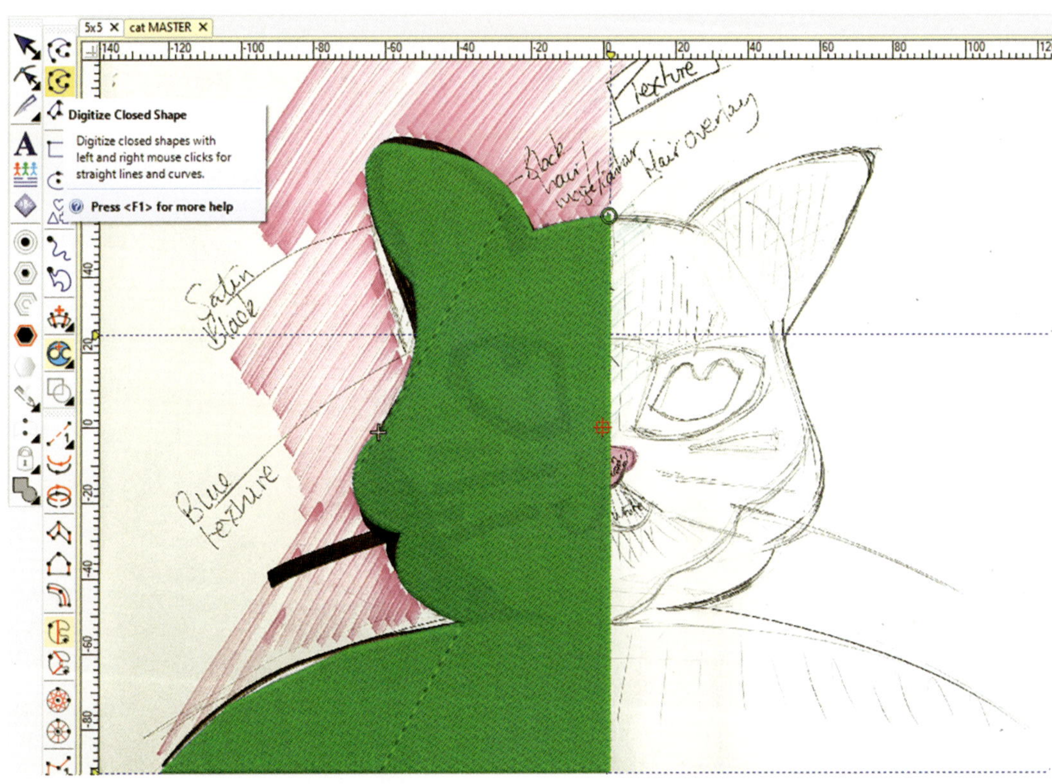

Digitising in progress - half the design digitised using the *Digitise Closed Shape* tool.

Reshape tool used to refine the digitised shape.

The original shape being copied, pasted, and mirrored.

Step Seven

Use the *Reshape* tool to refine your new shape. (Remember you do not have to follow your drawing exactly, use your aesthetic judgement on this.)

Step Eight

Select your shape, Copy and paste. Select the new shape and click on the *Mirror Reflect* tool (horizontally.)

Step Nine

Move your new shape to align on the centre front and the bottom.

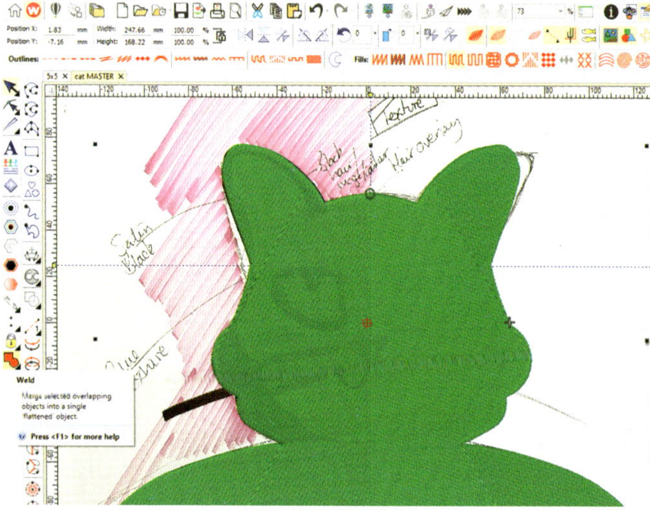

Step Ten

Ensure *both* the left- and right-hand side shapes are selected and merge (weld) together to form one shape.

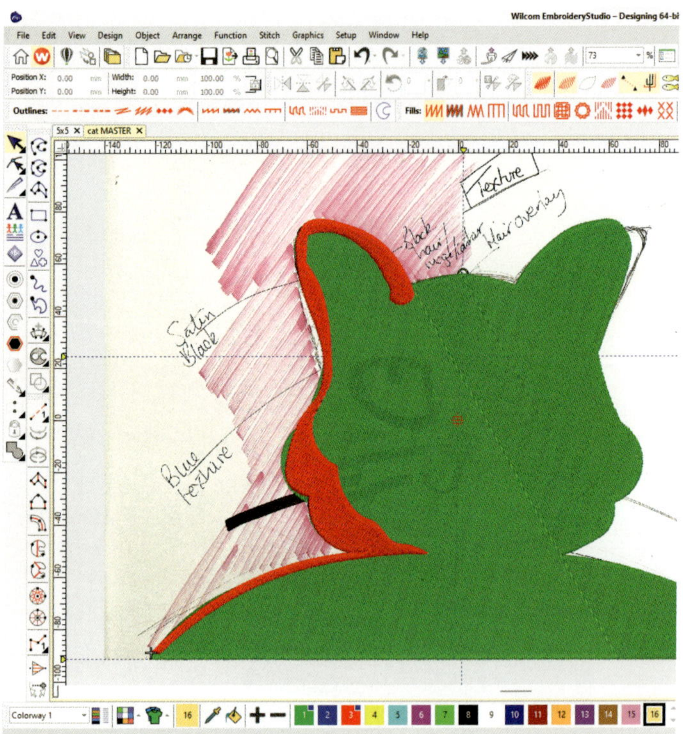

Addition of a new layer on top of the background layer.

New layer refined and repeated on the opposite side.

Step Eleven

Hide the background layer and trace the black edge shape using the *Digitise Closed Shape* tool. Make sure the two layers have different colours assigned to them so you can clearly see them both. *Unhide* the background layer.

Step Twelve

Reshape the top layer shape so it matches the background shape around the edge. **Copy and paste. Mirror and move** into place on the opposite side of the head.

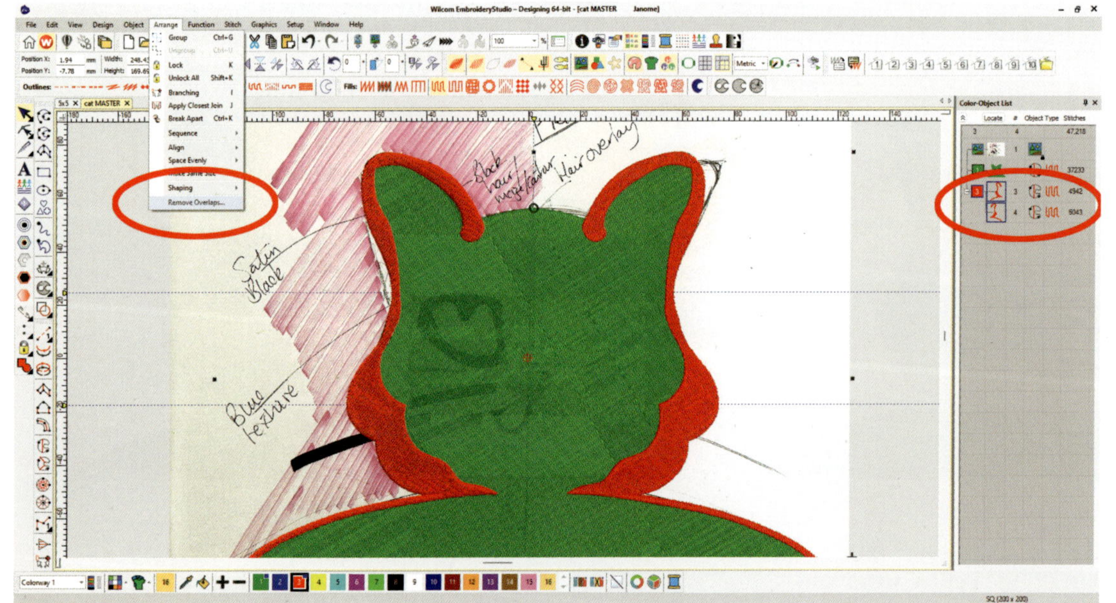

Step Thirteen

Ensure both the top layers are selected and then go to **Arrange** in the menu and select, **Remove Overlaps**.

Click ok using default setting.

Step Fourteen

Ensure there is sufficient overlap, thus preventing a gap appearing. I generally stick with the default settings that appear in the pop-up window as they are often very reliable.

Step Fifteen

Take a look at the *Color-Object List* window as sometimes objects will appear that are hidden behind the upper layers and hidden from view. The *Remove Overlaps* feature can be a little unpredictable. Select each of the hidden layers and delete. For this graphic, I should only have three objects in the window at the moment. Keeping unneeded layers will add extra thickness to the piece and thus increase the risk of fabric distortion.

Step Sixteen

Hide all the objects so only your artwork is visible. Repeat the process (11–14) for the left eye. For the whiskers and mouth, I would follow the above procedure but not the *Remove Overlaps.* For the nose, I would trace it as one complete shape.

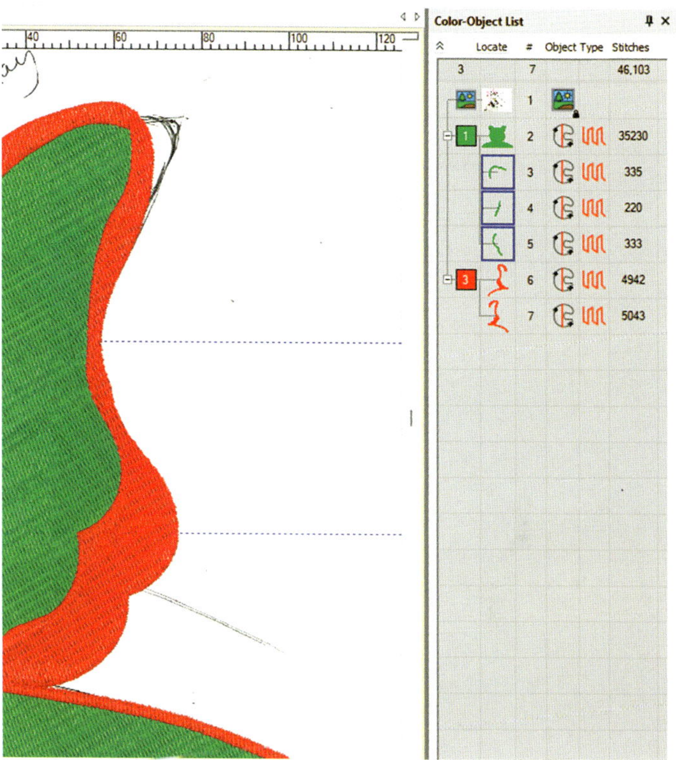

Unneeded objects in the *Color Object List* window after the *Remove Overlaps* feature has been applied.

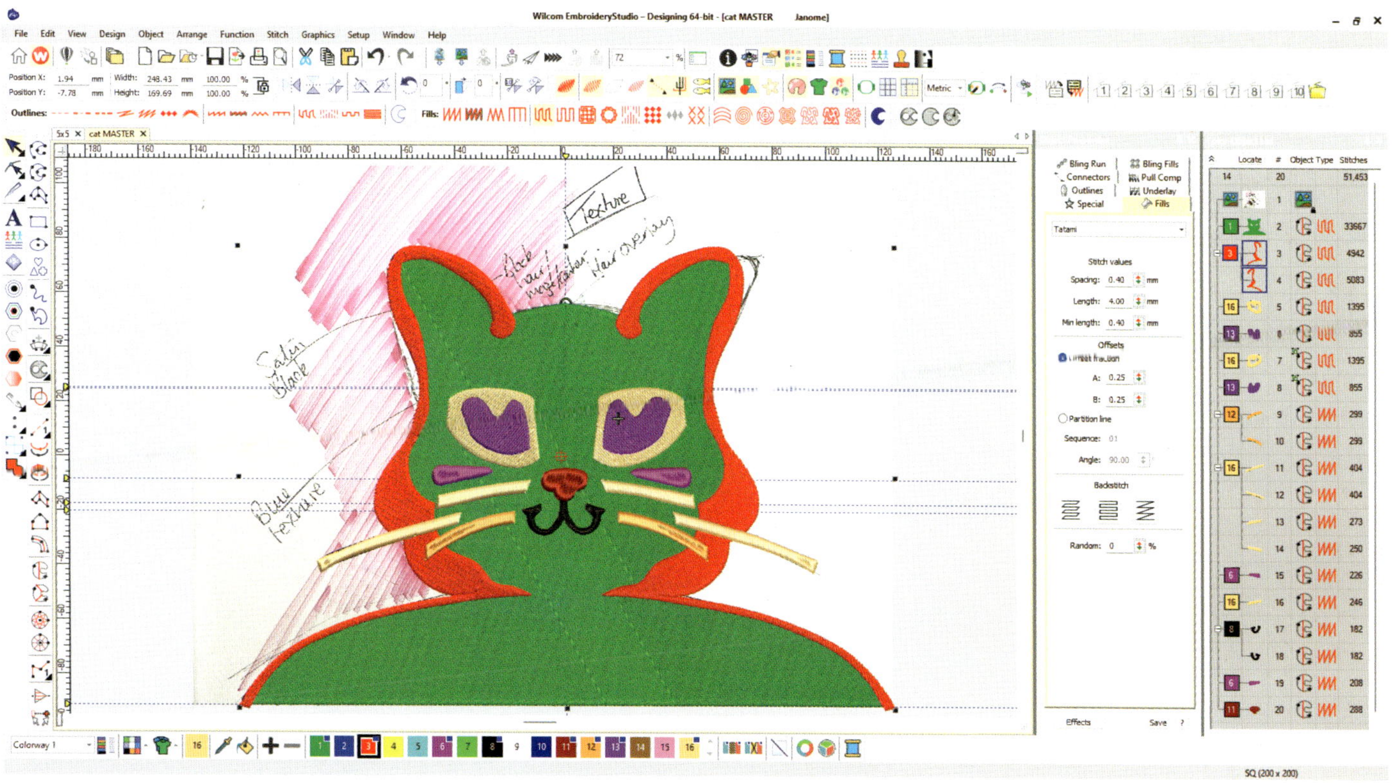

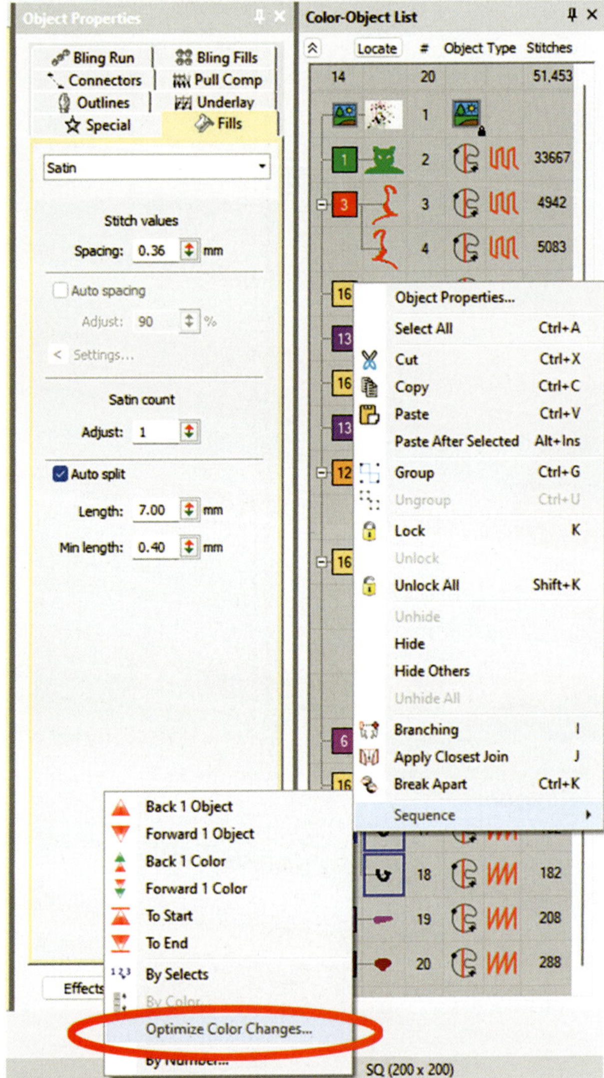

Optimise Color Changes feature in Wilcom.

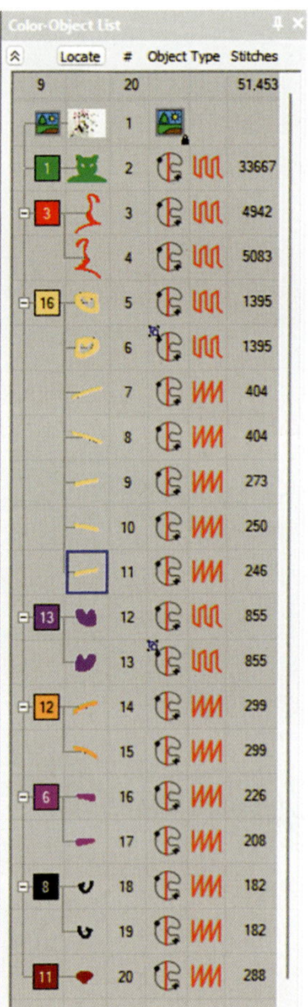

Result of the *Optimise Color Changes* once applied.

All new objects appear in the *Color-Object List* window. However, the sequence order is very inefficient, meaning that if I embroidered it in its current state, I would have a lot of colour changes to make. Re-sequencing can solve this issue and speed up the embroidery process. The aim is to group shapes of the same colour together, without changing the visual appearance of the graphic. The Wilcom software allows the user to *Optimise Color Changes*, which can do this for you; however, you may still need to check this and manually move objects up or down the sequence.

Reviewing the result of the auto colour optimisation, I noticed the whiskers are different shades of orange, which was not intentional. I will change the colours of objects 14 and 15 and manually move them so they are grouped with objects 5 to 11. (Click, drag and release).

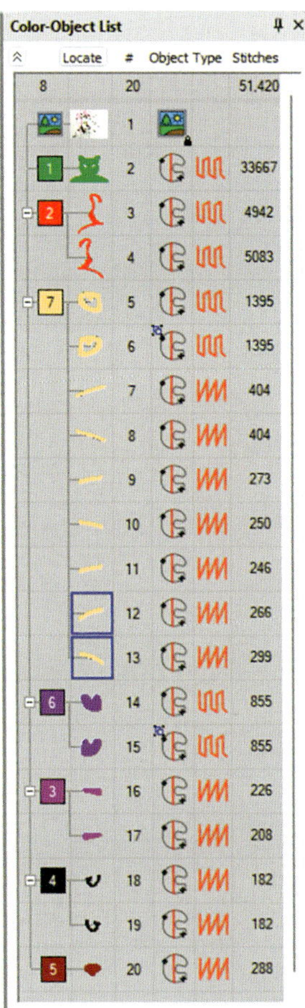

Result of manually refining the sequence order.

Tatami fill with 0% random applied.

Tatami fill with 50% random applied.

Tatami fill with 100% random applied.

Tatami fill with handstitched effect applied.

Step Seventeen

Now I am happy with the sequence, I will look at the stitch fills for each shape. I would like to create a sense of texture and will look at fills that can give a fur-like feel and also a sense of 3D body form. For this, I will look at the direction of the stitches and utilise the *Florentine* feature.

Starting with the background, I will keep the tatami stitch, but explore applying a hand-stitched feel. In the Wilcom software there is a *Hand stitch* option, which I will experiment with, but I can also get a similar result by increasing the *Random* percentage amount in the *stitch fill* window.

There is very little difference between the hand stitch tool and the *Random* feature in this case, so it doesn't really matter which I choose.

Step Eighteen

I will amend the fur direction adding a *Florentine* effect to replicate the roundness of the cat's head. The start and end points will be relocated to avoid any visible join lines.

Step Nineteen

I will explore all the shapes in the same way, until I am happy with the overall look.

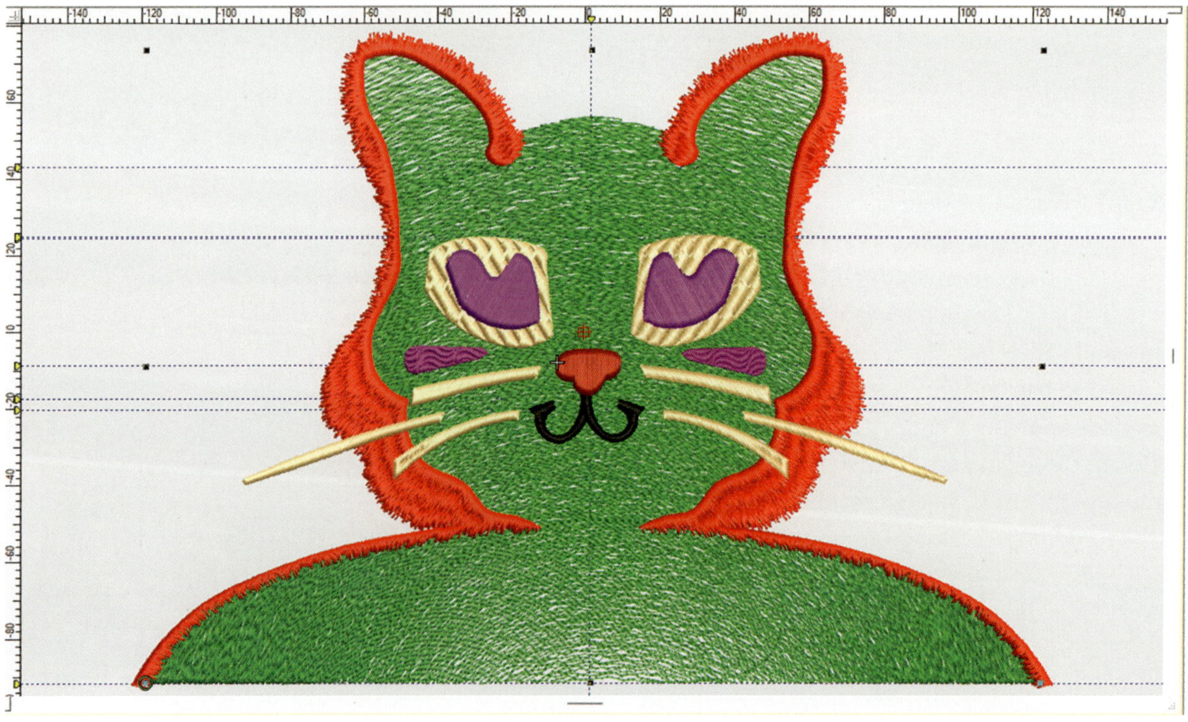

To finish the overall look, I applied the following settings:

- an *accordion* effect to the green background shape
- a *satin* fill with a *Jagged Edge* effect to the red outline shapes
- a *Program Split – Ziggy pattern* to the orange of the eyes
- a *satin* fill to the purple of the eyes
- a *satin raised* fill to the nose
- normal *satin* fill to the mouth and whiskers
- changed the colours.

The original artwork also had more fur detailing in the ears, forehead, under the nose and the main body. I will explore recreating this using the tatami fill with a spacing and the contour fill.

Digitised outcome of my cat design for Kim Joy. As per project one, I hide the other shapes and focus on each one individually.

Checking the pull compensation setting. For the underlays, I will apply an edge run for the first underlay and a tatami underlay for the second underlay.

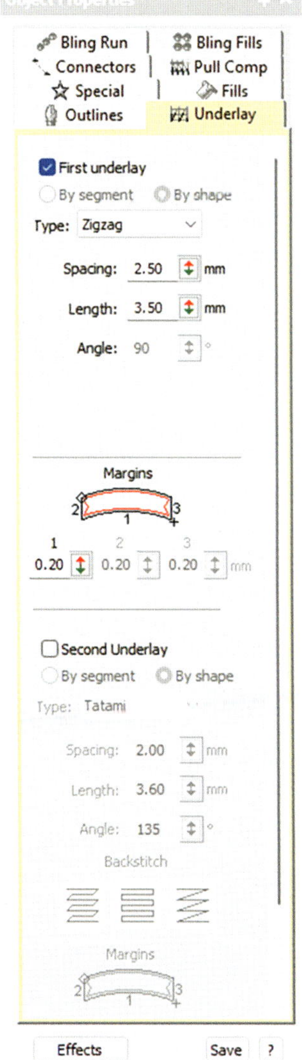

Underlayer settings for satin fills.

Underlayer settings for tatami fills.

Finally, to see contrast I am going to change the background to replicate the colour of the sweatshirt (pink). This virtual rendering gives me an as near as possible idea of how the embroidery will appear in reality, without actually embroidering it.

Virtual rendering of my final digitised cat ready to embroider.

Once I reach this stage, I normally send the virtual rendering to the client for feedback and make any changes accordingly. Whilst waiting for feedback (this is often an unknown and can range from hours to weeks), I sample the design on spare fabric to check the accuracy of the settings. As this is a real client project, I will send the rendering to my client and ask about any text they may like adding.

Three cats looking upwards at different text phrases.

Step Twenty Two: Adding text

My client has suggested three potential phrases or words to consider adding. Using the *type* tool, I have added all three options to the image, applying an arc stylisation to enable the text to bend around the image. As it looks like the cat is looking upwards, it makes sense to have the text above the image to suggest the cat is looking at it. The three phrases are 'Bake me a Cat', 'Meow' and 'Purrfect'.

Changing the text is a relatively quick process, so in this case I tried all three suggestions and sent them via my smart device to Kim-Joy. Seeing the text with the design helps with decision-making and is an opportunity to involve the client in the design process. Kim-Joy chose the design on the left-hand side, as she feels it best relates to the new cookbook that she is writing at the time.

Sampling (Stitch-out)

The final design will be embroidered on a pink medium-weight cotton sweatshirt. However, to sample I don't really want to be using the actual garment as it could go horribly wrong, and I would need to buy a replacement. Instead, I will use a similar fabric to the actual one, even though it might not be in the same colour. What I am keen to find out is: Is the design the correct size? Are the colours ok? Are there any unsightly stitch errors and could anything be improved?

Once sampled, I will show Kim-Joy for her feedback and make any changes before carrying out the final embroidery on the actual garment.

Step Twenty-Three: Hooping

For this project I will use the *floating technique* to attach the fabric to the hoop. There are two ways you can do this; either use a specialist adhesive backing which is trapped in the frame and sticks the wrong side of the fabric, or use a non-adhesive backing which is trapped in the frame and pin the fabric on top. I will be using the second technique for this project.

Using a medium-weight cut-away backing, trap in the appropriate hoop big enough for your artwork. In this case, my image is 19.5cm (7¾in) wide, so I will be using the Janome SQ (200 × 200mm) hoop, which is perfect. Ensure the backing is trapped to drum tension.

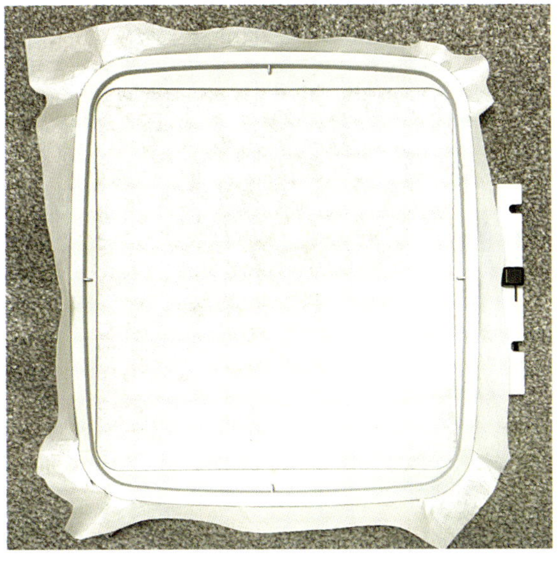

Stabiliser secured in the embroidery hoop.

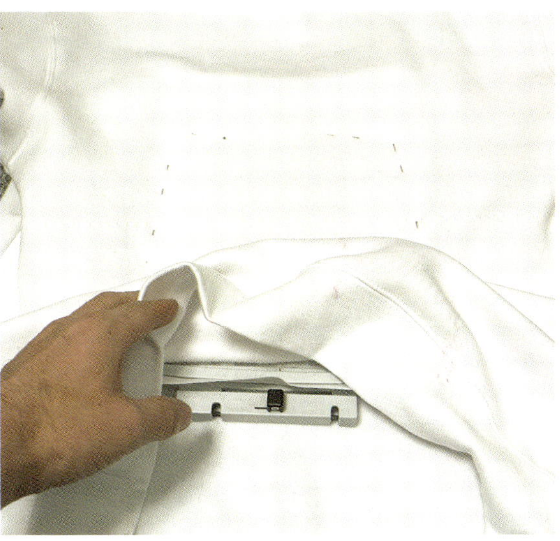

The hoop inside the garment, with the garment pinned to the stabiliser.

Step Twenty-Four

Place your fabric on top of the hoop and pin around the edge, being careful not to stretch the fabric as you do so. Here I am using an old sweatshirt. Due to my machine (Janome MC550e), I have to make sure that I am physically able to attach the frame to the machine once I have attached it to the garment. Garments, since they are 3D (circular) can be problematic to embroider in certain places, often restricted by the machine bed. Sleeves, for example, are impossible to embroider on this machine without opening the sleeve along one of the seams. It you are embroidering on a garment, be prepared to have to unpick a few seams in order to gain access and to allow for machine movement.

Step Twenty-Five

Based on my machine arm being on the right-hand side of the embroidery hoop and how I have attached the garment to the hoop, it now means that when I embroider, the image will be facing in the wrong direction. To counteract this, go back to your computer and digitised file, select all your image and rotate it until you are sure that it will embroider in the correct direction. This may take a little working out, but if you get it wrong it can be disastrous, so take your time and double-check.

Digitised design rotated on the computer to cater for the hoop and machine configuration.

Step Twenty Six

Attach the hoop (with the garment attached) to the machine, making sure you are not restricting the embroidery arm when it moves. When dealing with garments it is very easy to accidentally catch another part of the garment underneath the hoop and embroider through, often ruining the piece if it's not spotted quickly. Keep checking as you embroider to make sure this does not happen.

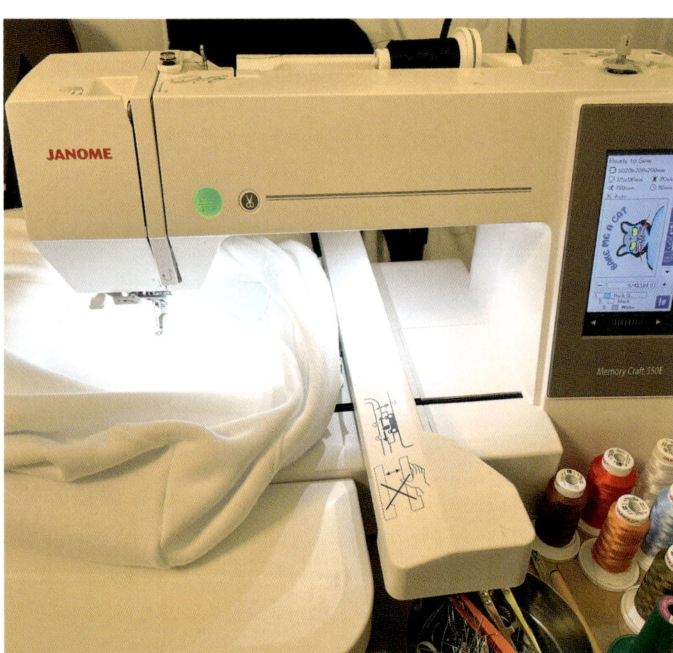

Embroidery machine with garment and hoop attached ready to stitch out.

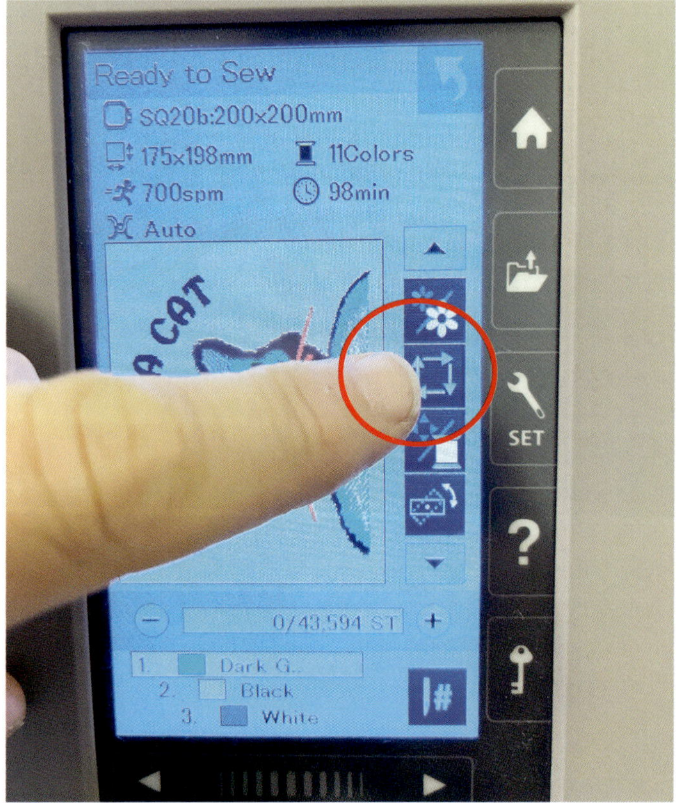

Basting feature icon on the Janome Mc550e embroidery machine.

Step Twenty-Seven

To further secure the fabric to the hooped backing, preventing unwanted movement, I add a basting stitch around the edge of the area to be embroidered. My machine has a setting feature that makes this process easy.

Step Twenty-Eight

Begin embroidering, following your machine's instructions to change colours. As this is a sample, keep an eye on the underlayers, sequences and any areas you feel could be improved. Make a note of anything that needs changing.

Completed design, basting and hoop removed.

Looking closely at the stitched-out sample, I am very happy with the textures, composition and overall feel of the image. There are minor areas that can be improved. The top layer on the forehead shows an unsightly stitch run on the right-hand side (I will relocate the start and end points for this shape). The top layer on the nose is too overpowering, so needs a colour rethink. The orange top layer on the chest has an additional vertical stitch run that needs removing (check *Color Objects* window and delete additional running stitch). The text needs to be bolder and the underlayer and sweatshirt can be seen through the black stitching (I will reduce the underlayer spacing, increase the pull compensation and increase the satin fill density). I will sample the text only before attempting the final embroidery on the pink sweatshirt.

These two projects are good starters to help you become confident at tackling more ambitious challenges. As you produce more and more, you will begin to find your own style, likes and dislikes and discover new and exciting ways of working.

RESULT

time to be critical and not precious. Look for areas that can be improved and refined. I am 95 per cent happy with this sample and would be happy to show my client. If the sample was a total disaster, I would re-do before showing my client.

kimjoy

Kim-Joy wearing the sweatshirt with her cat. (Photo: Kim-Joy)

je t'aime
oui oui oui

CHAPTER 6

ADDING DECORATION AND EFFECTS

Don't be afraid to try new techniques to add intrigue to your work.

As you learn more about digital embroidery, you might want to try new materials or methods to push your skills and add more variety to your work. This chapter will guide you through some easy projects that will introduce you to how to make patches, use the appliqué technique and work with foam. These techniques will help you add a three-dimensional look to your embroidery, making it feel more tactile and giving it a sense of depth.

PROJECT THREE: MAKING A PATCH

There are several methods you can adopt for creating a patch; however, here is my step-by-step guide you can follow to get you started. See how you get on and feel free to experiment to develop your own method if this does not work for you. For this project, I am going to use the ***RIA BELLE*** graphic I digitised in Chapter 5.

Step One: Design Preparation

1. Create your design using your embroidery software. Ensure it fits within the size of your machine's embroidery hoop.
2. Most patches have a satin boarder to give it a neat, refined edge.
3. When digitising, create a running stitch around the edge of your patch; this will be used to help identify the embroidery area. Ensure this stitch line is placed first in the sequence order. Allocate a totally new colour to separate it from the rest of the design.
4. Duplicate this new stitch line and place it second in the sequence, and assign it a double or triple stitch attribute (this stitch will be used to secure the fabric to the stabiliser). Assign it a totally new colour to separate it from the rest of the design.

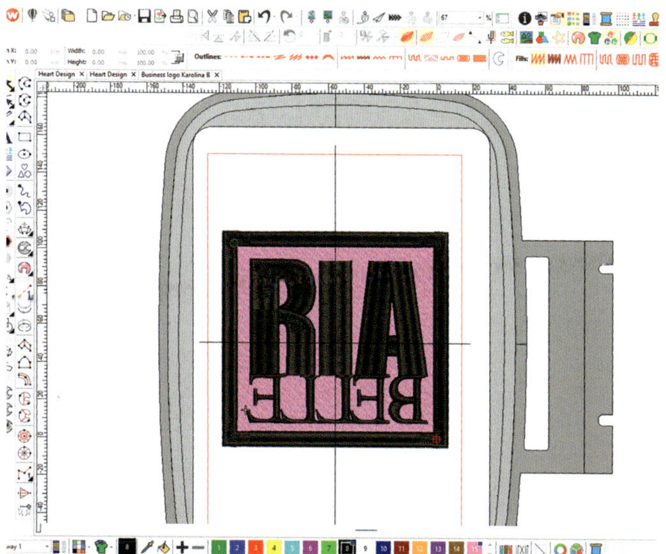

Graphic logo to be embroidered as a patch.

OPPOSITE: Embroidery art piece with textures and effects.

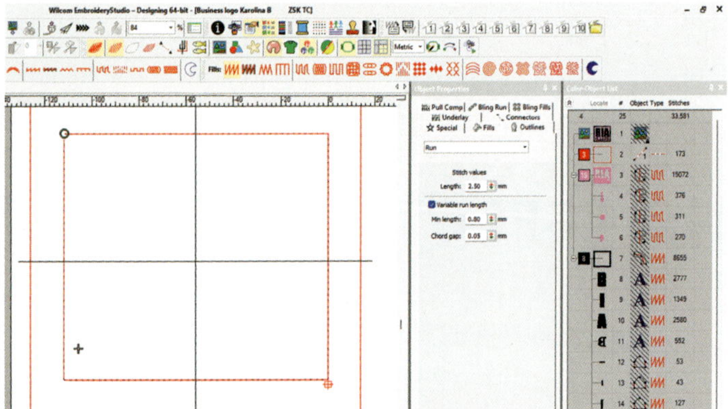

Single stitch edge border around the inner square, first in sequence order, allocated red colour.

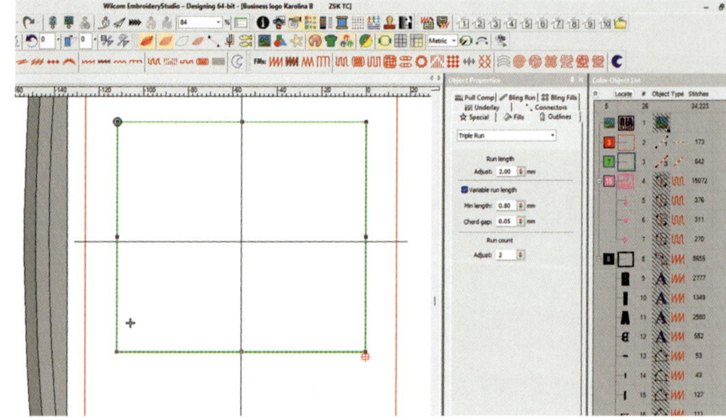

Triple stitch edge border, second in sequence order, allocated green colour.

Step Two: Material and Machine Setup

1. Select the fabric for your patch. Something sturdy like twill or canvas works well.
2. Cut a piece of medium or heavy tear-away stabiliser larger than your embroidery hoop.
3. Hoop the stabiliser tightly, making sure it is smooth and without wrinkles.

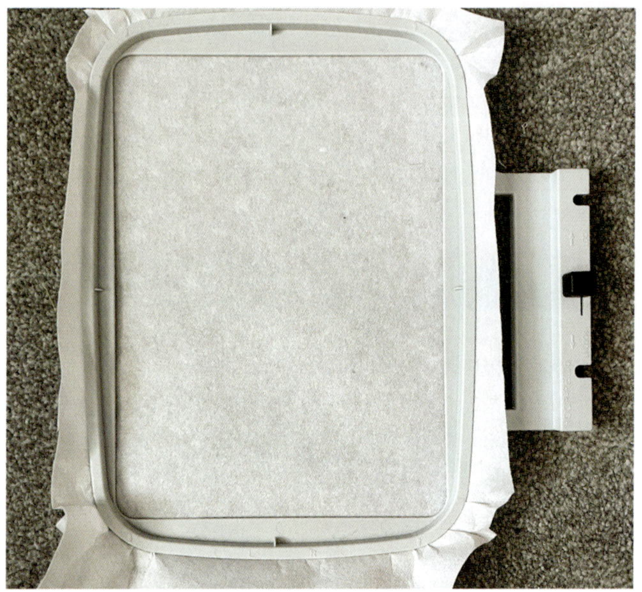

Single sheet of heavyweight tear-away stabiliser hooped on its own.

Step Three: Embroidery Start

1. Thread your machine with your first colour thread for the top and appropriate colour thread for the bobbin.
2. Attach the hoop to the machine.
3. Load your design onto the machine using a USB drive or direct connection, depending on your model.
4. Use the machine's on-screen editing features to position the design as needed.
5. Begin the embroidery and stop the machine after the first edge border has completed (shape one in the sequence order).

Outline edge stitch sewn onto stabiliser only, to mark location of the patch area.

6. Place your fabric over the sewn outline edge and use temporary adhesive to hold it flat if needed (some fabrics tend to move).

Fabric placed on top of the stabiliser covering first stitch outline area.

7. Embroider the second edge border and then stop the machine once completed. This stitch should help to hold your fabric in place (shape two in the sequence order).

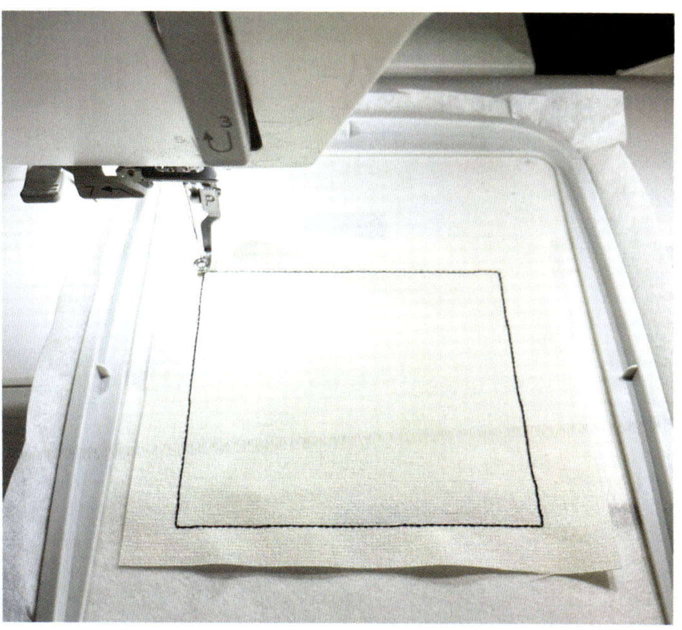

Fabric stitched to stabiliser with a triple running stitch.

8. With a pair of scissors, carefully cut the fabric around the stitch line as close as possible, ensuring you do not cut the stitch line or stabiliser.

Fabric sewn in place and being trimmed close to stitch line.

9. Continue stitching as normal.

Trimmed fabric ready for embroidering the patch design.

Tear-away stabiliser being torn away from the finished patch.

Step Four: Colour Changes and Trimming

1. When the machine stops for a colour change, clip the thread, re-thread with the next colour, and resume the embroidery.
2. Trim any jump stitches if your machine does not do it automatically.

Step Five: Finalising the Patch

1. Once the embroidery is complete, remove the hoop from the machine and the fabric from the hoop.
2. Carefully tear away the stabiliser from around the edges.

A heat source being used on the edges of the patch to remove any traces of stabiliser or fabric fibres.

Completed patch.

Step Six: Finishing Touches

- If desired, seal the edges of the fabric by carefully using a heat source like a soldering iron or lighter flame (being careful not to burn yourself), to gently remove any trace of the stabiliser or frayed fabric fibres.
- Add an iron-on backing if you want an iron-on patch, following the manufacturer's instructions for application.

Step Seven: Patch Application

- Your patch is now ready to be sewn or ironed onto your garment or accessory.

PROJECT FOUR: APPLYING APPLIQUÉ

Applying appliqué to digital embroidery involves combining pieces of fabric on a base fabric to create designs, adding texture and colour. The process is very similar to creating a patch in the previous project, with some minor differences. Appliqué is a quicker and more economical way of decorating a large fill area, compared to filling with embroidery stitches.

Design Preparation

Select a Design: choose or create a digital embroidery design that includes appliqué elements. Create a running stitch outline of the appliqué shape and place in the correct sequence order for your art piece. Repeat the running stitch outline and sequence directly after the first outline (you should have two identical outline running stitch shapes in your sequence window).

Choose Fabrics: select the base fabric and the appliqué fabric(s). Consider colour, texture and weight compatibility.

Apply Fusible Interfacing: if necessary, iron a fusible interfacing onto the back of the appliqué fabric to prevent fraying and to add stability.

Hoop the Base Fabric

1. **Stabilise:** place a suitable stabiliser under the base fabric to prevent puckering and ensure smooth embroidery.
2. **Hoop Tightly:** hoop the base fabric with the stabiliser, ensuring the fabric is taut without overstretching.

Appliqué outline stitches in *Colour Objects List* window, for the three hearts.

First Stitch-out

1. **Placement Stitch:** load the design into your embroidery machine and start embroidering. When you get to the appliqué object, stop the machine after the first outline placement stitch has completed. This outlines where the appliqué fabric will be placed on the base fabric.
2. **Place Appliqué Fabric:** apply temporary adhesive to the fabric and lay the appliqué fabric piece over the placement stitches, ensuring it covers the entire outlined area.

Selected fabrics for appliqué. Left to right: wool hooped in frame, red satin, pink spectrum printed velvet, pink worsted wool.

Appliqué placement outline stitches for the three hearts.

Fabric placed in location, larger than shape size, covering stitching.

Secure Appliqué Fabric

1. Stitch the second outline stitching to hold the fabric in place.

2. **Trim Excess Fabric**: carefully trim the excess appliqué fabric around the outline stitches, leaving a small margin to prevent fraying.

Complete the Embroidery

1. **Final Embroidery:** continue with the embroidery design. The machine will embroider the remaining details and edges of the appliqué, securing it further and adding decorative elements.
2. **Remove Stabiliser:** once complete, carefully remove the stabiliser from the back of the embroidery. If using a water-soluble stabiliser, follow the manufacturer's instructions to remove it.

Finishing Touches

1. **Press:** lightly press the finished piece with an iron, protecting the embroidery and appliqué with a pressing cloth if necessary.
2. **Inspect and Trim:** check for any loose threads or fabric edges and trim as needed for a clean finish.

PROJECT FIVE: USING 3D FOAM

Creating 3D embroidery with foam involves a technique where foam is placed under the embroidery stitches to create a raised effect, enhancing the texture and dimensionality of the design. Here's how to achieve this with digital embroidery.

Design Selection

Select a design with bold, wide stitches, as fine details won't effectively cover the foam. Designs specifically created for 3D foam work best. For this project we are going to use the capital letter T.

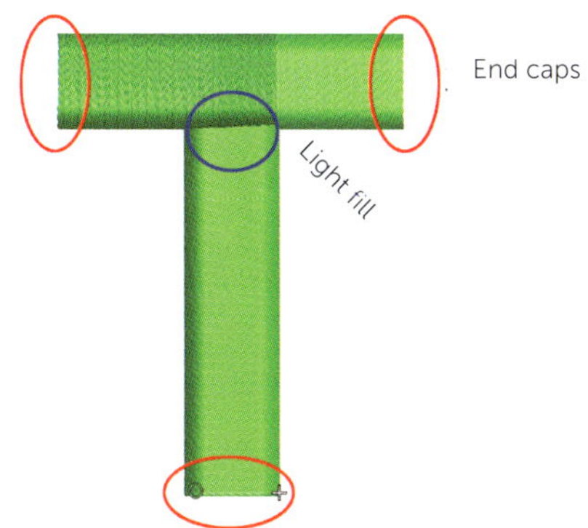

Showing areas for end caps and light fill for the letter T.

Digitising Your Design

This is a really important stage in order to get a good quality stitch-out. Foam has unique properties, and these settings are unique for this material. You cannot simply digitise as normal and just add the foam to the top of the fabric – it simply won't work, as the foam will be visible, bulging out in various places.

The letter T, showing exposed foam under the stitching, caused because of no end caps added when digitising.

Step One: Change Your Default Settings

1. **Remove all underlayers**: we do not need this for foam as we want the foam to puff up, forcing the stitches to rise and giving a 3D effect. Underlayers can prevent this from happening.
2. **Select satin stitch fill**: It is the only stitch than can work with foam due to its ability to travel a long distance without penetrating the fabric, allowing it to go up and over the foam.
3. **Adjust the pull compensation** to 0.10mm and satin stitch density to 0.19mm; this increases the number of stitches, which compensates for the foam's rise and prevents any foam showing through, whilst at the same time cutting the foam around the edges to allow for easy removal.
4. Instead of an underlayer we are going to add a running stitch up the centre of the shape using the running stitch, set to a run length of 0.40mm. This will hold the foam in place.

A foamed shape end point with end caps added, showing a tidier finish.

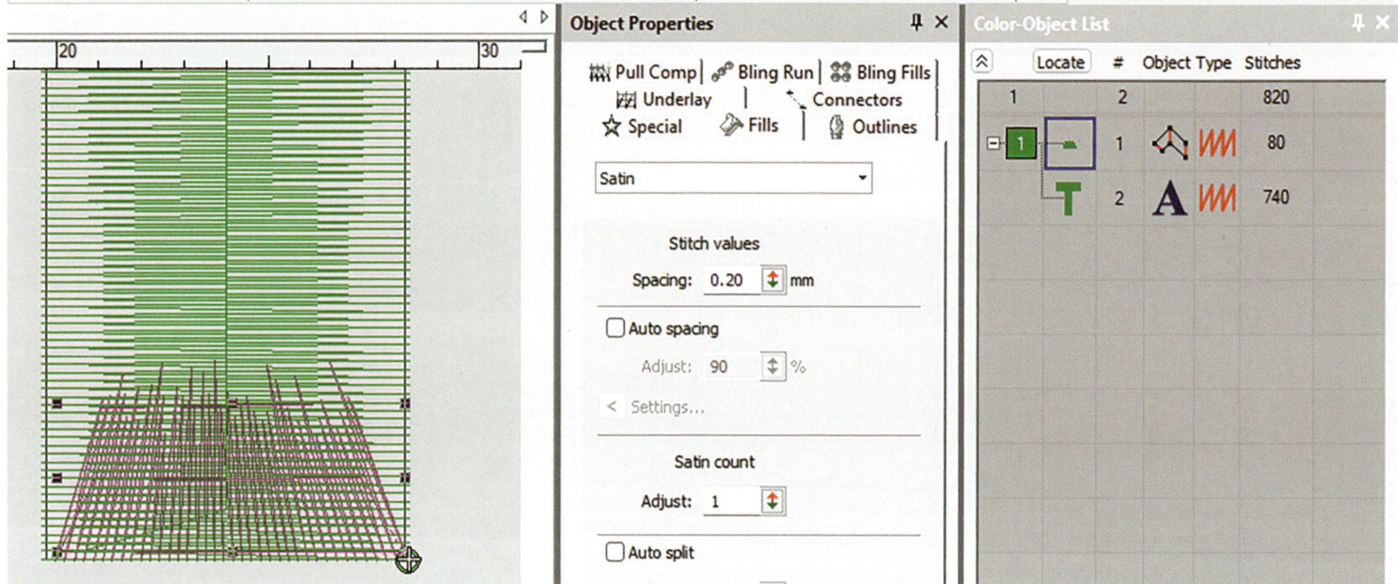

End cap added to digitised design.

Step Two: Adding End Caps

End caps prevent the foam showing through once stitched. We need to add end caps to the end of a shape to stop the foam sticking out, and a light fill where shapes overlap to stop the stitches splitting apart.

1. **Using the shape tool**, create a rectangle that is at 90 degrees to the end of the foam end. Taper it more narrowly on the top edge to prevent it forcing out the sides. Ensure the above settings are applied.
2. **Add a 'Jagged Edge'** effect to the top edge to stagger the stitches, preventing it cutting the foam.
3. Once you have created one end cap, copy and paste it to any other areas needing end caps. In the case of the letter T, you should have three end caps.

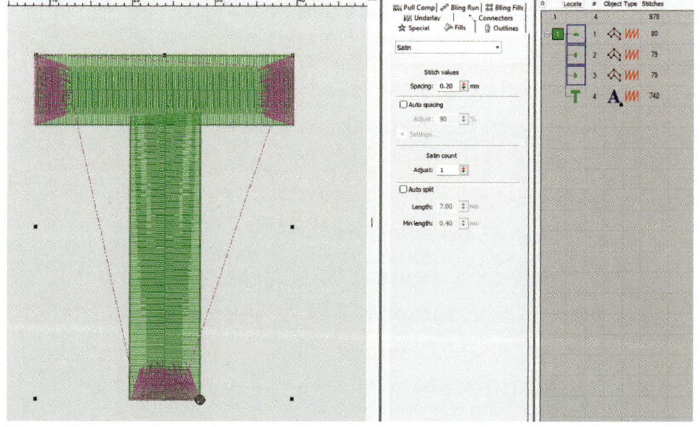
All three end caps added to letter T and the *Color-Object List*.

Step Three: Adding Light Fill Area(s)

The letter T is made up of two rectangular shapes, one horizontal running across the top and the other a longer vertical rectangle making the upright column of the letter. Where they join will need a bit of extra support to prevent any visible join gaps.

- **Use the shape tool** to create a small rectangular shape that covers the join line. Increase the stitch density to 0.4mm, as we only need a light fill.

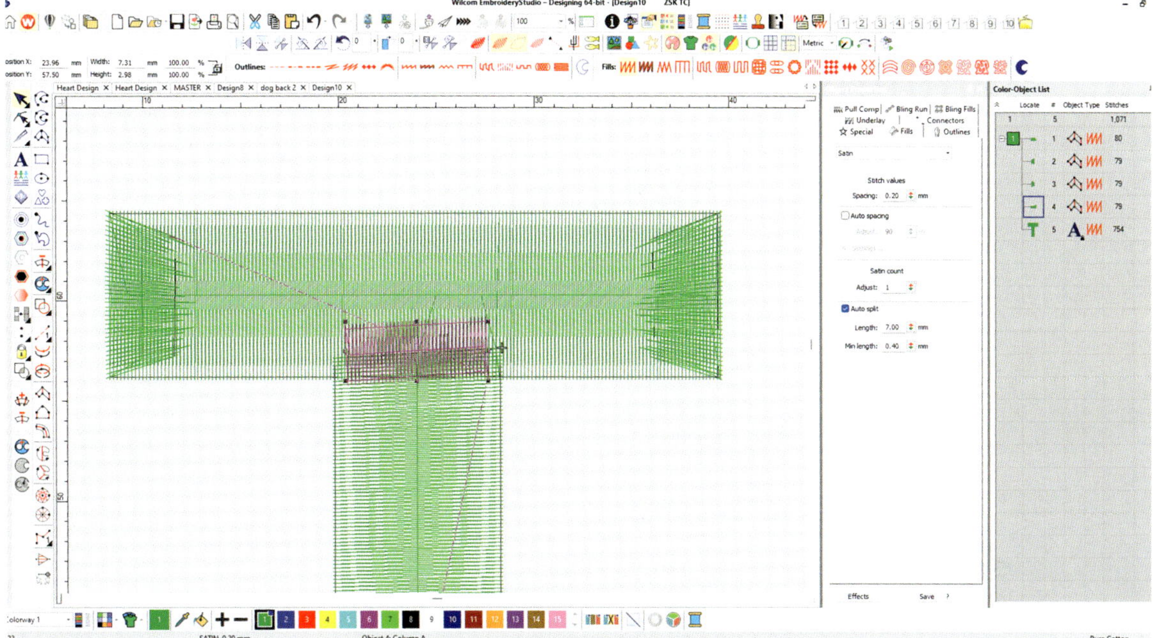

A light fill rectangle added to a weak area of the letter T.

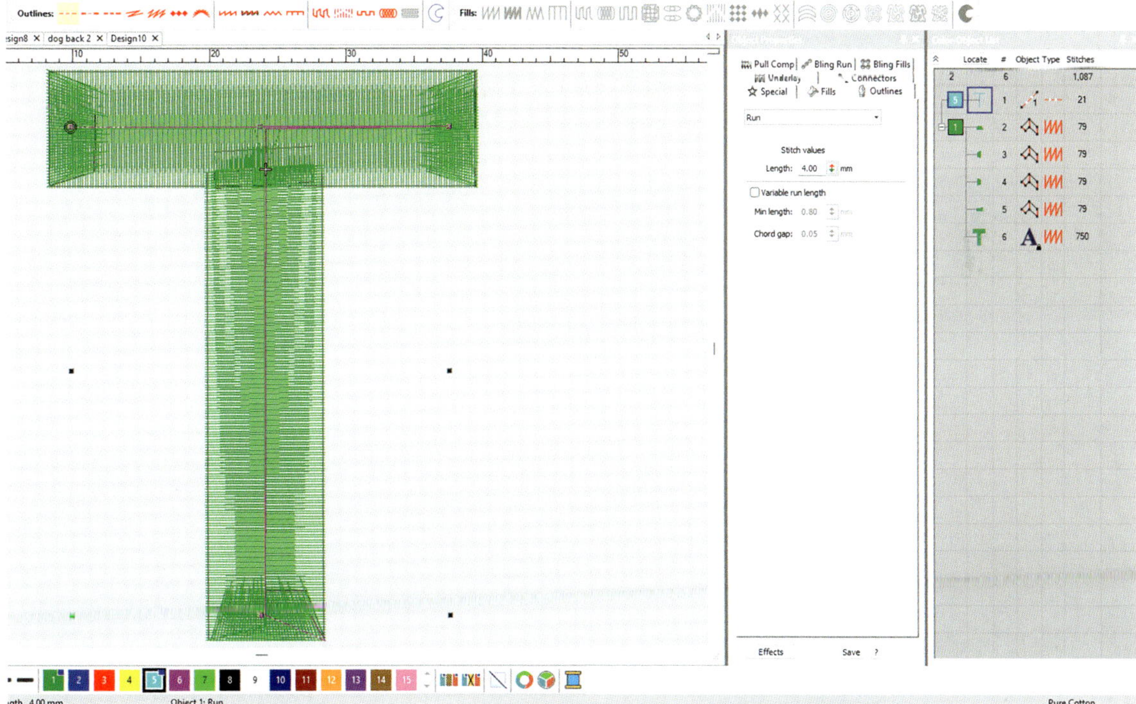

Running stitch applied and moved to the start of the sequence order.

Step Four: Adding the Running Stitch

The running stitch will ensure the foam sticks to the fabric and setting a large stitch length of 0.4mm will ensure it doesn't cut the foam into two.

1. Starting at the end cap, create a running stitch up the centre of the column and across the top.
2. For beginners this should be ok; however, for more advanced digitisers, you will want to sequence the end caps, fill area and running stitch for efficiency purposes, making the underlayer process continuous.

Step Five: Adding the Satin Decorative Top Layer

Once you have digitised the underlayer (end caps, light fill areas and centre running stitches), you can now add the top decorative layer, the satin stitch.

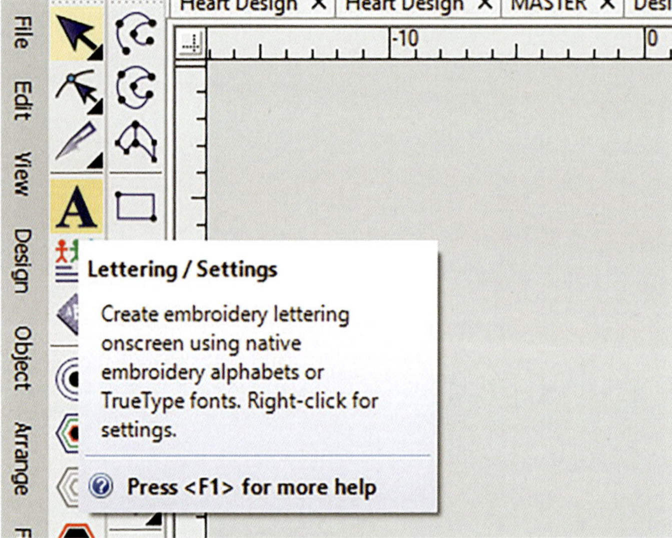

Lettering tool icon.

Satin stich applied to horizontal and vertical sections of letter T.

There are two ways to do this: **Manually and using the Lettering tool**.

If you use this tool, make sure you change the underlayer and pull compensation settings afterwards.

Manual Method (not using lettering tool)

1. Select the *closed shape* tool or *column A* tool if your software has this feature.
2. Start with the upright shape and work from the bottom towards the top, ending slightly past the join line.
3. Repeat for the horizontal rectangle.

We are now ready to export the file to the machine.

Materials Preparation

Gather all your materials for this project. You will need embroidery foam that is compatible with your project, embroidery thread, stabiliser and your fabric.

Choose the Right Foam: select foam that matches the height you desire for the 3D effect, typically 2–6mm ($^{1}/_{16}$–¼in). Foam can come in a range of colours, so pick one that best matches your main colour, as this will also help to hide it once stitched.

It is possible to use multiple layers of foam to create interesting effects and it is worth experimenting with the foam and your machine to see what it is capable of producing.

Foam embroidery sheets.

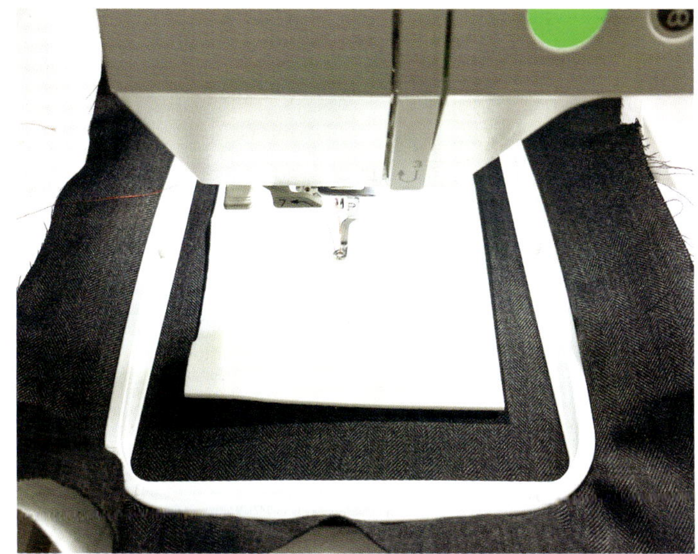

Foam sheet sitting on top of fabric, covering area to be foamed.

Machine and Fabric Preparation

Hoop your Fabric: securely hoop your fabric with an appropriate stabiliser. Use a stabiliser that supports the weight and density of the stitches.

Thread Selection: use a thicker embroidery thread (like polyester or rayon) to ensure the stitches fully cover the foam.

Foam Placement: position the foam by placing it over the area where the 3D effect will be, covering the section completely.

Embroidery Process: begin embroidering your design. The underlayer should hold the foam in place and the satin decorative layer will cover the foam and cut the edges around the shape's edge.

Foam Removal

After the design is complete, carefully remove the excess foam from around the embroidery. Use tweezers for precision.

Clean Up: gently pull away any visible foam pieces that protrude from under the stitches. A heat source like a hairdryer or heat gun can help retract any small foam remnants, but use it cautiously to avoid melting the thread or fabric.

Final Touches

Inspect your Work: check the embroidery for any missed areas where the foam might not be fully covered. If necessary, go back and add stitches.

Finishing: depending on the fabric and design, you might want to add a backing to cover the stitches and make the final product more comfortable to wear or use.

Hairdryer applying heat to foam to soften and shrink it, removing visible evidence from around the edges.

Holding running stitch, end caps and light join fill sewn into foam, seen from above.

Foam being pulled away after stitching is completed.

Stitched out letter T with foam, creating a raised 3D effect.

PROJECT SIX: COLOUR BLENDING

In the Wilcom software there is an accordion feature which, when applied to a fill, will vary the stitch spacing and density. This can create interesting outcomes that have a sense of depth and movement.

Overlapping and layering two accordion shapes can blend two colours together. You can do this manually; however, your software program may have an automatic feature. This is how it works using the Wilcom software.

Step 1: draw a shape and apply a tatami fill.
Step 2: click on the *colour blending* tool.
Step 3: Select the accordion types and colours you would like to blend from the pop-up window.
The shape will now consist of two layers grouped together. If you ungroup them, you can see what has happened to the shape after you click the *colour blend* tool.
Step 4: Stitch out to see the full effect.

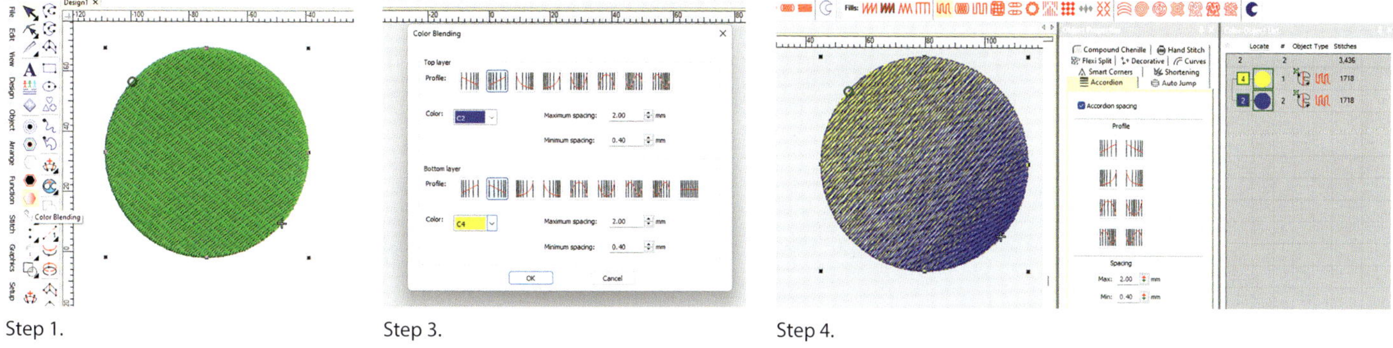

Step 1. Step 3. Step 4.

TROUBLESHOOTING

ISSUE 1: Parts of the foam peek through the stitches, leading to an uneven or patchy appearance.

This is quite common and can be solved by:

- increasing the stitch density to ensure complete coverage of the foam.
- using a matching foam colour to make any small imperfections less noticeable.
- use a gentle heat source to help retract any foam.

ISSUE 2: My patch is not stiff enough.

The following can help to stiffen a patch:

- use a heavier weight, stiffer stabiliser or additional layers.
- use a heavier weight fabric as a base or add an interfacing to stiffen.
- for any tatami fills, reduce the underlayer spacing and stitch length, to add more stitches to the fabric.

As we conclude this chapter on advancing your digital embroidery skills, you now possess the knowledge to create vibrant patches, apply intricate appliqués, and bring your designs to life with dynamic 3D effects. Each project has not only equipped you with specific techniques, but also opened the door to endless creativity and customisation in your future embroidery projects. Remember, the journey of mastering embroidery is ongoing and filled with opportunities for personal expression and innovation. As you move forward, let your imagination guide you, and don't hesitate to experiment with the skills you've acquired. The projects in this chapter are just the beginning – each piece you create is a step towards refining your craft and discovering your unique embroidery style. Keep pushing the boundaries of what you can achieve with thread and fabric, and most importantly, enjoy the process of bringing your artistic visions to life.

KISSES
DM

CHAPTER 7

ADVANCED PROJECT TECHNIQUES

Working in 3D opens a whole new world to discover and explore.

As you become more confident and familiar with the software, embroidery techniques and your machine, it won't be too long before you start to become more ambitious, wanting to experiment further and push the boundaries, to see what is possible. Two of the most common questions I get asked are, 'How do I design and digitise an image to fit a specific pattern shape?' and 'How do I embroider a large image using a small embroidery hoop?' Often these are referring to the application of the embroidery design onto a fashion garment, where the embroidery fits into a specific part of the garment and the complete image is on a larger scale.

In this chapter I will be demonstrating the processes I utilised in creating bespoke designs for a stunning evening dress and a denim jacket. These designs were challenging for several reasons:

- Designing on a 3D object to complement existing garment features.
- Transferring a design concept from a 3D physical product into the digitising software.
- Physically embroidering the garment when the design was far larger than the hooping area.

PROJECT SEVEN: EMBROIDERING IN A DEFINED AREA AND APPLYING MORE DECORATIVE FILLS

I created this jacket for the Australian pop star, DJ and TV personality Danni Minogue. The brief was to design an image for the top half of an existing denim jacket that used symbolism to reflect her personality and life. The jacket was to be worn by Danni when interviewing people on her radio show and podcast, focusing on 90s fun pop music. As Danni sits down during the show, only the upper half of the jacket is visible and occasionally the back, therefore the key focal areas are the shoulders, collar, upper sleeves, front and back yokes, and the back of the jacket.

Things to Consider:

1. I will be working on an existing 3D constructed jacket, not flat fabric. This brings with it accessibility issues when machining an image across panels and seams.
2. Denim jacket seams are likely to be thick, preventing hooping and possibly causing embroidering issues; careful needle and thread selection is required and I need to identify areas to avoid.
3. The garment may contain rivets and other fastening details that may not be able to be removed; careful consideration of design is needed around these areas.
4. The machine used is a domestic single needle Janome MC550e, which has a flat bed, preventing me embroidering on tubular garments. I will need to unpick seams to allow me to embroider on the sleeves

OPPOSITE: Close-up of embroidered jacket shoulder and colour.

AIM:

Only unpick the essential seams to allow the garment to lay flat and open on the machihine bed using the floating method.

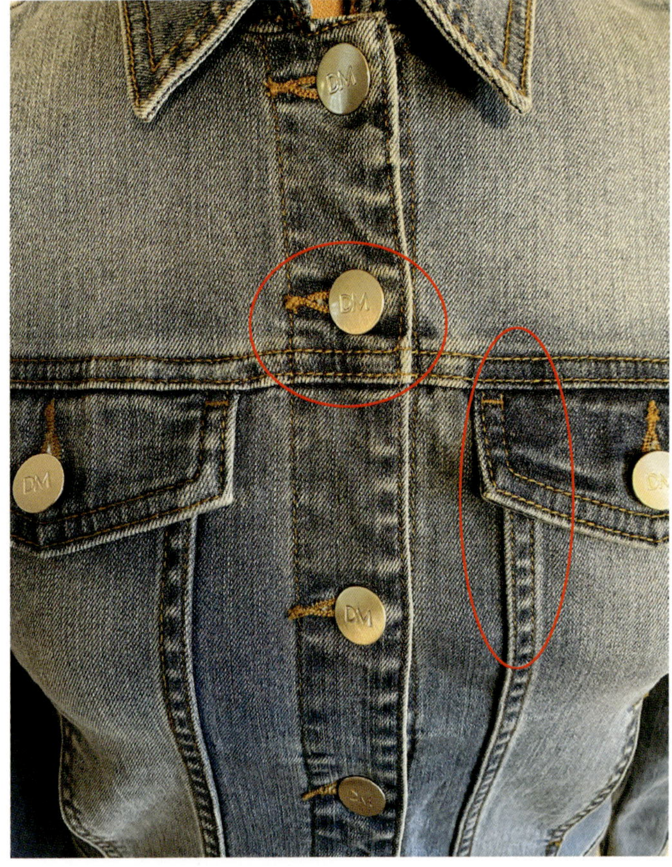

Areas to avoid on the denim jacket.

Step One: Preparing the Garment for Design

Place the actual jacket on a body form (mannequin). This allows for easy viewing from all angles to ensure the design flows around the body and is balanced.

Jacket on the mannequin showing 360° rotation.

Step Two: Creating Embroidery Work Areas

Select the areas that are going to be embroidered and add paper, pinning in place. Use the seams of the jacket as reference guides, and draw with a pencil to transfer the seams to the paper. Cut the paper along the drawn seam lines to replicate the jacket panel shapes. Repeat for all the garment areas required.

What you have created is your embroidery work areas, which we will use later in the software.

Step Three: Design

How you design is up to you. For this project I researched Danni's life history and picked out key events, images and facts. I realised Danni is very pro LGBTQ+ and therefore the rainbow colours needed to be present. Also, 90s fun music came through in the music cassettes, gold discs and the reference to her own radio show was captured by the headphones and music notes. The hummingbird is her personal logo and the letter E referenced her son, Ethan, who means the world to her. I collected and created a range of images on separate sheets of paper that I could refer to. Using pencils and felt tip pens, I drafted a rough sketch of my design idea onto the paper patterns, whilst still in place on the garment and mannequin. I was careful not to damage the garment itself with the felt pens.

Design drawn on paper panels using felt pens; top, back and front views.

Working in this way enabled me to design whilst keeping the 3D aspect in mind. It can be very difficult to design around an object when only working in 2D, but using this method I was able to view and amend the design as I rotated the mannequin to ensure curves and details were placed in the most aesthetically pleasing way and remained fluid around the form. If I decided I did not like anything, I simply drew over the areas or replaced sections with new paper and redesigned.

Step Four: Photograph Paper Pieces

Once you are happy with your design draft, remove the pattern pieces and lay them one at a time on a flat surface. Take a photo directly from above with your camera, ensuring you capture all the pattern pieces.

> TIP: Using a contrasting background will help to enhance the shape of the pattern piece, making it easier to work with.

Front yoke pattern piece with design drawn, photographed from above on a contrasting background, allowing clear view of the pattern piece shape.

Step Five: Import into Digitising Software

Open your digitising software (I am using Wilcom E4.5 as my go-to software program). Open a new file and upload or import your photograph.

> **IMPORTANT**
>
> The photograph will not necessarily be the correct size – do not assume it is. Always measure the actual pattern piece with a tape measure and then adjust your photograph to match. I always digitise at 100 per cent scale where possible, so I can best apply the most suitable design settings without having to rescale and readjust.

Step Six: Template Tracing

Lock your photograph so it cannot be selected, moved or adjusted. With the digitising tools available to you, start creating your design stitches, using your locked design as a template (in essence, you are tracing the original design). Repeat for all the pattern pieces.

Digitised front and back yokes.

Step Seven: Master File

Once all the separate pattern pieces are digitised, I find it useful to copy and paste them all onto one master file, placing them in their correct positions.

By doing this, it enables you to spot any discrepancies in design flow, colour allocation or pattern shaping.

Digitised master file, showing all the pieces laid flat in correct position to each other.

Step Eight: Sampling

For this project, I decided to embroider the front yoke onto a scrap piece of denim in order to analyse the digitising settings I have applied. The sample will be used to determine if any of the settings need adjusting at all. The main setting I will mostly likely amend is the pull compensation, if I spot any gaps appearing between shapes.

If I decide to change any settings based on the embroidered sample, I will then amend all the other pattern pieces to match. If in doubt, I may sample other pieces.

I often keep referring and comparing the physical samples and the digitised panels to determine if the design needs any amendments.

Test sample on a scrap piece of denim cloth.

Comparing the stitched-out sample with the opposite digitised yoke panel, checking for design flow.

Step Nine: Floating the Garment

When you are happy with the sample and digitised settings, you are then ready to embroider onto the garment itself. Using the floating technique, place and secure the garment on top of the hoop and stabiliser, ensuring it is in the correct position.

TIP: Use the plastic grid and trace the design from the computer screen onto the acetate grid. Use the grid in the hoop to locate the correct position the garment needs to be.

Plastic acetate grid with design drawn on, used to locate embroidery position on jacket.

Step Ten: Embroider

Begin embroidering with care. Repeat this process for all pattern pieces.

Embroidering the front yoke onto the jacket.

Jacket side view.

Full jacket back.

Jacket detail 3.

FINAL OUTCOME

Full jacket front.

Jacket detail 1.

Jacket detail 2.

Dannii Minogue wearing the finished jacket. (Photo: Dannii Minogue)

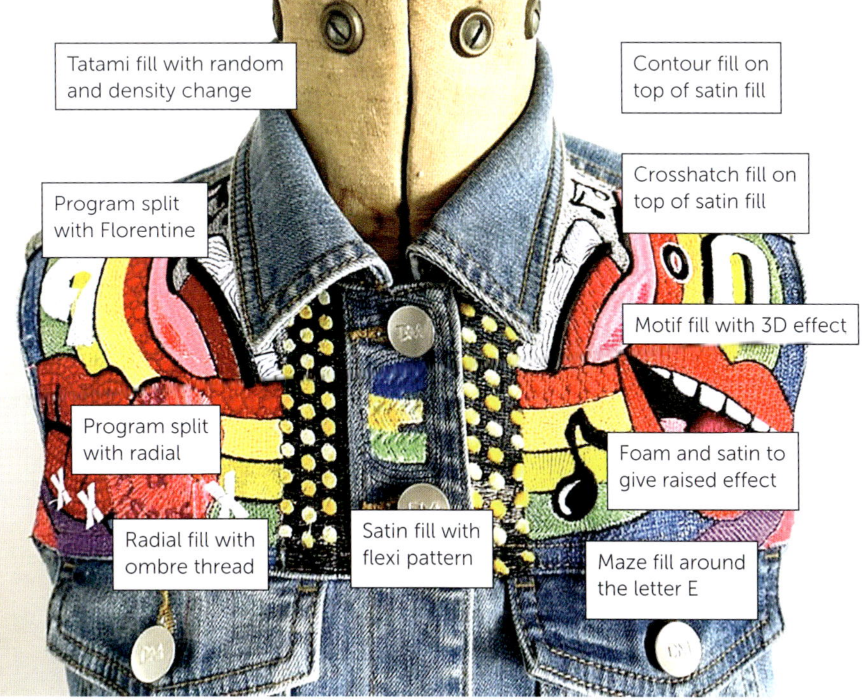

Jacket with fill types labelled.

PROJECT EIGHT: WORKING WITH LARGER DESIGNS – SPLITTING, MATCHING AND EMBROIDERING TO HIDE JOINS

Sometimes, designing can get tricky when your idea is too big for your embroidery hoop. It's frustrating and you don't want to make your design smaller – so what can you do? Some digitising software programs can split your design into smaller parts automatically, but this doesn't always work well and can make the final result look patched together, with visible join lines. I'm going to show you a manual method that I use to split a larger design into smaller sections, that can be performed on any digitising software program. Then, I will show you how to stitch the pieces together so it looks smooth and seamless, like putting together a jigsaw puzzle where you've made all the pieces yourself.

For this project I will demonstrate the technique I use, applying it to create the front section of this dress. The rest of the dress was carried out in exactly the same way.

Le Fil wearing an embroidered white dress made for *Ru Paul's Drag Race*, UK series 4. (Photo: Scallywagfox)

MASTER & HOOPINGS

When I digitise a large design, I do it as one whole image, and call this file the *master***.** Once happy, I then split it into smaller sections (each section should fit into your selected hoop size). I call each section a *hooping***.** This image, once split, will contain four *hoopings* and one *master* file.

Dress front pattern piece with embroidery design in position.

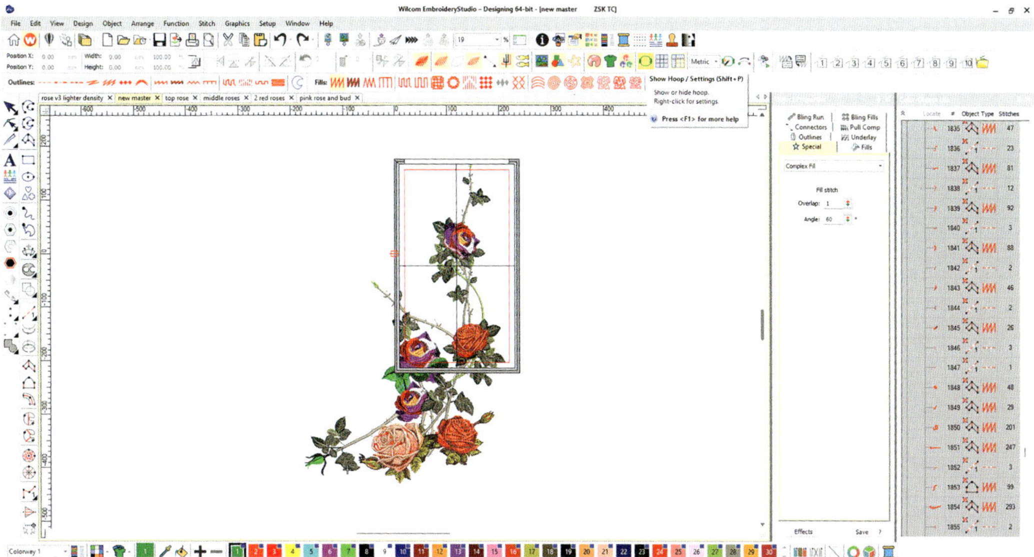

Step one: Setting your Hoop

Select your hoop from the preset menu of your software program (I am using the Wilcom E4.5 digitising software). Alternatively, add in the measurements as a new custom hoop – make your hoop visible so you can see the difference between your design and the hoop area. This hoop is 36 × 20cm and is the maximum hoop size for the Janome MC550e machine I will be using.

Step Two: Identify Split Areas

Study your design and try to identify the best places to split your design, trying to identify areas that are easy to hide when embroidered – think layers and overlapping.

AIM: is to embroider with no visible join lines

Whole shapes are better than cutting through shapes and trying to match back up, if possible. With the *freehand selection* tool, I click and drag over whole shapes that sit within the hoop area. The top rose and stems should easily fit into one new hoop. Once happy Edit > Cut.

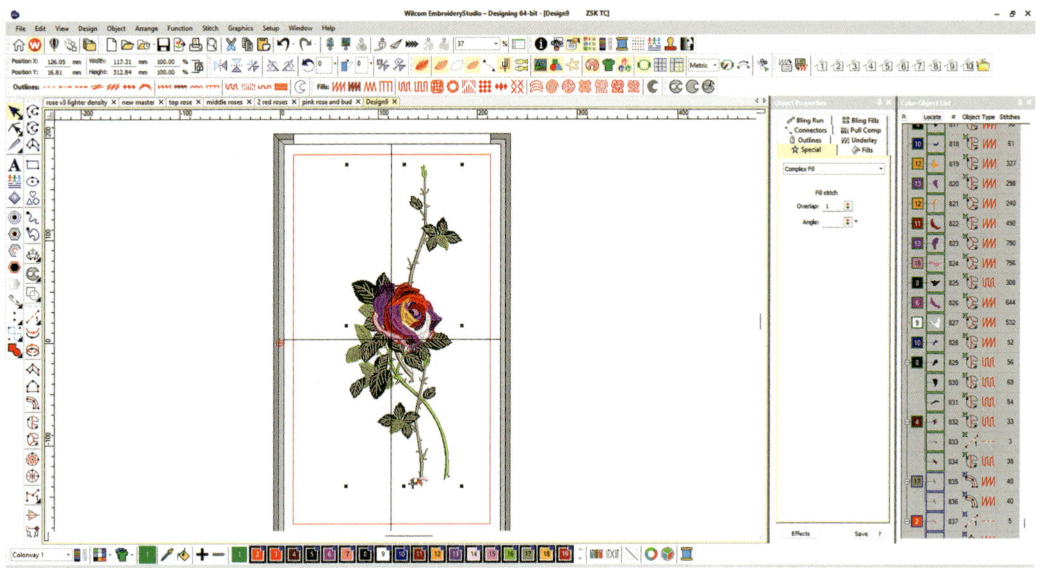

Step Three: Create New File

File > New > Edit > Paste.

You have created a new file for the top section of your design – save it with an appropriate name. I often use numbers to determine the embroidery hoop order followed by a two- or three-word description. As this is the first hoop to embroider, I have named it, '**1 – top rose and stems**'.

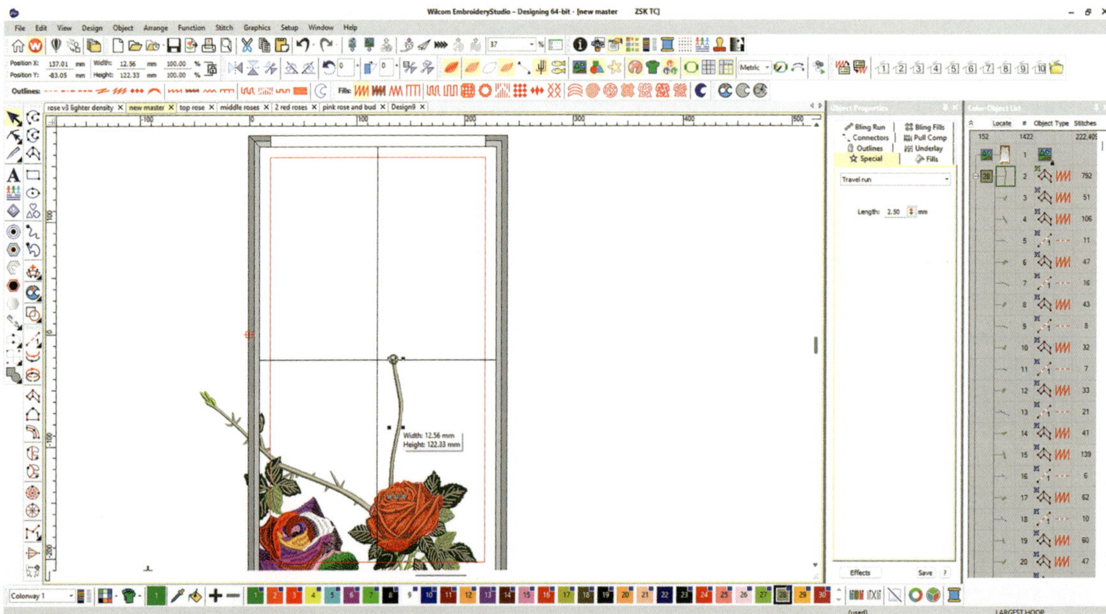

Step Four: Selecting Remnants

Notice that not all the stems transferred across from the original file. This sometimes happens, so you need to manually select the remnants, **Cut & Paste onto the new file**. You may need to re-sequence the objects after pasting so the design looks correct. If you did not move the first image when you pasted it on the new file, then the new pasted remnants should be in the correct place in relation to it. If you did move it, then you will need to move the remnants so they are in the correct place.

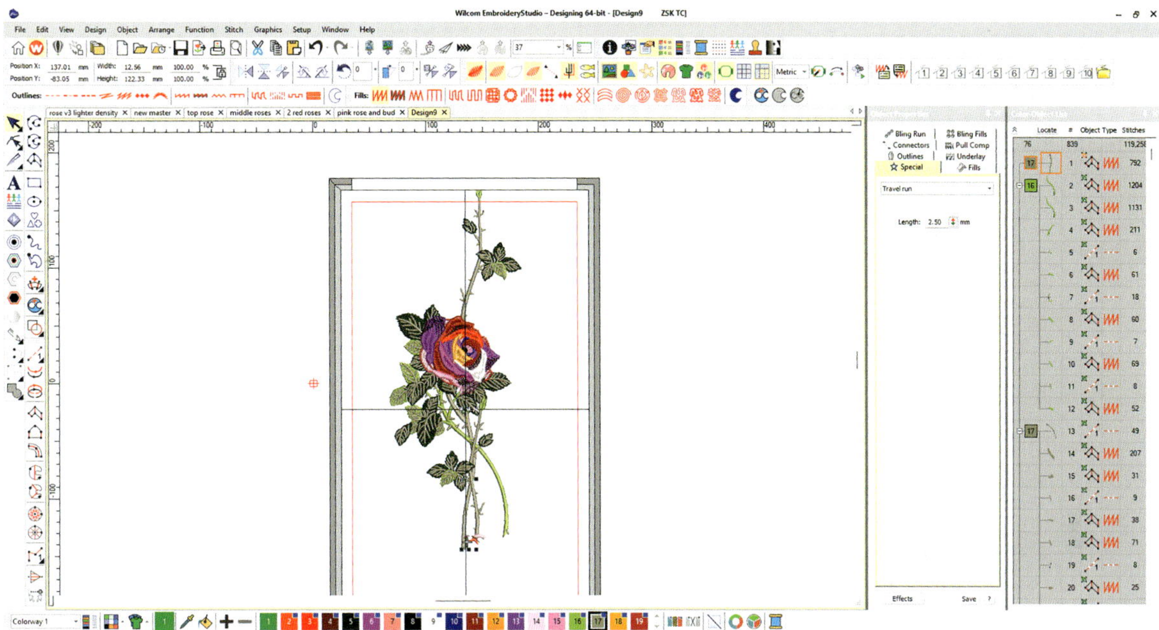

Step Five: Complete Hooping Number 1

The top section is now fully separated. I will often spend time working into the section, refining, re-sequencing and making sure all the settings are correct (underlayers, pull compensations and so on).

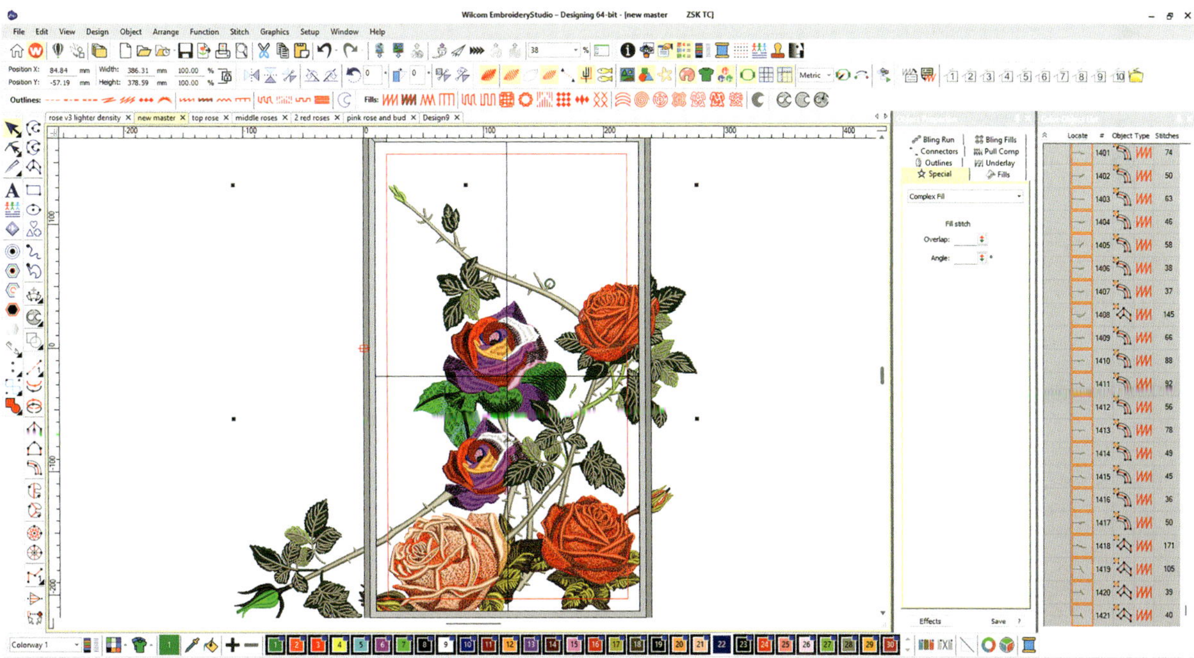

Step Six: Moving Hoop in Master

Go back to the **MASTER** file.

Select all and move the image into the hoop area. Again, look for large whole sections you can cut out with ease.

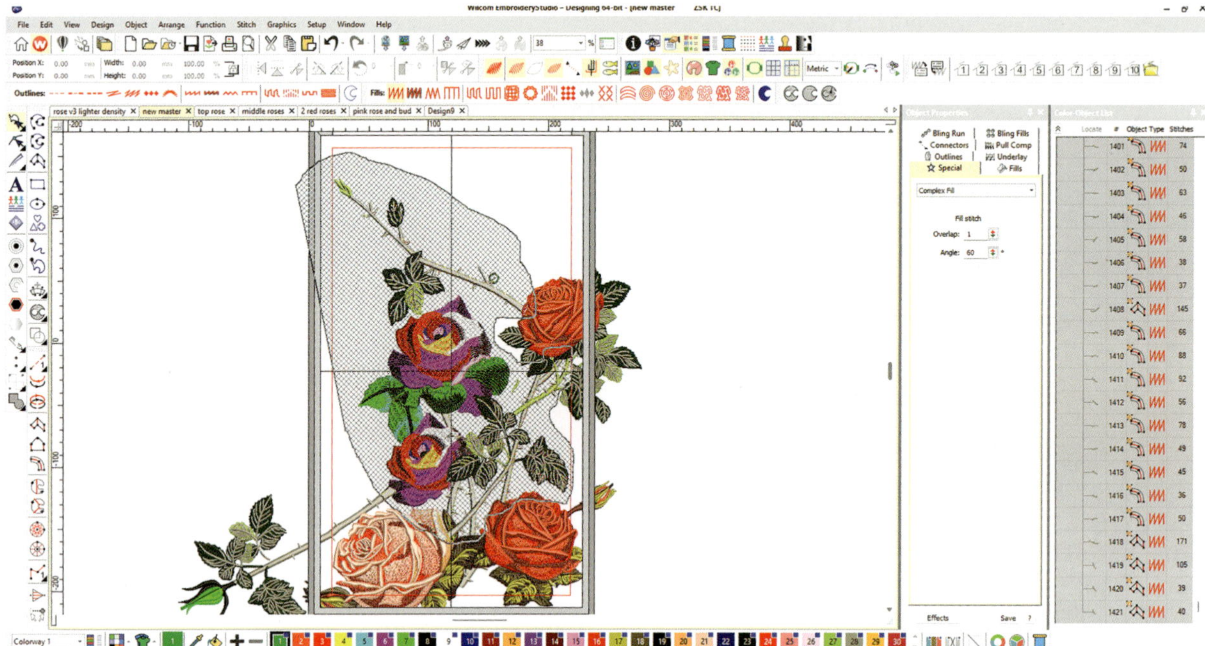

Step Seven: Freehand Selection

Freehand selection tool, select area.

Here, I can see the central stems and two roses are all comfortably within the hoop. The top red rose sits over the right-hand side edge so I will leave this for now. I don't really want to be splitting a rose head if it can be avoided.

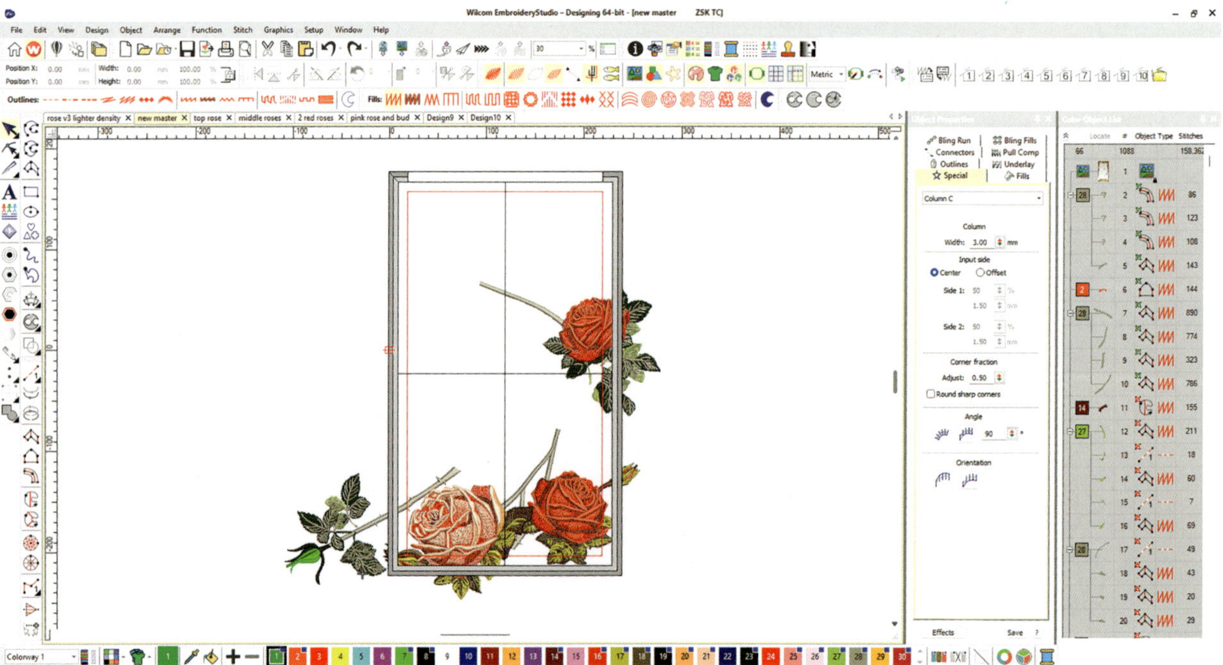

Step Eight: Cut

Edit > Cut

If there any remnant remaining, don't forget to Cut & Paste them aswell.

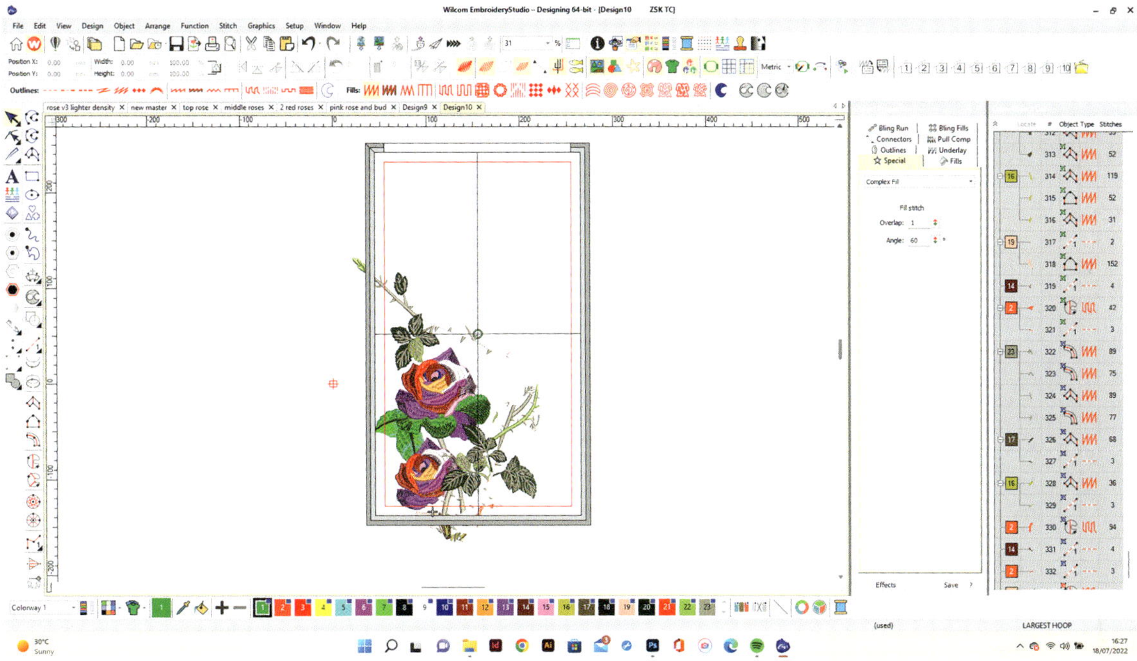

Step Nine: Creating Hooping Number 2

File > New

Edit > Paste

You may need to change your hoop settings to get your design to sit centrally in your hoop.

File>Save. I have called this one, **"2-two central roses with stems"**.

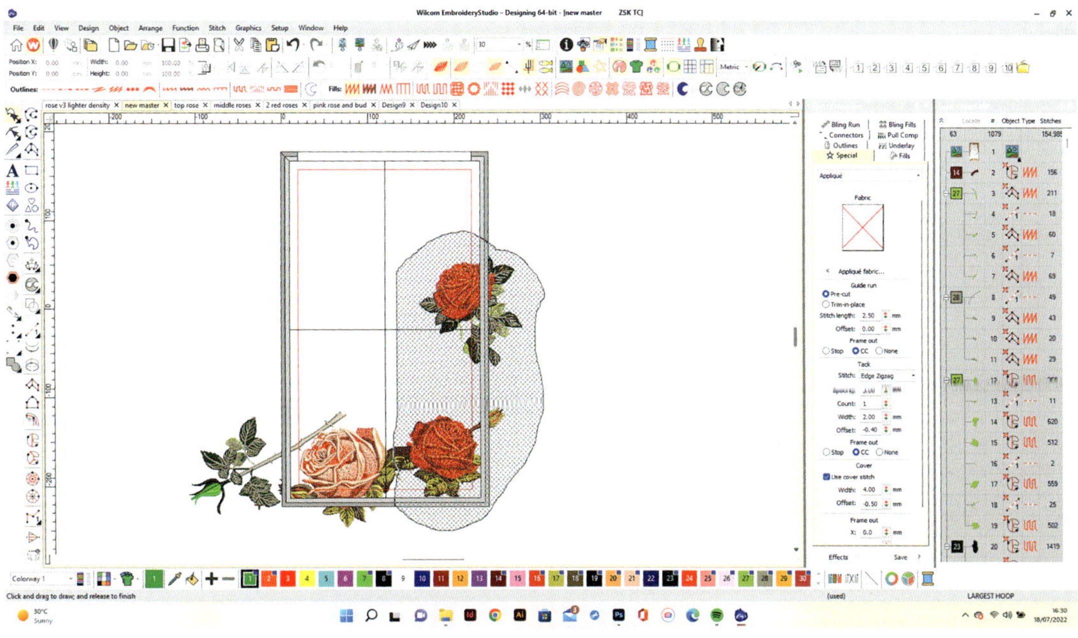

Step Ten: Searching for hoop number 3.

Back to MASTER-look for next hoop split.

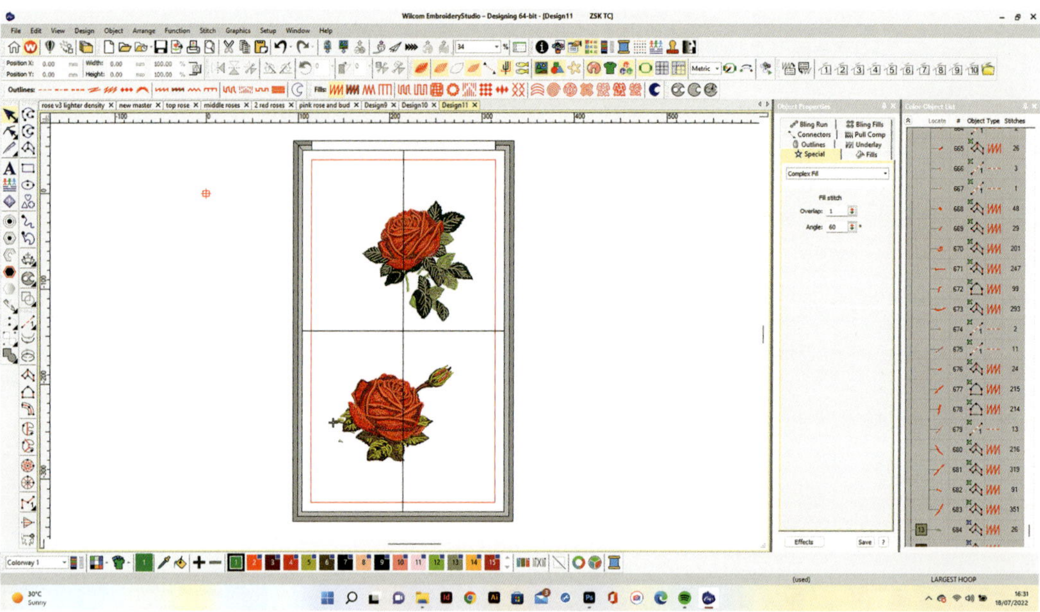

Step Eleven: Selecting hoop 3.

With the Freehand selection tool, select area.

Edit>Cut

File New>Edit Paste

File>Save. I called this one"**3-two red rose vertical**."

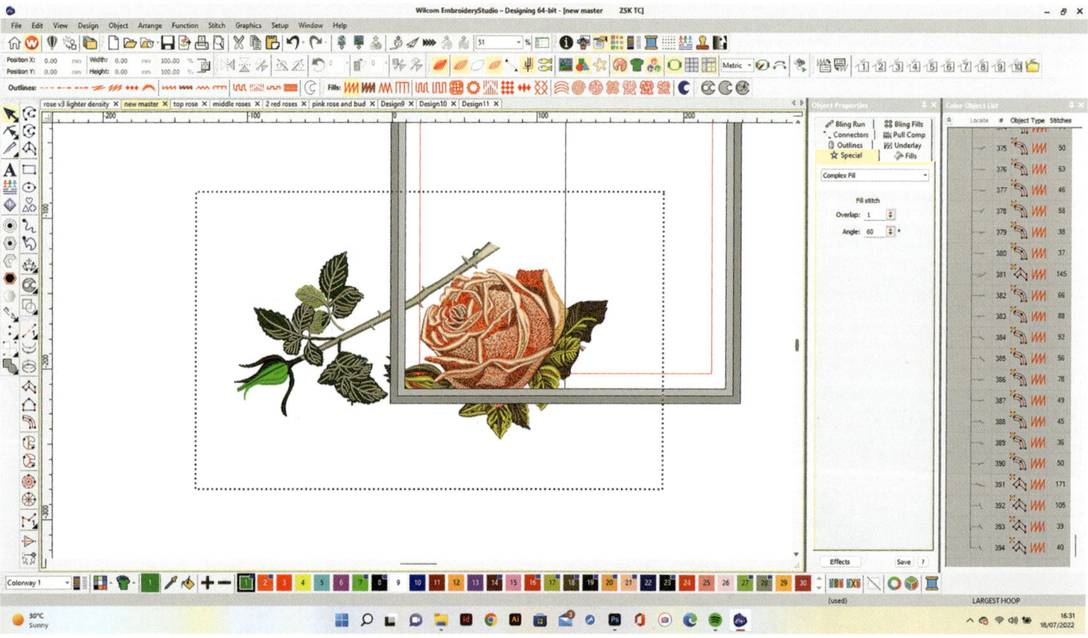

Step Twelve: Selecting hoop 4.

Return to the Master file and Select the last remaining image content. Here I used the standard rectangular selection tool.

Edit>Cut

File New>Edit Pate>File Save "4-Bottom Pink Rose."

Step Thirteen: Creating a NEW MASTER file

Once I have created each individual hooping and feel happy that all the image content has been captured and allocated to one of the hoops, I then create a new master file which is not only used as a good reference point, but also helps me when tracing the design onto the acetate grid in order to accurately position the design and hoop on the fabric.

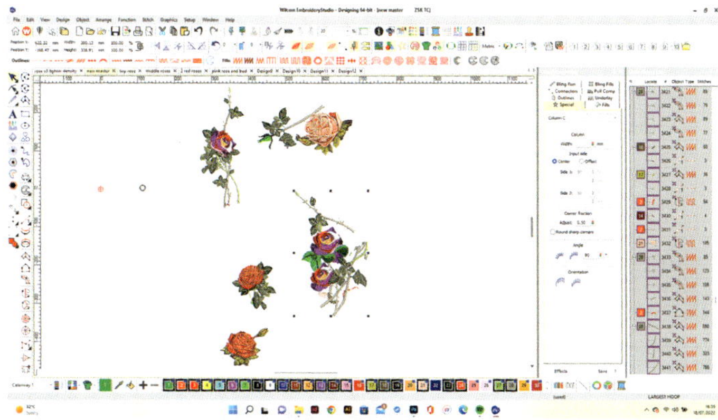

The four individual hoopings pasted in the master file.

File > New Save as "Master File New".

1. Goto Hoop number 1 – **File > Select All > Edit > Copy**
2. Return to the MASTER file.
3. **Edit > Paste**
4. Select all of hoop number **1 – Edit > Group.**

When you now click on any of the parts of the design that fall in hooping number 1, all the hoop will be selected. This makes moving the hoop around easier if you need to.

REPEAT steps 1 to 4 for the remaining three hoops.

This also keeps your sections separate for ease of working. When I work into each individual hoop section, I will replace the relevant hoop in the master. The master gives me an overall view of the design.

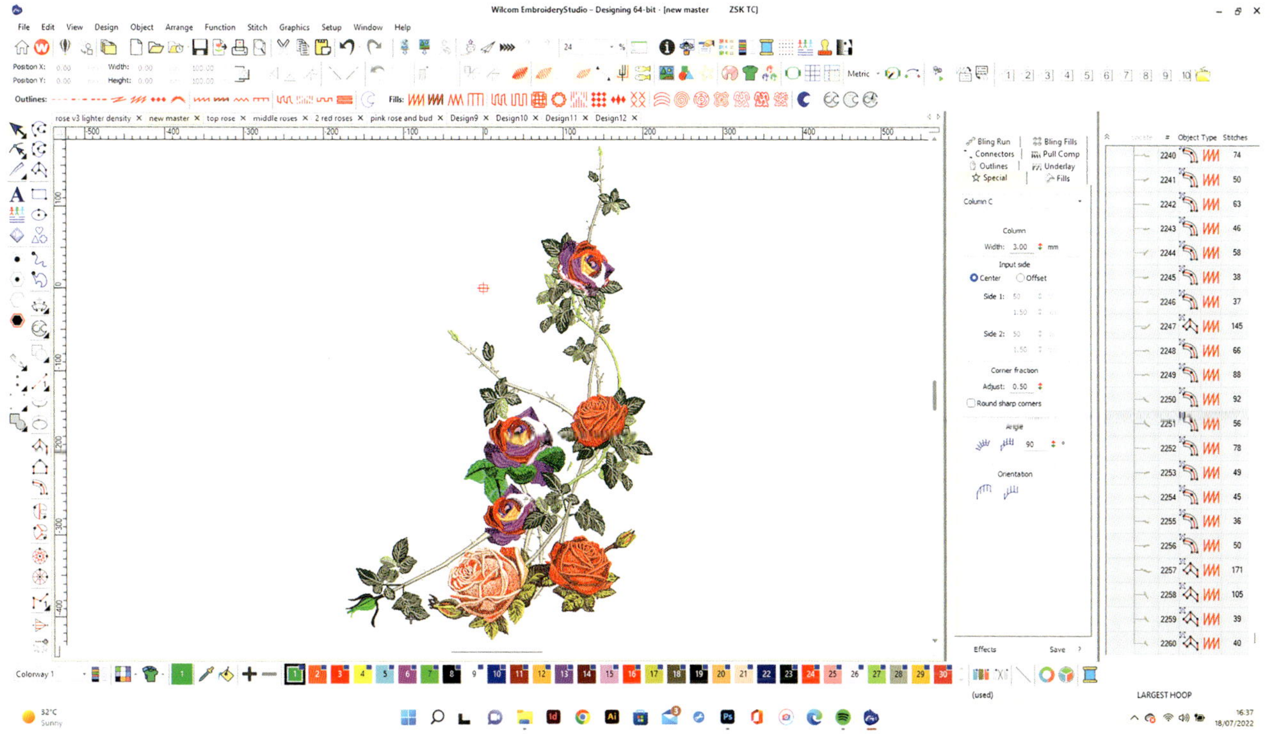

Completed new master file, with individual sections moved into place to create full design.

Step Fourteen: Refine Each Hooping

Continue working on each section until you are happy. Remember to update the master file and keep the hoops separated.

Files

For this design I have managed to split the full design into four smaller hoops. There are five files in total including the master file. I will now embroider each hoop separately on the fabric, trying to hide all the joins and ensuring the hoops are in the correct place relative to each other.

Some of my very large design may require 50+ separate hoops! My Hand & Lock, Wilcom award-winning piece took 65 hoopings in total and measured over 1.5m (5ft) in length.

Screenshot showing the four hoopings and master file.

PROJECT NINE: EMBROIDERING A MULTI HOOP DESIGN WITHOUT VISIBLE JOIN LINES

So you have created your design, digitised it, split it into smaller hoopings,. and you are now ready to stitch out. This is where the magic happens! I have used and developed this technique over time. Other people may have alternative ways to match multiple hoops, but this technique has worked for me many times and it is a method I have come to trust.

The trick is to ensure you have split the design into suitable hoopings. The more time you spend on accurately cutting up your design, the better the results when it comes to embroidering them together.

For this method you will need:

- The plastic square grid for your hoop (often comes with the hoop on purchase)
- A Sharpie pen (black and another colour)
- A Frixion pen (the ink disappears with heat) and/or pins.

I will demonstrate the matching method using the floating technique on an adhesive backing stabiliser.

Step One: Embroider Hooping Number 1

Embroider your first hoop onto your fabric as you normally would. As this is the first section, you do not have to worry about matching it with the other sections. Your main concern should be its location. If it is on a large fabric piece, ensure you have enough space for the rest of the sections to fit. If embroidering in a specific area, you need to make sure the design is in the correct position (especially important for embroidering on garments). This hoop will determine where all the other hoops sit.

Step Two: Preparing the Frame

Place the plastic acetate square grid inside your embroidery frame. Notice that the grid has a centre hole and side notches. The notches sit into corresponding grooves on the grid.

I use the notches to ensure the design is located on the fabric in the correct place.

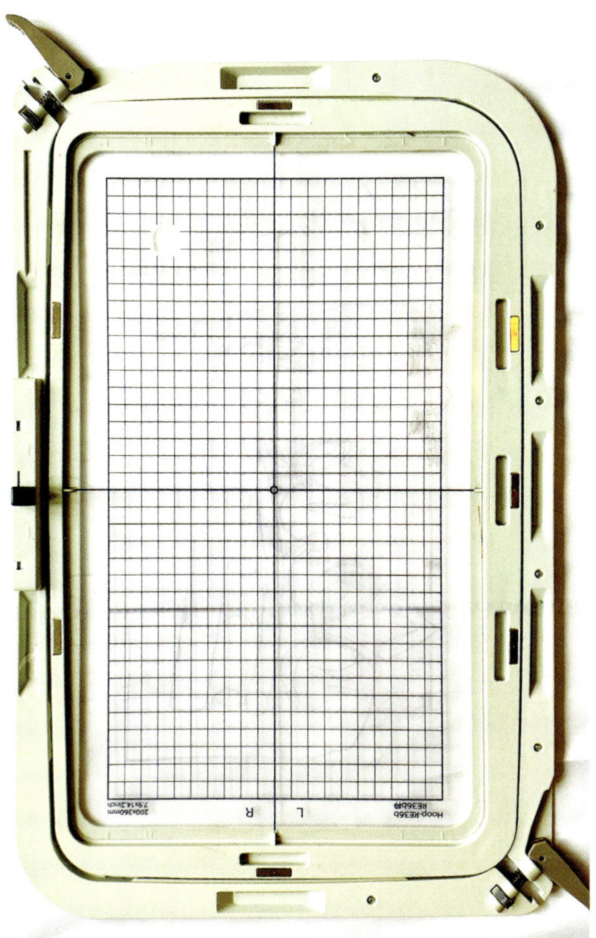

Square plastic grid in embroidery frame.

Hooping 1 embroidered on duchess satin fabric.

Step Three: View Hooping Number 2 at 100 Per Cent on Screen

On your computer screen, ensure your next hooping design is viewed at 100 per cent scale, with the virtual hoop and grid visible.

PLACE and HOLD the physical grid onto the computer screen, aligning the physical grid to the digital grid so they match (do not press too hard or you could damage your computer; you just want to prevent the physical hoop from moving). Using a Sharpie pen, trace the design onto the physical grid.

Tracing of the digital design onto the plastic grid using a Sharpie pen.

The traced design on the plastic grid.

Step Four: Traced Design on Grid

Admire your traced design on the grid.

Step Five: Tracing Reference Points from Master File

Using your **MASTER** file, trace elements of the first hooping onto the physical grid. This will be used to help ensure placement is as accurate as possible when you place the grid on the fabric. If it helps, you could change pen colour at this point, so the tracing differs between the hooping tracing and the master file reference point tracing.

Step Six: Final Traced Grid

Your grid will now contain a tracing of your next hooping image and some elements of your previous hooping (which you have already embroidered). If it is easier to distinguish between the two, you can use different coloured pens.

The grid on the master file screen, tracing off location reference points.

Prepared grid.

Step Seven: Placing the Grid on Fabric

Place the grid on the cloth and match the tracing on the grid to the embroidery on the fabric. Using the image you traced from the master file as a reference point, ensure the grid matches the physical embroidery.

The grid in its correct location with the top right section of the grid matching the physical embroidery on the fabric.

Step Eight: Mark Fabric Position

With the grid in the exact location on the fabric, use a temporary ink pen and mark the centre point and the side notches. I find using a Frixion pen where the ink disappears with heat works best on most fabrics. Pins can be used instead of a pen to mark the notches.

Centre location of the grid being marked with a disappearing ink pen on the fabric.

Step Nine: Marked Fabric

Your fabric should now be marked with a set of notches and centre point.

Marked fabric, highlighted by red circles.

Step Ten: Preparing the Hoop

In order to avoid damaging the satin, I am going to use the floating method for hooping. I have trapped an adhesive backing into the hoop frame, with the adhesive side facing upwards, towards the back of the fabric.

Remove any protective film to expose the sticky layer. Place the plastic grid in the hoop and mark the centre point on the adhesive backing.

Adhesive backing trapped in the frame with the grid on top.

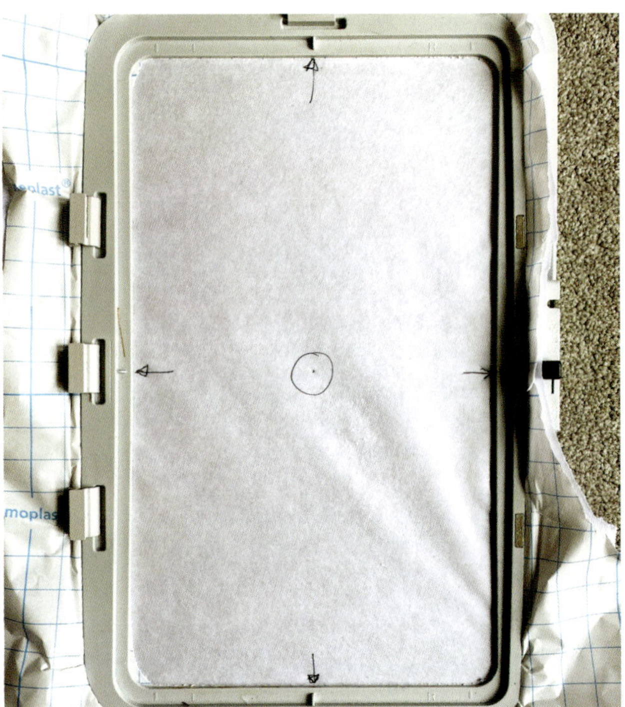

Marked stabiliser.

Step Eleven: Remove the Grid

Remove the grid.

Notice the side grooves on the grid; these will be used to align the fabric, matching the notches in step 9.

Step Twelve: Aligning Centre Points and Notches

Carefully place the fabric on the adhesive backing, matching the centre point of the fabric to the centre point of the backing (I use a pin to align the two centre points precisely).

Next, match the side markings of the fabric to the grooves on the grid and smooth the cloth flat. Try to avoid twisting or overstretching the cloth. Ensure the centre marks as still aligned.

Fabric placed and stuck on top of stabiliser and frame.

Step Thirteen: Double-checking Alignment

Place the grid in the hoop to check alignment is still accurate. If need be, carefully lift the cloth and move into the correct location. Use the tracing as a guide.

Plastic grid used to check alignment and ensuring fabric is in the correct position.

Step Fourteen: Stitch-out

Embroider your section.

Stitched-out hoop in fabric in the correct location.

Traced-out design on plastic grid for the next hooping.

Step Fifteen: Repeat for Remaining Hoopings

Repeat for remaining sections of your design – Steps 3–14.

Completed stitched-out piece with no visible join lines.

Close-up shot of the design on the garment from Le Fil's Instagram post. (Photo: Scallywagfox)

By David Morrish

DIGITALLY EMBROIDERED ART FOR FASHION & INTERIORS

SHOP NOW

CHAPTER 8

TALKING BUSINESS

People will always doubt you; stick by your vision and convictions, and shout very loud to be heard and seen by your people.

Embroidering can be a profitable hobby or business if you have the skills, patience and imagination to create unique and high-quality embroidered items. Here are some ways to make money from embroidering.

Sell embroidered products online: you can sell your embroidered products through online marketplaces such as Etsy or eBay. You can make and sell a variety of embroidered items such as hats, bags, clothing or home décor.

Offer custom embroidery services: you can offer custom embroidery services for individuals or businesses, e.g., you can embroider logos or names on shirts, hats or bags.

Create and sell embroidery designs: You can create and sell embroidery designs online. There are many websites that allow you to sell your embroidery designs, such as Etsy or Creative Market.

Teach embroidery classes: if you have advanced embroidery skills, you can teach embroidery classes to others. You can offer classes online or in person.

Participate in craft fairs or markets: this is a great way to showcase your work and connect with potential customers.

Collaborating with businesses: reach out to local businesses, such as clothing stores or boutiques, and offer to create custom embroidery designs for them to sell. You can agree on a commission or a fee for each product sold.

Commission work: you can also offer your services for commissioned work, such as creating a custom embroidery design for a wedding dress, or bespoke pieces of wall art.

Repair: embroidery can be used on garments to hide damaged areas. This repair service can be appealing to those who do not want to discard precious items of clothing and are willing to invest in sustaining their use.

WHAT TYPES OF EMBROIDERED PRODUCTS TO MAKE

Embroidery is a popular craft that can be applied to many different products. Here are some embroidered products that tend to sell well:

Apparel: embroidered clothing items such as hoodies, sweatshirts, hats, T-shirts, jackets and bags are popular items. Personalised and custom-designed embroidery on clothing items can be a great way to stand out and create a unique look.

Home décor: embroidered home décor items such as cushions, pillows, tablecloths and curtains are popular items. These items can add a touch of personality to any space and can make great gifts.

Accessories: embroidered accessories such as scarves, gloves, shoes, boots, bags and purses are also popular items. These items can be personalised and can be a great way to add a pop of colour to any outfit.

Baby items: embroidered baby items, such as blankets, bibs and onesies, are popular gifts for new parents. These

Kingfly shop website page.

items can be personalised with the baby's name or birth date, making them a special keepsake. Embroidered baby scans for keepsakes make for a truly unique and personalised present.

Pet products: items such as collars, leashes, and blankets are also popular items. These can be personalised with the pet's name or a cute design, making them a great gift for pet owners. Pet portraits makes for great art pieces.

When deciding which embroidered products to sell, consider your target market and what products they are most likely to be interested in. Also, consider the quality of the embroidery and the materials used, as this can affect the perceived value of the product.

Subject matter

You have identified your product type, but what about subject matter? What are the most popular subject matters to embroider? Here are some of the most popular:

Flowers and nature: this is a very popular, classic embroidery theme that includes natural elements; very popular subject matter for interior décor.

Animals: Designs of animals such as cats, dogs, birds and butterflies are popular and can offer a range of interpretations and styles.

Holiday themes: seasonal themes such as Christmas, Easter, Valentine's Day, New Year's Eve and Halloween are popular, but you will need to plan in advance to ensure your products are ready to send to the buyer in time.

Personalised designs: personalised embroidery designs such as monograms, names and initials are always in demand for customising clothing, accessories, and home décor.

Vintage and retro designs: these are becoming increasingly popular, and professionals use these designs to create a nostalgic effect on clothing, linens and other items.

Sports team logos: embroidered sports team logos are popular among fans who like to show their support at games or in everyday life.

Quotes and sayings: embroidered quotes and sayings can add a personal touch to gifts or home décor items.

MARKETING

So, you have created your embroidered product or decided to offer embroidery services, but how will you tell everyone you exist? How will you market yourself, to attract press, interest, following and sales?

Here is a step-by-step guide to help you market your embroidery business and reach your customer base.

Set goals: the first step to creating a successful marketing campaign is to set clear objectives. Determine what you want to achieve through marketing your business. Do you want to increase your customer base? Promote a new product? Increase sales?

Define your target audience: who do you want to reach with your marketing campaign? Identify your target market and tailor your marketing messages and strategies to their preferences and needs.

Develop a brand identity: develop a recognisable brand identity for your embroidery business through a logo, colour palette, website, social media profile and other marketing materials. This will help your business stand out and create a lasting impression on potential customers.

Create a website: a professional website is an essential part of your marketing strategy. Customers want to learn more about your business, view your products and services, and contact you quickly and easily.

Use social media platforms: social media is a powerful tool for promoting your embroidery business and reaching potential customers. Identify the social media platforms your audience uses the most and create profiles on those sites. Regularly post content, share your embroidery work, and engage with your customers. Instagram, TikTok, YouTube and Facebook are the most common at the time of writing.

Offer special deals and discounts: encourage customers to purchase your products or services by offering special deals and discounts. This can include a percentage off their first purchase, seasonal sales or clearance items.

Attend local events and trade shows: attend local events and trade shows to promote your embroidery business and meet potential customers. Make sure to bring business cards and samples of your work.

Consider paid advertising: paid advertising can be a powerful way to reach new customers quickly and easily. Options for paid advertising include Google Ads, social media advertising, and local print ads.

Ask for referrals: lastly, don't be shy about asking happy customers for referrals; word-of-mouth is still one of the best ways to promote your business and gain new customers.

SUSTAINABILITY

You may have decided that sustainability is an important factor of your business model, but how can digital embroidery be sustainable? Here are some ways you can make your embroidery business sustainable and environmentally friendly:

Use eco-friendly materials: use sustainable and organic materials for your embroidery projects such as bamboo, organic cotton and hemp. These materials are biodegradable and produce less waste when discarded. There are sustainable and recycled embroidery threads on the market these days that perform as well as their counterparts. The Sensa range by Madeira is one example.

Reduce waste: avoid throwing away fabric scraps by implementing a zero-waste policy. You can use scraps to create smaller embroidery projects such as patches, earrings and hair accessories.

Use environmentally friendly packaging: use biodegradable and compostable packaging materials such as paper or cardboard boxes and avoid using plastic packaging.

Use energy-efficient equipment: use energy-efficient embroidery machines and equipment to reduce your energy consumption.

Recycle and reuse: recycle or donate used embroidery equipment and textiles instead of throwing them away.

Support eco-friendly suppliers: choose suppliers who are environmentally conscious and use sustainable materials and production processes.

Educate your customers: educate your customers about your eco-friendly practices and encourage them to recycle or reuse your products.

Made to order: adopting this model means all goods have a home before they are made; no overproduction or worries about unsold stock going to landfill.

PRICING

How do you price your embroidery work? Pricing can be tricky but consider the following essential factors:

Material costs: include all the materials used, that is, threads, fabric, needles and stabilisers.

Labour: determine an hourly wage for yourself and multiply it by the number of hours spent on the piece.

Overheads: factor in costs like electricity, equipment wear and tear, and any rented workspace.

Profit margin: ensure you add a profit margin to cover your enterprise and allow for business growth. (I often work on a × 3 markup.)

Postage and packaging: don't forget to factor this in your costs as bigger or heavier pieces can be quite costly to send to a customer. Remember also that posting internationally is usually more expensive and you may have to factor in customs, shipping taxes or exchange rates.

Other factors to consider that may have a significant impact on your pricing strategy include:

Skill level: if your work reflects a high skill level or is particularly unique, this should be reflected in the price.

Demand: if your work is in high demand, you may be able to price it higher.

Size and complexity: larger and more complex pieces generally warrant higher pricing.

Emotional value: sometimes a piece may have a special value that can be reflected in the price.

Presentation: if your work is framed or presented in a certain way, this should be added to the cost.

Market research: investigate pricing for similar pieces in your market. This will give you a ballpark figure to work from. Ensure your pricing is fair to both you and the customer, reflecting your skill and time without being prohibitively expensive.

RAISING YOUR PROFILE AND REPUTATION

Being featured in magazines and books, celebrity association, success in competitions, featured on podcasts and blogs, TV, presenting at big events, giving talks, panel discussions, judging competitions, accreditations and joining art or craft associations can all help to raise your public-facing profile. Becoming established as a household name and a leading expert can help you strengthen your business and firmly cement your place in the market, as well as build consumer faith and demand. All this, however, can take many years to achieve, but if you are patient, strategic and maximise opportunities it is perfectly achievable.

USEFUL RESOURCES

I hope this section will help save you time and you may learn from my experience and findings. Here is a list of producers, suppliers, courses and useful reading that you may wish to refer to or familiarise yourself with as you continue on your digital embroidery journey.

DIGITISING SOFTWARE

Bernina Embroidery Software: www.bernina.com/en-GB/Software-GB/
Brother PE-Design: https://sewingcraft.brother.eu/en/products/machines/pe-design-software
Design Doodler – The Deer's Embroidery Legacy: https://www.digitisingmadeeasy.com/embroidery-software-design-doodler/
Embird: www.embird.net
Embrilliance: https://embrilliance.com/
Floriani Total Control U: https://rnk-floriani.com/products/Floriani-Software/Floriani-Total-Control-U
Hatch: https://hatchembroidery.com/
Janome Artistic Digitiser: https://www.janome.com/products/software/artistic-digitiser/
Pulse ID: https://www.tajimasoftware.com/
Wilcom E4.5: https://wilcom.com/embroiderystudio/designing

MACHINE SUPPLIERS

Bernina: https://www.berninasewingshop.co.uk/
Brother: https://www.brothermachines.com/
Digitek: https://digitek.me.uk/
GS-UKdirect.com: https://www.gs-ukdirect.com/
Janome: https://www.janome.co.uk/
Midwest: https://midwestworld.com/
Stocks Embroidery and Sewing Solutions: https://www.stocks.co.uk/

THREADS, BACKINGS AND MORE

Barnyarns: https://www.barnyarns.co.uk/
ETC Supplies: https://etcsupplies.com/
GS-UKdirect.com: https://www.gs-ukdirect.com/
Madeira: https://www.madeira.co.uk/
Somac Threads: https://www.somac.co.uk/

COMPETITIONS AND EXHIBITION CALLS

Hand & Lock – Prize for Embroidery: https://handembroidery.com/the-prize/
Loewe Craft Prize: https://craftprize.loewe.com/en/craftprize2024
Madeira Embroidery Competition: https://www.creativecraftshow.co.uk/competitions/
Royal Academy (RA) Summer Exhibition: https://summer.royalacademy.org.uk/
Royal Society of British Artists: https://www.mallgalleries.org.uk/open-calls/royal-society-british-artists
The Broderers' Exhibition: https://broderers-exhibition.co.uk/
The Mr X Stitch Contemporary Needlework Prize: https://www.mrxstitch.com/needlework-prize/?utm_content=cmp-true

USEFUL WEBSITES

Crafts Council: https://www.craftscouncil.org.uk/
Diana Springall Collection: https://dianaspringallcollection.co.uk/
Embroiderers' Guild: https://embroiderersguild.com/
Mr X Stitch: https://www.mrxstitch.com/
QEST: https://www.qest.org.uk/

Royal School of Needlework (RSN): https://royal-needlework.org.uk/

The Sunbury Embroidery Gallery: https://www.sunburygallery.org/

MAGAZINES AND BOOKS

Embroidery The Textile Art Magazine: https://embroiderymagazine.co.uk/

Love Embroidery: https://www.ourmediashop.com/products/back-issues/craft/love-embroidery-magazine

Images magazine: https://www.images-magazine.com/

Stitch magazine: https://embroiderersguild.com/stitch-magazine/

Digitising Made Easy: Create Custom Embroidery Designs Like a Pro – John Deer – Available on Amazon.co.uk

TRAINING

Digitek: https://digitek.me.uk/

EMBROIDERY PRODUCERS

Hand & Lock: https://handembroidery.com/

Hawthorne & Heaney and London Embroidery School: https://londonhandembroidery.com/

GS-UK Ltd: https://www.gs-uk.com/

ABOUT THE AUTHOR

David Morrish is the founder of Kingfly, a brand that weaves together contemporary art and digital embroidery to breathe life into fashion and interiors. Twice winner of the Hand & Lock Wilcom Digital Embroiderer of the Year award in both 2019 and 2021, David then went on to gain an Embroiderer's Guild Scholarship in 2022. He also appeared on the Bafta-nominated craft to business TV series, *Make It at Market*, captivating millions of viewers on a global scale.

In 2023, David secured a prestigious QEST scholarship (Queen Elizabeth Scholarship Trust), which allowed him to delve deeper into the realm of hand embroidery techniques, with online teaching from the Royal School of Needlework and workshops carried out with leading embroiderers of differing styles and techniques. In 2024 David was awarded the Madeira Embroidery overall winner's prize for his tactile *Vision of Paris* art piece, displayed and judged at the Sewing for Pleasure event at Birmingham NEC.

Beyond his creative endeavours, David's influence extends to the academic realm as Senior Fashion Academic at Sheffield Hallam University, Fellow of the Higher Education Academy and External Examiner. His dedication to teaching stems from a place of pure passion, as he takes immense pride in passing on his invaluable knowledge and experience to the next generation of creatives.

Make It at Market presenter Dom Chinea (left) with the author and one of his digital embroidery pieces.

INDEX

First published in 2025 by
The Crowood Press Ltd
Ramsbury, Marlborough
Wiltshire SN8 2HR

enquiries@crowood.com
www.crowood.com

British Library Cataloguing-in-Publication Data
A catalogue record for this book is available from the British Library.

ISBN 978 0 7198 4464 5

Cover design by Sergey Tsvetkov

Typeset by Envisage IT
Printed and bound in India by Nutech Printing Services

Acknowledgements
The path to writing this book has been more challenging than I anticipated. When embarking on this endeavour, the scale of the undertaking wasn't entirely clear to me. These three years have been a profound learning experience, enriched by both the trials faced and the knowledge acquired from numerous sources — the vast digital library at our fingertips and the valuable insights from the digital embroidery community.

I am particularly grateful to Pete Tarrant, whose mentorship post my Hand & Lock, Wilcom Digital Award win in 2018, has been invaluable. Pete's expansive knowledge and willingness to support others are extraordinary and incredibly motivating.

My deepest appreciation goes to my wife, Alison Morrish. Her unwavering support was the bedrock upon which this journey was built. Her encouragement kept me going, even when the goal seemed unreachable. I hope to have made her proud.

Special thanks to Deborah Shepherd from Janome for her enthusiastic support, providing me with equipment and opportunities to exhibit my work. To Pete Tarrant and Rob Smith from Wilcom for recognising my creations with the Hand & Lock Prize and for their ongoing support with exceptional digitising software. My gratitude extends to GS-UK Ltd for their vast array of vibrant threads, The Embroiderer's Guild for welcoming me into this incredible community, supporting my growth, and offering numerous opportunities to present my work. The QEST (Queen Elizabeth Scholarship Trust) has been instrumental in advancing my skills with funded training at renowned institutions and with master embroiderers across the UK.

Finally, I must thank the Sunbury Embroidery Gallery for the honour of hosting my first exhibition, a memorable showcase that I will always cherish.

And finally, a massive thank you to Sheffield Hallam University for supporting me and encouraging me to keep on growing as an academic and creative visionary.

I hope this book helps many people as they explore the incredible world of digital embroidery.